A

DECADE

OF

MUSIC

BOOKS BY B. H. HAGGIN

A Book of the Symphony (1937)
Music on Records (1938)
Music on Records (1941)
Music for the Man Who Enjoys "Hamlet" (1944)
Music in The Nation (1949)
The Listener's Musical Companion (1956)
Conversations with Toscanini (1959)
Music Observed (1964)
The Toscanini Musicians Knew (1967)
Ballet Chronicle (1971)
The New Listener's Companion and Record Guide (1971)

B. H. HAGGIN

A
DECADE
OF
MUSIC

HORIZON PRESS  NEW YORK

Foreword

I heard my first major concert in Carnegie Hall and my first performance of opera at the Metropolitan in January 1914. And what I heard in the sixty years that followed led me to conclusions I think of as Haggin's First and Second Laws of Esthetic Dynamics: the First, that artistic gifts do not always, necessarily, inevitably, produce valuable art; the Second, that you cannot keep a bad man down.

The operation of the First Law I began to perceive in the thirties—in what was produced by men with the gifts of a Stokowski, a Horowitz, even a Furtwängler—and began to report in the writing collected in *Music in The Nation* and *Music Observed*. And the collection in this book has reports of the continued activity of Leonard Bernstein, Rudolf Bing, Julius Rudel, Daniel Barenboim, among others, that in recent years has revealed the operation of the Second Law.

But in addition this collection, like the earlier ones, has reports of occasions when great artistic gifts did achieve great art. In these reports I attempted to repay my debt—to Berlioz and Musorgsky, to Toscanini and Cantelli, to Cliburn, Ashkenazy and Michael Rogers, to Colin Davis, Boulez and Michael Tilson Thomas, to Janet Baker, Marilyn Horne and Fischer-Dieskau, to Balanchine, Verdy and Villella—in the way open to a critic, which is to inform others of the great artistic achievement he has experienced.

Contents

Music Criticism Today [1]

A few years ago, when I published a collection of my writing on music, an English reviewer of the book mentioned my "undisguised loathing" for some of the writings of other critics. I hadn't realized it was that apparent; but since it is, I may as well admit it and explain it. The explanation is that I care intensely about music, and therefore about what is done to it, not only by performers but by critics. Bernard Shaw once wrote about the people who pointed to the evidence of strong personal feeling in his concert reviews as though this were a misdemeanor, and contended that the true critic is a man for whom good or bad art *is* a personal matter, and who becomes a personal enemy on the provocation of a bad performance. I feel as Shaw did about the damage done to music by a bad performance; and I feel just as strongly about the damage done to it by a piece of bad criticism —the damage first to the reader in giving him wrong ideas about the music or the performance, and then in this way to the composer and the performer. As I see it, such damage is done by most of what is written about music in newspapers from *The New York Times* down, in magazines ranging from *Harper's*, *The Atlantic Monthly* and *The New Yorker* to *Esquire*, in the news weeklies, and in the magazines devoted to records. And of what I see, I propose to give some examples.

The critic's operation is performed with a specific equipment for the purpose—the specific gifts of perception, judgment and taste which enable him to hear what is placed before him and to evaluate it. [2]

[1] Adapted from an opening statement at a session of John Simon's *Prospects of Criticism* series at the Poetry Center of the Y.M.H.A.

[2] See pages 192-4.

And most criticism of music is done by people who write as though they have these gifts, but who actually do not have them. They don't have the judgment and taste with which to evaluate correctly what they hear; they don't have even the perception with which to hear it correctly. And my first examples are concerned with this lack of mere perception—perception of what I think may be considered simple fact: the fact, say, that one voice is ravishing to the ear, and another is unpleasant; or that one voice is steady, and another is afflicted with tremolo; or that one singer's—or one pianist's—phrasing is simple, and another's is fussy.

Thus Angel issues a new recorded performance of Mozart's *Così Fan Tutte;* and right at the start, in the opening trio, one is struck by the unpleasant and straining tenor voice of Alfredo Kraus, as against the ear-ravishing and easily flowing voice of Leopold Simoneau in the earlier Angel performance, and by the unattractive bass of Walter Berry in the new performance, as against the superb voice of Sesto Bruscantini in the earlier one. But Roland Gelatt of *High Fidelity*, reviewing the new performance in *The Reporter*, writes that Berry is a "decided improvement" over Bruscantini, and Kraus is up to the standard of Simoneau. And the result is damage to the readers who are persuaded to acquire this new performance with poorer voices, and to think these voices are good.

Nor is this deficiency in mere perception exhibited only by writers for record magazines. Harold Schonberg reports in *The Times* on two recorded performances of a Schubert sonata which are strikingly dissimilar: one by Friedrich Wührer, which is simple, straightforward and lifeless; the other by Wilhelm Kempff, in which he keeps fussing with tempo and phrasing. And he writes that "Kempff and Wührer are pianists very much in the same style. Both exhibit the Teutonic style of playing; both work in broad, massive strokes"—which actually neither of them does. And again the result is damage to the readers who are persuaded to acquire one or the other of these poor performances and to hear it as something it isn't. (Since Schonberg's preoccupation as a reviewer is with this placing of the pianist or singer or conductor in such nonexistent "styles", "traditions" and "schools" his readers learn also of the "Austro-German tradition" in conducting exemplified in the completely dissimilar practice of Furtwängler, Klemperer and von Karajan; and of Fischer-Dieskau's singing of *Lieder* being "of the Elena

Gerhardt school", when in fact it offers the antithesis of Gerhardt's.)

But it isn't only people like Gelatt and Schonberg. Winthrop Sargeant of *The New Yorker* is a professional musician who played in the New York Philharmonic with Toscanini, and whom one would expect to be able to hear that Patricia Brooks, in the New York City Opera's *La Traviata*, chews up the music in explosions of tremulous vocal sound, but who instead writes that her singing, done with a voice that is "pure and well-produced", is that of the greatest Violetta he has ever heard—which is damaging to the readers whom it persuades to attend a performance of *La Traviata* with her bad singing and to think it is good singing. So again at a concert performance of Gluck's *Orfeo*, where one would expect Sargeant to be able to hear that Elisabeth Schwarzkopf's phrasing of recitative is unbearably mannered and affected, and that in the arias she produces not a sustained melodic line but explosions of shrill sound—instead of which he writes that Schwarzkopf "is perhaps the most sophisticated of living sopranos" and that "a more stylish and appropriate Euridice would be hard to imagine." And so again when Sargeant hears a Serkin performance of Beethoven—the frenetic belaboring of music and piano—and reports its "scholarly meticulousness"; or he hears Barenboim's undisciplined playing in Beethoven's *Appassionata*—the expressive crescendos that are too violent, the retardations that linger too long, the pauses that are too great, the *Andante con moto* theme of the variation movement that is excessively slow, the first variation that is too fast after the slow theme, the feathery playing that is ludicrously unsuitable in the impassioned finale—and writes about the "extraordinary musical taste and intelligence", the "fine sense of repose", the "infallible sense of form", the "use of *rubato* in precisely the right way" that make Barenboim "one of the world's important artists of the keyboard".

But most astounding are the instances involving conductors. For Sargeant, as I have said, played in the New York Philharmonic with Toscanini, and came to know the plastic shaping of the music, the sensitive phrasing and rhythm, the grace that were characteristic of Toscanini's performances; and one would expect him to recognize that the stiff, insensitive, hard-driven, graceless performances of Szell today are as unlike Toscanini's as any performances could be; instead of which he writes on one occasion that "Szell's performances are of all contemporary ones the most apt to resemble Toscanini's," and on another occasion credits Szell with "exquisite taste, a grasp of a vast variety of musical styles, and a profound comprehension of form, climax and what the Germans call *Aufbau*"—all of which he says are reminiscent of Toscanini and make Szell "more like this fabulous predecessor of his than any other conductor who has been heard here in recent years". This is damaging to the readers who not only are persuaded to listen to Szell's bad performances and think they are good, but are given the idea that such stiff, graceless performances were what Toscanini produced.

And they are given this false idea of Toscanini's performances explicitly when Sargeant, describing the excellences of Zubin Mehta's *Aida*, cites in particular its lack of rigidity, which one would expect him to consider a point of resemblance to Toscanini, but which instead demonstrates to Sargeant that Mehta is refreshingly unlike the other younger conductors of today who imitate Toscanini's "adherence to rigid and speedy tempo". This reveals an astounding failure to hear the actual lack of rigidity that is strikingly evident not only in Toscanini's recorded *Aida* but in all his performances—and not only in the expansive, flexibly paced performances of the Philharmonic years which Sargeant himself played in,[3] but in the performances of the later NBC years that got to be simpler and faster but even then didn't lose the plasticity and grace that were characteristic of his operation.

But it isn't only in performance that Sargeant exhibits this deficiency in mere perception; it is also in music. A few years ago Stravinsky created a sensation in one of his books of conversation with Robert Craft by attacking the music critics as a group, and two critics—Sargeant and Paul Henry Lang—in particular. His point about the group was that they were incompetent because they didn't know how music was written; his specific point about Sargeant was that his giants were Menotti and Giannini, and his dwarfs were Schönberg and Stravinsky. I pointed out at the time that what criticism requires is not the knowledge of the composer, the doer, the insider, but instead the perception, judgment and taste of the non-doer, the outsider, the listener—which is to say, the professional listener, the critic. And so what made Sargeant contemptible as a critic was not his lack of the composer's knowledge

---

[3] For example, the performance of Mozart's *Haffner* Symphony in which Sargeant played in his very first week with Toscanini—with its striking expressive distention of the initial basic tempo in bars 6-9—which can be heard on Victor M-65 and Camden CAL-326.

of how to write music, but first of all the deficiencies of taste that Stravinsky had pointed out. On the one hand there was Sargeant's high regard for the worthless unoriginal pseudo-music—what Shaw called second-hand music—of Menotti, Barber, Giannini, Douglas Moore and the rest. And on the other hand there was what Sargeant thought of Stravinsky's music—not the recent *Movements* and *Variations*, which one could understand Sargeant's finding inaccessible and non-communicative, but the early works that are twentieth-century classics —*The Rite of Spring*, for example, which to Sargeant's ears was "that most famous of all musical conversation pieces" that "is beginning to sound dated." To him these powerfully original works revealed Stravinsky's "lack of creative capacity", which he covered over with his "mastery of the artificialities of music", like orchestration. This was a failure of taste; but it involved also again a failure of mere perception.

That is, for Sargeant the only works of Stravinsky that were likely to survive were things like *Pulcinella* and *The Fairy's Kiss*, "because their basic inspiration is not Stravinsky's own. They are . . . Stravinsky orchestrations of music written in the styles of others"—i.e., music in which Stravinsky merely imitates those styles of others. This represented the misunderstanding that has existed from the start about Stravinsky's practice of letting his mind play with the substance and styles of other composers; but it also revealed a remarkable ability not to hear what actually happens in *The Fairy's Kiss*. In this score the fragments Stravinsky uses from Tchaikovsky's piano pieces and songs are reworked by him, and are integrated into contexts of his own invention, some of it in styles that are his reworking, his extension of Tchaikovsky's style; and in the reworking of the Tchaikovsky fragments, as in the Stravinsky contexts, one hears constantly the operation of the Stravinsky mind—just as one hears the operation of the Beethoven mind in his variations on an aria from Mozart's *The Magic Flute*. And Sargeant's description of *The Fairy's Kiss* as a mere Stravinsky imitation of Tchaikovsky was damaging to the readers whom it kept from experiencing and appreciating what is actually Stravinsky's most masterfully and beautifully wrought, most imaginative and expressive, most affecting score.

Similar deficiencies not only of taste but of mere perception appear in what Sargeant writes about Berlioz—all the old clichés about extravagances, rhetorical flourishes, ingenious and dazzling orchestration covering the poverty of the melodies that for Sargeant are no better than Massenet's and often not even as good. And it is damaging to the readers whom it keeps from discovering that the man Sargeant is talking about is the composer of the exquisitely delicate, wonderfully imagined orchestral magic of *Capulet's Garden* and *Queen Mab* in *Romeo and Juliet*, of the impassioned and heart-piercing melodies of the *Love Scene* in that work, of the delicate and beautiful writing in the first three movements of *Harold in Italy*, the first three movements even of the *Symphonie Fantastique*, of the great melodic writing and marvelous supporting orchestral writing in the songs *Les Nuits d'Eté*.

The deficiences of perception and taste I have been talking about are those of equipment that contribute to making most music criticism as bad as it is. But there is another important deficiency that contributes to this result—the deficiency in discipline. I once pointed out that what made Shaw a great music critic was not just his equipment of perception and taste, literary brilliance and wit, but the discipline that caused him to use the literary brilliance and wit strictly in the service of the perception and taste for the critic's task of describing and evaluating accurately the piece of music or the performance before him. And what makes most critics bad is their lack not only of his equipment but of his discipline. They think to themselves not "'What can I write that will describe most accurately what I heard?" but instead "What can I write that will impress my readers with my knowledge, my perception, my cleverness, my charm?"—which is likely to produce faulty criticism even when they have knowledge, perception, cleverness and charm, since the critic's eye that is partly on the effect he wants to make is that much less on the object before him and less likely to see it accurately.

Thus a critic as well equipped as Joseph Kerman, who in the early years of *The Hudson Review* was content at times to write perceptive criticism of particular pieces of music, felt impelled at other times to put on acts of pretentious intellectualism that would impress the readers of a literary quarterly, with results similar to those in his recent book on Beethoven's quartets, in which the music is presented to the reader as, in effect, seen through the distorting lenses of Kerman's pretentious intellectual constructions—the last three Op. 18 quartets, for example, as being made radically different from the first three by certain "disruptive forces", when in fact no such differences are heard by someone who listens to the works with ears unaided by Kerman.

Another fairly perceptive critic, Michael Steinberg of *The Boston Globe*, has a Ph. D. in music which gives him a great deal of knowledge; and so knowledge-dropping—sometimes relevant, sometimes not—is one of his ways of impressing his readers. Occasionally the knowledge-dropping is part of an operation of one-upmanship in relation to the performer, also to impress his readers; and in this operation he sometimes uses the immaturity ploy that is so plausible and so profitable. Thus, reviewing the first RCA record of the extraordinary Guarneri Quartet, whose members are remarkably young, Steinberg writes that the group's immaturity is evident in, among other things, its failure to vary recurrences and repetitions—specifically the repetitions of the minuets after the trios in the Mozart quartets on the record. Here the knowledge Steinberg is dropping—which does apply to the repetition of a section in a keyboard piece by Couperin or a *da capo* aria by Handel, in which variation was customary—does not apply to the minuet in a symphony or quartet by Haydn or Mozart, in which the composer has written out all the notes and the layout of dynamics for their performance, and his direction to repeat it after the trio is a direction to repeat it as he has written it. And the Guarneri Quartet, in doing this, doesn't exhibit immaturity any more than Toscanini and the Budapest Quartet did.

On occasion, moreover, the knowledge isn't knowledge at all. Reporting on Boulez's superb performance of Debussy's *Ibéria*, Steinberg singles out two details: the transition from the second movement to the third, in which Boulez, by preserving continuity, passed "a crucial test . . . failed by all other conductors", presumably including Toscanini; and "another notorious problem spot", the accented chord of the downbeat of the very first bar of the work, "usually converted by conductors [again presumably including Toscanini] into a ponderous thump", but not by Boulez, who "gave it as an upbeat," so that "it had force, but with spring rather than weight." The problem spots I was made aware of at Toscanini's rehearsals of the work did not include the two mentioned by Steinberg; listening to Toscanini's performances I never heard the first accented chord made into a ponderous thump, but heard it given the spring Debussy asked for in the direction *dans un rhythme alerte;* nor did I hear a loss of the continuity so characteristic of Toscanini's operation in his handling of the transition

from the second movement to the third. And listening to Boulez's
performance I didn't hear anything different from Toscanini's at either
point (also, watching him I didn't see the first chord on the downbeat
given as an upbeat); nor did I hear anything different at the two points
when, later, I compared a Boulez performance of *Ibéria* on a tape with
the Toscanini performance on the Victor record. Thus Steinberg's
statements turn out to be an example of the practice of making imagined
points about imagined facts.[4] It is the normal practice of the man
who cannot hear and describe what is actually before him; but it is
indulged in also by competent critics—Steinberg being one example,
and the most notable being Virgil Thomson.

An other example of imagined facts was the obituary article on Fritz
Reiner in *The New York Herald Tribune*, entitled *A Titan's Last Bow*,
in which Alan Rich described Reiner as one of the last of what he
called the "German-classic" school of conducting, whose earmarks
included "probity, self-effacing eloquence, clarity of stick technique",
as against what Rich called "the Italian school of Toscanini and De
Sabata, or the Franco-Russian school of Koussevitzky, Monteux and,
by adoption, Stokowski". If one thinks of the sober, self-effacing conducting of Monteux with its clear stick technique, and then of the
contrasting operations of Koussevitzky and Stokowski, and then of
the probity, self-effacing eloquence and clear stick technique of Toscanini, and then of the flamboyance of De Sabata, one realizes that
Rich's categorizing was pure invention and nonsense which diminished
his readers' understanding of the subject. Moreover, when Rich went
on to say that "as an interpreter of the German classics Reiner was
above reproach"—his Beethoven *Eroica* being "next to unapproach-
able"—he was indulging in a flight of obituary rhetoric about imagined
Reiner performances, not describing the actual Reiner performances
of Beethoven, which, like his performances of other music, did leave
him open to reproach for the erratic details of tempo that flawed the
musical objects he was producing.

An unforgettable example was Irving Kolodin's statement once about

---

[4] A recent Steinberg review of the Guarneri Quartet's first recordings of Beethoven
quartets contained several examples of the superhuman Steinberg ear hearing what to
the normal ear is not there to be heard—e.g. the cellist's alleged breaking the opening
melodic line of Op. 59 No. 1 with the "gap" Steinberg hears between the A at the
end of bar 7 and the G at the beginning of bar 8, when in fact the two notes are
connected.

Beecham's ponderous recorded performance of Mozart's exquisite Symphony K.201: "It has been my reaction, after hearing Beecham's more recent performances of this work, that the interpretation he recorded was a transitional one, tending toward the conception he holds today." I knew of no "more recent performances" that Kolodin could have heard, and I was able to ascertain from Beecham, at an accidental meeting, that there had been none. But there may be no more connection with reality in what Kolodin writes about something he does hear; for his criticism is a churning up of turgid verbiage, supposedly for the purpose of informing his readers about the music or performance, but actually for the evident purpose of impressing them with Kolodin—with what he mistakenly thinks is fine writing and impressive ideas, or with the accumulated Kolodin experience and expertise which enables him to perceive in Cantelli's performance of a Mozart divertimento that "that degree of musical culture and experience which can settle, almost instinctively, on proper tempi and sonorous values for such works as the Mozart, are not yet his"—when in fact it is Kolodin who lacks that degree of musical culture and experience which would enable him to perceive in the performance Cantelli's sure instinct for right tempos and sonorities.

The lack of discipline I have been talking about can reach an extreme—and on occasion an ugly and outrageous extreme—which may leave one amazed that such writing is published. But the fact observed by Shaw—that "editors, by some law of Nature which still baffles science, are *always* ignorant of music"—doesn't only make editors incapable of recognizing a music critic's deficiencies in his special knowledge, and in the special perception, judgment and taste necessary in addition to make a musically educated writer a good critic: Shaw's point was that editors are so overwhelmed by a display of the knowledge of music they lack as to be unable to recognize in a piece of music criticism the mere bad thinking and bad writing they would perceive immediately and not tolerate in an article on any other subject. And so it was not surprising that the editors of *The Herald Tribune* published Alan Rich's review of Menotti's opera *The Last Savage*, with its pseudo-boyish gushing about how "all the things that are wrong with it just don't seem to matter," since "there comes a time when high aesthetic principles must be thrown to the winds, and this, dear reader, is the time"; about how the eclectic Menotti has this time "made the whole

continent of Europe his oyster. America too, for that matter; didn't
we hear Sardula's Act Three aria in *The Sound of Music?* Of course
we did. But how seductive it all is! . . . Only a churl could cavil
at such treasures, hollow as they may be"; and about the production
that is "gorgeous beyond dreams", the cast that is "glorious", the
orchestra that is "right on its tippy-twinkletoes". Nor was it surprising
that the *Herald Tribune* editors earlier accepted not only Paul Henry
Lang's deficiencies of perception and taste but his atrocious writing.
What *was* amazing was their toleration of the outrageous personal offensiveness Lang exhibited repeatedly in his references to Stravinsky's
collaboration with Robert Craft—in particular his repeated contention
that in their published volumes of conversations Stravinsky was a mere
ventriloquist's dummy speaking what a sinister Craft, with his loaded
questions, got him to speak; his statement that the collaboration had
reached the point where "Mr. Stravinsky should use the business designation 'A Division of Craft Products Inc.' "; and the later statement
that carried this offensiveness to the point of referring to Stravinsky's
"amanuensis, librettist, and *valet de chambre*, Robert Craft".

But it wasn't only the *Herald Tribune* editors who amazed one in
this way. The editors of *The Times* may have been incapable of recognizing Harold Schonberg's appalling deficiencies as a critic, the appalling
quality of his prose ("Every now and then Mr. Richter played a phrase
in the most ravishing manner possible. Then he would turn around
and play without apparent liaison with the previous phrase."), and
on one occasion his inadequacy as a mere reporter when he described
the eccentricities of tempo in Glenn Gould's performance of Brahms's
D-minor Concerto without placing them in their context of the impressive operation of Gould's powers, the beautiful playing he did, even
in that eccentric performance. But it was amazing that the editors
of a paper as concerned with propriety and decorum as *The Times*
should have tolerated a performance by Schonberg as unprecedented
in its ostentatious vulgarity and personal offensiveness as Gould's had
been in its slow tempos. Schonberg professed to be writing about
the performance to a friend named Ossip: "Such goings-on at the New
York Philharmonic concert yesterday afternoon! I tell you, Ossip, like
you never saw. . . . First the conductor comes out to read a speech.
He says that he doesn't like the way the pianist will play the concerto.
I mean this, Ossip. Glenn Gould is waiting in the wings to play Brahms,

and has to listen to Leonard Bernstein saying that this was a Brahms he never dreamed of. He washes his hands of it. . . . So then the Gould boy comes out, and you know what, Ossip? Now I understand. I mean, a conductor has to protect himself. You know what? The Gould boy played the Brahms D minor Concerto slower than the way we used to practice it. (And between you, me, and the corner lamppost, Ossip, maybe the reason he plays it so slow is maybe his technique is not so good.)" And much more of same.

One last point. I've been talking about the damage done by bad criticism to the reader in giving him incorrect ideas about good and bad in music and performance; and I said at the beginning that through these incorrect ideas damage was done also to the composer and the performer. Not to Stravinsky; but to some extent to Berlioz, whose music some people are still kept from appreciating by writing like Sargeant's. And certainly to Musorgsky, whose own *Boris Godunov* is replaced everywhere today by Rimsky-Korsakov's falsification because of the critics' failure to recognize themselves, and to proclaim to the public, that Musorgsky's *Boris* is the work of an extraordinary genius, not of a clumsy dilettante in need of Rimsky's assistance, and that it is as illegitimate for an opera company to produce his *Boris* rewritten by Rimsky as it would be for a museum to exhibit an academician's repainting of a work of Picasso. And though the career of an established celebrity like Glenn Gould couldn't be damaged by Schonberg's arrogant sneering; nor the career of another such celebrity, Vladimir Ashkenazy, by Schonberg's nonsense about his performance of Schubert's Sonata in B-flat;[5] the career of an outstandingly gifted but uncelebrated young pianist like Michael Rogers, which depended on the reviews he got in *The Times*, was damaged right at the start by what one unperceptive *Times* reviewer wrote about his debut, and again by what other unperceptive *Times* reviewers wrote about his later recitals.[6]

This, then, is the situation I see in music criticism; and I think I am justified in feeling so strongly about it. Actually I have felt slightly better since last spring, when *Commonweal* began to publish the occasional writing of a young critic, Harris Green, who seems to be able

---

[5] See page 145.
[6] See pages 139-40.

to hear correctly and to want only to describe what he hears.[7] (*Commentary*, October 1968)

Postscript 1973 In a lifetime devoted to the thinking up of schematizing ideas that wrapped artistic phenomena in neat packages (e.g. "the improvisatory aspect of jazz is remarkably adapted to the musical needs of a pragmatic, pioneering people" [what about the improvisatory aspect of Hindu music?]; and the inconclusive end of a jazz improvisation, like the "indefinite upward thrust" of the American skyscraper, represents the typical American's dislike of endings because "he is an incurable progressive"), Winthrop Sargeant's ceaseless pondering on what was wrong with Berlioz and his music achieved the staggering conclusion that it was his inability to play the piano. For it had struck him that the great composers up to and during Berlioz's time had been pianists or organists who therefore had "had an extraordinarily intimate knowledge of the relation between music as played and music as written"; whereas Berlioz, since he was "unable to perform his own gigantic works by himself with the aid of a keyboard, often miscalculated his effects." Actually the magical *Queen Mab* Scherzo was the writing of a man who did his musical thinking directly in terms of the orchestra, and therefore calculated his effects with absolute accuracy without the aid that a piano couldn't give him in such music. Moreover, what was performed had first to be rehearsed; and it was the rehearsals that provided Berlioz with the necessary opportunities to correct miscalculations; so that what Sargeant heard as miscalculations Berlioz presumably heard as exactly what he wanted.

I should have mentioned Kerman as another competent critic who sometimes indulged in the practice of making invented points about invented facts—his writing about the changes caused by "disruptive forces" in the last three of Beethoven's Quartets Op. 18 being one example. Another was his first article in the first issue of *The Hudson Review* in 1948, about the invented deficiencies of the invented writing of an invented B. H. Haggin, who was "simply not to be taken seriously as a critic of music" because much of the time he didn't write about music, and when he did write about a composer or a work he

[7] (1973) *Commonweal* didn't publish Green's writing very long; and he now makes an occasional appearance in the Sunday Arts and Leisure section of *The Times*.

didn't do so in detail. This was after the actual Haggin had written about the detail of pieces of music not only in *A Book of the Symphony* (1937) and *Music for the Man Who Enjoys "Hamlet"* (1944) but occasionally in *The Nation*—about Shostakovitch's *Leningrad* Symphony, for example, when it was first performed here by Toscanini in 1942, and Mozart's Concerto K. 503 when Schnabel introduced it in 1944; and there was, moreover, no validity in Kerman's idea that my summary statements about composers and particular works could not be considered criticism. Kerman's invented Haggin provided his readers with nothing but a "catalogue of generally accepted prestige tastes"; but the actual Haggin's *Music on Records* (1938 and 1941) and writing in *The Nation* had offered his independently arrived-at dissents from the generally accepted prestige tastes that he had thought overestimated some of the works of Bach, Beethoven, Brahms and Wagner and those of lesser figures like Rachmaninov, Puccini, Sibelius and Ravel, and underestimated Schubert, Berlioz, Musorgsky, Tchaikovsky and Verdi. (I never read Kerman's 1948 article: what I have reported is what he repeated from it in a letter to *The Hudson Review* in 1959, with the explanation that he did this because "nothing has changed," and also because "I have other ghostly fathers to exorcize.")

And on the other hand I should have cited a critic *without* real perception who trafficked entirely in invented facts—Albert Goldman, whose elaborate constructions of ideas about "generations", "forces", "crises" and the like had no connection with the realities of what he professed to be discussing, and who on one occasion wrote about the invented deficiencies that made an invented Haggin unequal to an invented "crisis of taste today".

Three Mozart Andantes

One important aspect of Mozart's piano concertos is left undiscussed in Girdlestone's monumental book about them. "The theater," says Dent in his book on Mozart's operas, "is the sphere in which Mozart is most completely himself; his concert works—concertos, symphonies, quartets and sonatas—are all fundamentally evocations of the theater." This is one of the most illuminating statements about Mozart; and it is most evidently true of the piano concertos: as I have pointed out elsewhere, the circumstances which produced them made them the most explicitly dramatic in character of Mozart's instrumental works, as well as the richest in substance, the most elaborately organized, the most fascinating and exciting to listen to. For he produced most of the great ones for the occasions at which he presented himself to the public as the greatest musician of his time—the greatest performer, exhibiting his powers in music written for the purpose by the greatest composer. He wrote a concerto, then, as an actor might write a play to act in; and he produced a musical equivalent of a play, in which the orchestra, which we hear first, creates suspense in anticipation of the moment when the piano makes its first entrance—to hold attention with lovely melodies, dazzling passage-work, lively exchanges with the orchestra, and eventually to work up to a brilliant exit; at which point the orchestra prepares for the piano's next entrance—its last such entrance being made for the solo cadenza that originally exhibited Mozart's powers of improvisation, after which the orchestra brings the curtain down on the movement. I have been speaking of the dramatic alternation of orchestra and piano that occurs within the sonata-allegro structure of the first movement, complicating it and making it the most elaborately and fascinatingly organized of Mozart's instrumental forms. But similar alternation complicates and elaborates whatever structure Mozart uses in the meditative slow movement, the high-spirited finale. And I will be concerned here with three of the slow movements—the tremendous Andantes of the Concertos K. 482, K. 453 and K. 467.

The purpose of the work being to impress the listener, the fascination of a particular concerto is in what Mozart contrives for this purpose. But in the succession of the concertos there is additional fascination in the endlessly new contrivance with which Mozart, in one work after another, fills out his established scheme in the achievement of his purpose. And my concern here is with the extraordinarily different ways in which Mozart, in those three Andantes, achieves his purpose of overwhelming the listener.

Girdlestone, as I said earlier, leaves undiscussed the dramatic aspect of the musical progressions he writes about with such love, perception and exhaustive knowledge. Actually, one doesn't always get a clear idea of the course of events in a movement as one pushes through the luxuriant thicket of his emotionally warm but diffuse, involved and unclear writing on the detail of the movement. And one is astonished —in view of this concentration of attention on detail—to find him missing the significance and effect of two enormously important details: the concluding master-strokes of the Andantes of K. 482 and K. 453.

The effect of those two concluding details—as of the sublime *Contessa, perdono* passage near the end of *The Marriage of Figaro*—comes from where they are placed, what they follow, refer to, derive their expressive meaning from. We must, then, consider the course of events in each movement.

In the Andante of the Concerto K. 482 the dramatic alternation of orchestra and solo piano takes place within a structure of theme and variations, with the variations separated by episodes of contrasting material. The orchestra plays first, in preparation for the piano's entrance—the muted violins beginning what develops into an unusually long, eventful and poignant statement in the key of C minor:

This is the theme; and when the piano enters it is to play the first variation on that theme—i.e. to elaborate on the notes of the statement and in this way to intensify its poignant expressive effect:

At the end of this variation the orchestra takes over with the first episode, which presents the contrasts of its key of E-flat major, its instrumental colors of wind instruments, its light-hearted expressive character. It is in two parts, the first of which ends with

in the dominant of E-flat, and the second with a similar statement in the tonic.

After this episode the piano enters again, to play the second variation, again in C minor, with the original melody in the right hand over left-hand passage-work creating a context of agitation and urgency:

At the end of this variation the orchestra again takes over with the second episode, an animated and gay dialogue of flute and bassoon in C major. Then the piano enters again for the third variation—this one a powerful dialogue of orchestra and piano, again in C minor:

The end of this variation brings the coda—the section of concluding summation. Concerning this, Girdlestone does remark on the feeling we have that the supreme moment is at hand; he does characterize what begins here as one of the most magical passages in all Mozart, in which the passion rises to tragic intensity; and he does direct attention to the desolate statement by clarinet and bassoon:

with which the coda begins. But then, having described the repetition of [6] by the piano, he speaks of the closing statement that follows as unfolding wearily, with all feeling of tragedy gone and only saddened resignation remaining. And this, for me, is an astonishing failure of perception; for actually that closing statement brings back [3], originally part of a light-hearted episode, but now—restated, after all that has intervened, in C minor—overwhelming in its poignancy:

It is the climax of the movement, achieved by a concluding master-stroke.

As with the Andante of K. 482, so with the Andante of K. 453: the substance, the organization of substance in structure, the scale of the operation, of the resulting musical object, of its expressive effect—all these make it one of the greatest of Mozart's utterances. The substance is of course different; and its organization—which builds up tremendous expressive force to another overwhelming concluding master-stroke—is unique.

The movement is organized by the several appearances of what is heard at the very start—a wistfully pensive statement which comes to a stop without attaining a conclusion:

Each time it is heard [1] is followed, after a pause, by a different sequence of ideas, which eventually leads to its next occurrence. Complicating this essential arrangement is the fact that [1] is heard alternately from the orchestra and from the piano; the further fact that of the sequences of ideas which take off from [1] the first comes from the orchestra, but all thereafter from the piano; and the further fact that although each of the piano's sequences begins with a new idea, as it continues it brings in ideas from the orchestra's first sequence.

We get, then, this course of events. It is the orchestra again that plays first, and at length, in preparation for the entrance of the solo piano—the violins beginning with the inconclusive statement [1], followed by a pause, after which the first sequence of ideas begins with this passage:

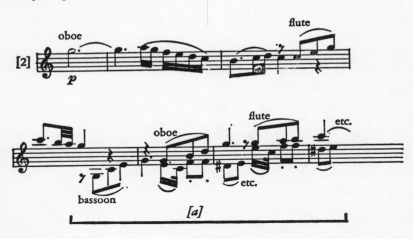

It leads eventually to this forceful statement:

and this eventually to a poignant conclusion:

Now the piano enters, first to play [1], then, after the pause, to take off in a sequence of ideas that begins with this impassioned statement:

The sequence becomes calmer with [2a] from the orchestra's first sequence, which the piano carries further in an ornate style with great expressive intensity. Eventually it leads to the conclusion [4] of the orchestra's first sequence, which this time continues on and builds up to the next appearance of [1], this one coming from the orchestra's flute.[1]

Again, after the pause, the piano takes off, beginning with this quiet statement:

---

[1] A strength of Girdlestone's writing is exhibited by the beginning of a sentence about the inconclusive statement: "A question it certainly is, and incomplete"; a weakness by the conclusion of the sentence: "and, later, when it is given to the flute, a forsaken faun in the light of a sun-bathed, empty 'afternoon'." The mere fact of its being played by the flute is enough to "remind" Girdlestone "of an *Après-midi d'un faune* in 18th-century idiom", when actually it hasn't the slightest similarity to the flute's statement in Debussy's piece. Similarly, the mere fact that both works are in G major is enough for Girdlestone to "see in Beethoven's [Piano Concerto No. 4] a spiritual offspring of Mozart's [K. 453]", when actually there isn't the slightest stylistic or expressive resemblance between them. And the fact that bars 65-8 of Mozart's work and bars 60-2 of Beethoven's go from a D to a G and back to the D is, for Girdlestone, a "likeness" that makes Beethoven's passage "a variation of Mozart's", when actually the going from D to G to D, in the two passages, occurs within two markedly different sequences of notes that are given markedly different shapes by the markedly different rhythms—the differences being enough for the passages to be obviously unrelated and dissimilar.

and then answering the woodwinds' phrases in an increasingly florid style with great expressive intensity. Eventually the orchestra takes over, building up to the next appearance of [1]—this one, more forceful, from the piano.

And again, after the pause, the piano takes off, beginning with this powerful statement:

The sequence becomes calmer, once more bringing in [2a] from the orchestra's first sequence, but then continuing with forceful [3], which the piano carries to a conclusion—at which point the orchestra builds up to the pause on the anticipatory six-four chord that is the signal for the piano's entrance alone to reflect in a cadenza on the happenings of the movement.

The end of the cadenza brings the orchestra in with the last appearnce of [1], beginning what Girdlestone recognizes as the "finest [bars] in the movement". But then, quoting this final appearance as follows:

he says that it is no longer a question, but finds its answer in [4] of the orchestra's first sequence. And this is an antonishing misreading of the passage and missing of its point. For the initial statement that has attained no conclusion each time it has been heard is what is played by the flute and oboe in [8], with the affecting changes in the melody (marked by asterisks) and underlying harmony; and the tremendous thing that happens now is that this time, at last, the statement does attain a conclusion—the few measures added in [8] by the piano, which, after all that has happened in the movement, constitute an overwhelming conclusion of summation, resignation, sublimity. Those few measures of the piano are the climax of the movement, achieved by another master-stroke.

In the Andantes of the Concertos K. 482 and K. 453 Mozart offered his audiences impressive examples of great cumulative force and impact being built up by elaborately, intricately organized musical structures; in the Andante of K. 467 he offered something even more remarkable—an example of equal cumulative force and impact being built up by a musical structure that was quite simple. Again the orchestra plays first in preparation for the entrance of the solo piano, stating a succession of ideas; then the piano enters to discourse for the rest of the movement on these ideas and additional ones that it introduces as it goes along. Up above the piano's melodic discourse moves on—with tensions and involvements which build up cumulative force—endlessly and with the utmost calm; while down below there is the agitation of the faster-moving triplets, the powerful effect of the plucked bass-notes; and at certain points the melody's expressive effect is intensified by poignant phrases of the orchestra's woodwinds. All these, working together, cause the movement, as it proceeds and develops, to build up tremendous tension and impact, so that with all its quiet it is one of Mozart's most powerful utterances, and this power achieved in quiet makes it one of the most extraordinary pieces of music he ever wrote. *(The Sewanee Review,* Fall 1965)

Rudolf Bing's Metropolitan

Bernard Shaw's explanation of his failure to attend a performance of Brahms's *German Requiem* was that listening to this work was one of the sacrifices which should not be demanded twice from any man; and that was the way I felt about Strauss's *Die Frau ohne Schatten*, which the Metropolitan produced this year. But I contend further that there are some sacrifices which should not be demanded of a critic even once; and after Samuel Barber's opera *Vanessa*, nothing could get me into the Metropolitan for his *Antony and Cleopatra*. This was true even before I read what was written about it; and when I read Stanley Kauffmann's report in *The New Republic* I accepted his characterization of the work as a "pseudo *Aida*" produced by the "unmemorable operatic talent" that had produced "the MGM soundtrack score of *Vanessa*", since I knew that pseudo music in every genre was what Barber had produced all along—not only the pseudo opera *Vanessa*, but the pseudo Piano Sonata, and the pseudo Piano Concerto that placed him, for the ears of Winthrop Sargeant, "head and shoulders above all the other American composers whose work one is likely to encounter on current symphonic programs".

Commenting further, Kauffmann thought the primary point was not Barber's lack of talent but "the very idea of commissioning an American opera". For "there has never been an American opera composer of consequence; there is no American operatic tradition of consequence; and, if socio-cultural history and portents can be read, we can say flatly there never will be an American opera of consequence." Certainly, nothing done by Virgil Thomson's predecessors provided him with a point of departure, a basis, for what he did; but with

30

complete disregard of Kauffmann's Law, Thomson's own gifts enabled him to envision his own untraditional objectives and realize them in two operas of consequence, *Four Saints in Three Acts* and *The Mother of Us All*. Nor were they the only ones: Aaron Copland's *The Tender Land* was another work of consequence in which he certainly did not take off from the worthless American operas that preceded his at the City Center and the Metropolitan, but which nevertheless, in the absence of an American operatic tradition, he was able to achieve with his own gifts. And so I don't think we can say flatly that such exercises of personal gifts will not occur again and will not give us additional operas of consequence—even, possibly, an opera in a style suitable for the Metropolitan, which Thomson's and Copland's operas were not.

Continuing, Kauffmann doubted that Bing and his associates "really believe that Barber is a valuable opera composer and that opera in anything like the tradition of European opera can be written in this country. . . . I do not think they are so ignorant. I think they commissioned Barber *despite* their knowledge of these matters: because they wanted an American work to open an opera house in America." And he was depressed by this act of "empty obeisance to presumed cultural and social demands". But Kauffmann was again speaking with disregard of the facts that contradicted him. The Bing who commissioned *Antony and Cleopatra* for the new Metropolitan was the Bing who produced *Vanessa* at the old Metropolitan, and not only Barber's *Vanessa* but Menotti's *The Last Savage*, and who produced these operas not in obedience to institutional demands, but because he himself believed Barber and Menotti were good composers and their operas were worth producing—which is to say, because he *was* as ignorant as Kauffmann thought he was not. A man with the "knowledge of these matters" that Kauffmann credited Bing with would have said: "It would be fine to open this American opera house with an American opera; but the only good American operas so far are not suitable for the occasion; and I don't know any American composer who would produce a good opera in a suitable style; therefore I must give up the idea of opening the new American opera house with an American opera." It was a man without this understanding who really thought that the idea of opening the new American opera house with an American opera could be carried out successfully by commissioning the composer of *Vanessa* to write

Antony and Cleopatra. Indeed, the point to make about Bing's commissioning Barber to write this huge empty work, and his getting Zeffirelli to contrive for it the monstrosity of designing and staging that Kauffmann described, was that they merely provided the most monumental demonstration of what Bing had demonstrated repeatedly in the past on a smaller scale: namely, that he is a man of no artistic understanding, judgment and taste.

I am, then, challenging the contrary image of Bing propagated by the writers who have accepted his own idea of himself and his operation and have embodied it in the ostensible news reports in weekly news magazines, articles in *The New York Times Magazine*, and profile in *The New Yorker*, that actually have been little more than publicity stories. These writers have used the technique I first encountered forty years ago in a *New Republic* article by Deems Taylor on the occasion of Walter Damrosch's resigning as conductor of the New York Symphony. Taylor's way of dealing with Damrosch's admittedly "listless performances of the classics" was to write: "He can sometimes make Tchaikovsky dull and Beethoven unbearable. But I have never heard him miss a cue, or allow wrong notes"; and also "I have never heard him give a bad performance of difficult or unfamiliar music"—which was to say, Tchaikovsky and Beethoven were at fault for being too familiar and easy.[1] And in his *New Yorker* profile Joseph Wechsberg wrote that Bing "has been known to deal quite roughly with some of his top stars," but that "he has rarely been accused of uncharitable behavior toward singers of lower rank" (who, he didn't add, were not in a position to make accusations), and that one well-known performer had said, "With Bing you always know where you stand, even if the knowledge is not always pleasant." Moreover the rough treatment, as Wechsberg told it, was a necessary disciplinary measure—for example, on the occasions when a singer reported himself or herself hoarse or voiceless and unable to sing. Wechsberg told it as Bing told it, recounting Bing's description of a typical visit to the singer, who is found "sitting next to a phonograph listening to an electronically beautified rendition of the glorious voice", and who "makes desperate, silent gestures

---

[1] (1973) "He never was a Karl Muck," Taylor wrote, "and I don't believe he ever wanted to be one. He seems curiously impatient of ultra-subtle readings of the classics."—by which Damrosch's inadequacy was converted into a defect in Muck.

intended to convey to Bing that . . . there is just no voice left", but who "in the end . . . may be persuaded to make a supreme effort to save the performance. 'Usually he or she sings very well,' Bing concluded acidly." Thus Wechsberg accepted Bing's contention that in the typical incident the singer's claim to be incapacitated was fraudulent. And he described actual incidents of such fraudulent claims— presumably told to him by Bing—in which Bing had acted with justified ruthlessness. I have no doubt that there have been incidents such as Bing described. But on the other hand I have no doubt that there were also the incidents described to me some years ago by a former member of the Metropolitan's administrative staff, in the course of telling me what had happened between Bing and Callas: incidents in which the singer did have laryngitis, and Bing used the decisive method of "persuasion" omitted from his description of the typical incident —that of taking out his watch and giving the ailing singer three minutes to decide whether to sing that night or not sing again at the Metropolitan.

"Bing is not offended," Wechsberg wrote, "when people say the Metropolitan is a dictatorship. He thinks it has to be one." But what my informant said about Bing's treatment of ailing singers, and of Callas, was not that he was a dictator, but that he was a bully. Wechsberg's statement about the Callas episode was "Bing fired Callas in 1958 after a feud that made front-page headlines in the *Times*"— which was not an adequate description of what my informant told me had happened. Callas was to sing in the Metropolitan's first production of Verdi's *Macbeth*; and Bing notified her, several months in advance of her arrival, that he was scheduling her also in *La Traviata*. She replied that she could not sing *La Traviata* in alternation with *Macbeth* because of the different demands they made on the voice. Her reason was a real and good one; she was telling him months in advance; and the situation, said my informant, was one that arose constantly in an opera company and was always dealt with in the same way: one waited for the singer to arrive, and settled the difference privately with persuasion and mutual accommodation. But Bing did not wait, and demanded Callas's submission; and when she refused it, he gave himself the satisfaction not just of the assertion of power in firing her, but of making the assertion of this power a public one. He could indulge himself in this way because he had another singer for *Macbeth*; when he has had to submit to the demands or the misbehavior of a singer he needed, he hasn't publicized the fact. Someone who was present told me how, as a rehearsal was about to start, Leonard Warren stepped forward and informed Mitropoulos that he had his own ideas about how to sing his aria in that act and would expect Mitropoulos to conduct in accordance with his singing—clearly a situation which called for Bing to make an appearance, take out his watch and give Warren three minutes in which to decide whether he would sing as Mitropoulos conducted or not sing at all; but Bing didn't appear. As the incident developed, the orchestra made a gesture of solidarity with Mitropoulos, angering Warren and causing him to express his disrespect for the orchestra, which thereupon left the pit. Clearly another reason for Bing to discipline Warren; but still Bing didn't appear; and it was a representative of the musicians' union who compelled Warren to apologize to the orchestra. Mitropoulos, who had only Bing to protect him from Warren's arrogance, got no apology.

With conductors too, as Wechsberg told it—which is to say, as Bing told it to him—what Bing did, he had reason to do. "He dismissed several conductors when he took over the Met, and others quit. One conductor wanted the right to cast a work (a prerogative that Bing has always claimed for himself); another wanted a première (which Bing was unwilling to give him); and a third wanted not only to conduct but to produce a very popular work (which seemed to Bing too much of a risk)." Casting—since it involves musical judgment, and Bing is not a musician—is something one would expect a conductor to have a say about; and it is extraordinary that Bing should claim all casting as his exclusive prerogative—one feature of the dictatorship that has him "personally involved in every major or minor decision" in the company's operation. But as Wechsberg told the history of opera, an opera director who was not a musician but nevertheless made the musical decisions had historical logic and inevitability, and made sense in the opera house of today. The era of singer-dominated performance was followed by that of conductor-dominated performance, inaugurated by Toscanini; but Toscanini, according to Wechsberg, "was interested mostly in the musical aspects of the lyric theater," and it was only in the early nineteen-twenties that stage direction became important, leading to the designer- and director-dominated performance of recent years. Hence, according to Wechsberg, there was need now of someone who was neither a conductor nor a designer or director to mediate disinterestedly between the two. Moreover opera production had become so complex that "the managing of a modern opera house requires not only artistic judgment and a sound knowledge of music but also a high degree of executive skill," which a conductor or stage director is not likely to have. Hence the present-day opera director—exemplified by Sir David Webster of London's Royal Opera and Rudolf Bing of the Metropolitan—who is neither a musician nor a stage director but a skillful administrator with the necessary knowledge of music and artistic judgment. And Bing was pictured as the administrator who not only ran the company's business operation efficiently and imposed on singers and conductors a discipline that substituted order for the earlier confusion, but was able to exercise over-all artistic direction—one important exercise of it having been his improvement of the staging of opera at the Metropolitan by bringing in prominent designers and directors from the dramatic theater, making them equal in rank and authority with the conductor, and retaining the final authority needed to decide conflicts between them.

Actually, Sir David Webster is General Manager of the Royal Opera with Georg Solti as Musical Director; and in the past Toscanini was Musical Director of La Scala with Gatti-Casazza handling its administration. Actually, too, the visual elements of an opera production had great importance for Toscanini and received his close attention; and he had strong convictions about them which not only were evident in his own productions but were expressed in his occasional comment on others. When he saw, in a 1934 production of *Falstaff* in Vienna, a first scene of Act 3 which had Falstaff warming himself not in the sun outside the inn but under a mountain of bedclothes in his bedroom, he denounced the *"criminali"* who changed the work of Boito and Verdi; and when that bedroom appeared again in Salzburg the following summer at a rehearsal of the production he was to conduct, he walked out of the theater, and came back only when the correct outdoor set was substituted. In other words, he applied to the visual elements the principle of strict fidelity to the composer's wishes that governed his treatment of the music. And his 1929 La Scala production of *Lucia di Lammermoor* exhibited in its naturalistic scenery, as well as in the musical performance, a fidelity to the style and conventions of the work which indicated his belief that it was possible and right to make such a work valid and convincing to an audience of today by respecting and giving effect to its own style and conventions—as against the contention that for an audience of today one had to give such a work a contemporary scenic style embodying a contemporary idea of its dramatic content (no more necessary with an opera of Donizetti than it is to modernize a novel or a painting of the same period). Moreover, Toscanini's 1929 *Lucia* exhibited in its stage action an understanding of the conventions imposed by the very nature of *dramma per musica*, as against drama through the words and action of a play—the most important being that an aria or ensemble in an opera is a point where action stops and music takes over. So with the *Falstaff*, *Fidelio*, *Meistersinger* and *Magic Flute* that Toscanini conducted in Salzburg: they were made unforgettable not only by his conducting of the music but by the staging that embodied his correct understanding of what the very nature of opera dictated in its presentation on the stage.

Undoubtedly, then, and rightly, Toscanini would have denounced what has been done by some of the stage designers and directors brought in by Bing who have regarded their task as being not to employ their skills in the effective realization of the explicit requirements of the opera, but instead to use the opera for the exercise of their skills in a striking or bizarre piece of stagecraft, without regard for the opera's requirements that it sacrificed. An early and extreme example was the Elson unit set for the 1953 *Don Giovanni*—with its house front on each side, and its rising and curving ramp filling most of the stage and impeding most of the action—which resulted in sheer absurdities like Don Giovanni giving a ball or having supper in the middle of the street. A recent one is the Dupont permanent sloping platform of the current *Faust*, which works for the several outdoor scenes but not for the three interior scenes of the last act, so that Marguerite is seen not hiding from her neighbors in her house but walking about in her garden, and finally imprisoned in a huge stage space open on all sides. In between there have been the earlier Gérard-Brook *Faust*, relocated in the early nineteenth century, with its garden scene lacking the house which Faust addressed as *"demeure chaste et pure"*, and which the action required, so that one did not, at the end of the scene, see Marguerite enter the house, open a window and sing dreamily of her love, while Faust watched and listened outside, but instead saw her merely hurry off the stage and then return to it; the Berman-Graf *Forza del Destino* with its three Velletri scenes combined into one, with the absurd result that one saw Don Alvaro carried out on a stretcher badly wounded, and a few minutes later saw him walk back into the same scene fully recovered; the Neher-Ebert *Macbeth* with its last two scenes combined into one, with the result that Macbeth heard the women's cries at Lady Macbeth's death not as he sat in an adjoining room but as he stood on the plain outside the castle; the modern-style arrangement of bare platforms and ramps in the final scene of the O'Hearn-Merrill *Die Meistersinger*, incongruous after the naturalistic sets of the preceding scenes, and necessitating changes in the stage action that made it less effective. And there have been productions exemplifying the tendency of present-day designer-director teams to concern themselves with ideas that never entered the composer's head, while they disregard his explicit demands. One of these was the Heinrich-Rennert *Salome* in which the "passage of the huge, carbuncular moon" was intended to suggest "not only the decline of Jochanaan's fortunes but the moment of transition from a pagan to a Christian era"—this seemingly requiring Herod to leave his banquet hall to sit not on the terrace of his palace, as Strauss writes, but in its back yard (a clutter of platforms and steps on which the sitting and all the action was difficult), and Narraboth to kill himself some distance away from Salome, in disregard of Strauss's directions and the dramatic point they are intended to achieve—that Narraboth's act is done before the eyes of Salome which, fixed on Jochanaan, do not see it. Another was the Colonnello-Wallmann *Lucia*, with its enormously cluttered stage pictures whose "architectural framework . . . mounted on mobile platforms which create continuously changing ambience and perspective [symbolize] the irrational element which parallels the transformation and final disintegration of Lucia's mind," and with its excessive stage activity introduced by the director, a former dancer and choreographer who, like the directors Bing brought in from the dramatic stage, did not understand that in opera action must stop when an aria or ensemble begins, and who—in the mistaken belief that there must be something happening on the stage at every moment—converted the famous sextet into an accompaniment for the continuing movement and grouping of lords and ladies and soldiers.

Toscanini would have denounced not only the designers and directors who presumed to change the composers' works in these ways, but the man who made it possible for them to do so. For Bing's operation has not been what he got Wechsberg to describe it as—the Diaghilev-like dictatorship of a man of artistic understanding and taste whose mediation between conductors and designer-director teams has produced examples of musical performance and stage production in ideal harmony. The productions I have cited show that he has sided with the designers and directors even in their worst extravagances; and the monstrosities he has presented prove him to be not only without understanding of the special requirements of opera but without taste. If anyone points out that there have been occasional beautiful productions, and argues that the man who gave us the marvelous 1957 *Don Giovanni* designed by Eugene Berman must be conceded to have taste, my answer is to insist that the man who gave us the monstrous 1953 *Don Giovanni* must be conceded to be without taste, and to point out how it was possible for this man without taste to give us the marvelous *Don Giovanni* of 1957. For as I see it, what Bing has done has been to engage all the prominent designers around, good and bad, and accept whatever they did—now something as monstrous as the *Don Giovanni* of 1953, and now something as beautiful as the one of 1957; or now this beautiful *Don Giovanni* and now the hideous *Salome;* or the incongruous mixture of naturalistic and modern styles in one production of *Die Meistersinger.* The same with the stage directors whom Bing has brought in from the dramatic theater, and from whom he has accepted now something as good as the Webster *Don Carlo*, and now something as bad as the *Lucia* or the Zeffirelli *Falstaff* or the Ritchard *Marriage of Figaro.* And the lack of understanding of the special requirements of operatic staging that caused Bing to accept these major examples of constant and excessive stage activity has led him to accept bad details of that kind. Toscanini—who would have understood that during *Non ti fidar*, in *Don Giovanni*, the audience's attention must be concentrated on the phrases that are being sung by the four principals in the foreground—would not have tolerated any stage business in the background that distracted this attention; but Bing, who doesn't understand, did tolerate the distracting coming and going of peasants during this piece. Toscanini—who would have understood that Verdi wrote the Prelude to Act 1 of *Aida* for the audience to hear while the curtain was down, to prepare its mind for what it would see and hear when the curtain rose—might have allowed the first scene to become visible during the piece, but would not have tolerated the distracting procession of priests across the stage; but Bing, who doesn't understand, did tolerate this meaningless and distracting stage activity. (And one didn't have to have the understanding of Toscanini to perceive and correct two absurd details after the curtain rose: Rhadames's exclaiming *"Dessa!"* supposedly at the sight of Aida, when she hadn't yet appeared on the stage, and then her entering at a point different from the one he was looking toward; but the Bing eye, for which we have been told no detail is too small, didn't perceive and correct these two.)

The Bing method applied to singers brought to the Metropolitan now a celebrated singer as outstanding as George London or Renata Tebaldi or Carlo Bergonzi, and now one as appalling as Mario Del Monaco. It didn't bring the celebrated Elisabeth Schwarzkopf until she had little left to make her worth bringing; and one news magazine reported her as saying that Bing had indeed invited her some years earlier, but to sing Tatiana in Tchaikovsky's *Eugene Onegin* in English—which, if true, provided only the most ludicrous example of his lack of competence for the casting he maintained as his prerogative. Another example was the choice he finally made of the singer for Tatiana: Lucine Amara, who was wholly unsuited for the role in appearance, personality and voice. Other major examples I recall were the repeated assignment of Margaret Harshaw to the role of Donna Anna, for which her unpleasant voice and her lack of the agility required by *Non mi dir* were disastrous; his similar persistence with the inadequate Mary Curtis Verna. And he continued for years to assign Zinka Milanov to Verdi roles for which she had only the tremulous, unpleasant shreds of her once beautiful voice.

As for repertory—outside of the main body of standard repertory, that is—Bing did give us Stravinsky's *The Rake's Progress*, Berg's *Wozzeck* (but in English), Musorgsky's own *Boris Godunov*. But he later replaced this *Boris* with the Shostakovitch version, which falsified Musorgsky's work no less than the Rimsky-Korsakov. And he produced other works beside Barber's *Vanessa* and Menotti's *The Last Savage* that should not have been produced: Flotow's *Martha*, which I doubt that one can hear even in a German opera house today; Cilèa's *Adrianna Lecouvreur*, for which Tebaldi's insistence was not sufficient justification; European operettas—Johann Strauss's *Die Fledermaus* and *The Gypsy Baron*, Offenbach's *La Périchole*—which are no more the proper business of an opera company than are *Show Boat* or *Brigadoon*. In reply to the newspaper reviewers who criticized him for not producing contemporary works, as even the smaller European opera companies did, Bing pointed out that government subsidies enabled the European companies to produce works which only a small part of the public was interested in, whereas the Metropolitan, without such subsidy, could invest the cost of a new production only in an opera which the public's interest would keep in the repertory eight or ten seasons. But what he said the Metropolitan couldn't invest in a contemporary work it invested in *Martha*, *Adrianna Lecouvreur* and *The Gypsy Baron*, which couldn't have been expected to last longer than the one season they did.[2]

What Bing did last September was entirely in line with what I have been describing. An opera director with knowledge and taste, looking for something special with which to inaugurate the new opera house, might have remembered Berlioz's *The Trojans*[3] and realized that this was exactly the work for the occasion. Bing carried his operation of the previous sixteen years to its logical climax by inaugurating the house with the Zeffirelli production of Barber's *Antony and Cleopatra*. (*The Hudson Review*, Spring 1967).

[2](1973) Incredibly, *Martha* and *Adrianna* were performed again.
[3](1973) It turned out later that Bing considered *The Trojans* "a bore".

The Imagined World of
Virgil Thomson

A clipping I have held onto all these years has the replies of the two American composers whom Olin Downes, early in 1934, asked for "their opinions apropos of last Sunday's leading article on this page, on the becoming attitude of the American critic toward the native composer and his works". Roger Sessions wrote about the relation of the critic to the composer; Virgil Thomson wrote about the proper way to set declamation in opera. And a few years ago there was occasion for me to speak of this and to comment that it enabled me "to understand those articles and reviews that have no connection with the concert or book they are supposedly concerned with. Thomson writes about what is in his mind at the moment; and it's up to the pianist or author to adjust himself to that—not the other way around." I mention this because it now turns out, in his memoirs, *Virgil Thomson*, to be true not only of his writing about music but of his writing about everything: he lives in, deals with, and writes about a world imagined as he would like it to be.

Not entirely, of course: the fascinating letters Thomson quotes—the ones from Gertrude Stein about their collaborations, the one from John Houseman about Orson Welles—actually were written by Stein and Houseman; some of the things Thomson says happened in the creation and production of *Four Saints in Three Acts* did happen. That is, in a matter like *Four Saints* Thomson *could* make reality conform to the idea of it in his mind. In 1926 he decided that Gertrude Stein was the one to write an opera libretto for him:

> My theory was that if a text is set correctly for the sound of it, the meaning will take care of itself. And the Stein texts, for prosodizing in this way,

41

were manna. . . . You could make a setting for sound and syntax only, then add, if needed, an accompaniment equally functional. I had no sooner put to music after this recipe one short Stein text than I knew I had opened a door. I had never had any doubts about Stein's poetry; from then on I had none about my ability to handle it in music.

In the winter of 1928-29, in New York, at a party where he played and sang the completed *Four Saints*, he met a Miss Ettie Stettheimer, who invited him to meet her sisters, one of them a painter; and "as soon as I had seen Florine's pictures . . . I knew we shared a view about the stage. So I besought her, should there be an American production of *Four Saints*, to consider designing its costumes and scenery." In 1932-33, during a visit to a small joint in Harlem "where Jimmy Daniels was just starting out as host and entertainer . . . I turned to Russell, realizing the impeccable enunciation of Jimmy's speech-in-song, and said, 'I think I'll have my opera sung by Negroes.' " Also, "I had early invited Alexander Smallens to conduct the work," and "I had looked around too for a stage director; but none of the old and famous ones was interested, and the young ones seemed to have no prescience about opera. . . . When I went back to Paris in April, I knew my décors and my music were in good hands; but I still had no idea what director or choreographer would add movement." However, in London that summer he met young Frederick Ashton, who was beginning to do choreography for the Sadler's Wells company, and for whom he played and sang *Four Saints*. " 'Could you imagine staging my opera?' I asked. 'O yes, and with delight,' was the reply." And back in New York in the fall of 1933, he met John Houseman, for whom he played the opera, and whom he told about his wish for a Negro cast and about Miss Stettheimer. "Did he think the work would interest him to stage? 'It would be fun to try,' he answered." All as un-Lincoln-Center-like as it could be; and it achieved not only the delightful work itself but the production that was one of the great events in American theater history.

On the other hand, somewhere around 1926 Thomson made "the very simple discovery that the classic masters, in terms of logic and syntax, did not always quite make sense," which "meant that I could . . . cultivate the discipline of spontaneity" in what developed into "the long-line nonrepeating continuity of the Violin Sonata and the First String Quartet". In these and other works of that period he felt, in 1932, he "had either broken new ground or brought something to term." Here Thomson could have his private idea of the music of the classic masters and of his own music, but he could not change the realities of the music as they were apprehended by others. For their ears the classic masters continued to make excellent sense in terms of logic and syntax; which is to say that what, in classical sonata form, Thomson later described as "the static rhetorical returns and recapitulations" that "depersonalize the expression", and the "structural continuity devices" that distract listeners' attention "from whatever direct and personal communication the music may have to offer them", were for others part of an ordered use of the medium for the purpose of "direct and personal communication". And to my ears—as I wrote once after a performance of the Violin Sonata—the "long-line nonrepeating continuity" that Thomson substituted for those devices sounded like a free association which produced a flow of undifferentiated, unshaped material without coherence. (I am, like Thomson, speaking here only of his internally organized instrumental works, not of his music organized by words.)

So with Thomson's writing about music. In his account of what he achieved *in* the writing, and *with* it, Thomson, like God, sees "everything that he . . . made, and behold, it was very good." And he can have this private idea, but he cannot change the known or ascertainable realities for others. Thus, in his mind his first book, *The State of Music* (1939), and the first collection of his *Herald Tribune* reviews and articles, *The Musical Scene* (1945), received "rave reviews". Having no recollection of any such enthusiasm for *The State of Music*, I looked up the review in *The Times Book Review*, which turned out to be a characteristic leaden performance by Howard Taubman: "Mr. Thomson has broken down the sources of a composer's income into a careful set of categories. . . . Mr. Thomson attempts to discover how each of these income-sources affects a composer and his music. He hits the mark often. Occasionally he is betrayed into some large generalization. . . . " But the review of *The Musical Scene* I didn't have to look up; I had described it in *The Nation:* "Reviews of books sometimes provide performances that are interesting or amusing to watch. Thus, Virgil Thomson's *The Musical Scene* being condescended to, in *The Times*, by Mark Schubart, and Mr. Schubart reminding the reader to take the book's contents as only the opinions of Mr. Thomson—that is something to hug one's sides over." As for my own *Nation* reviews, I recommended *The State of Music* "to a reader who has, to start with, a grasp of the facts about the musical world that will enable him to know when Thomson's acute, ironic, witty, eccentric mind offers a keenly and amusingly perceptive comment on the facts, and when, on the other hand, the writing is to be taken as a mere exercise of an acute, ironic, witty, eccentric mind, and as such enjoyable or fantastic or unintelligible." And concerning *The Herald Tribune* writing in *The Musical Scene* I wrote: "There are . . . in this volume constructions of thought . . . which deal with . . . things as they exist in a private world of Thomson's, and which are so remote from the realities of our world as to be worthless, and in some instances not to make coherent, understandable sense even in their own terms. . . . But there are also . . . occasions when his sharp ears and mind are applied to what is actually happening . . . and the results are superb pieces of criticism." I might say that I made the same comment about the collections of further *Herald Tribune* writing, *The Art of Judging Music* (1948) and *Music Right and Left* (1951); and I repeat it about the pieces reprinted from the earlier volumes, and the additional ones from Thomson's last years on *The Herald Tribune*, in the recently published paperback, *Music Reviewed*. Thomson evidently sees that they are all very good; but an outsider distinguishes the accurate descriptions of the singing of Flagstad and Tourel that he approved of, the playing of Heifetz and Horowitz that he disapproved of, from the writing like *The Toscanini Case*, whose inventions and schematizations have today no more connection with what the listener experienced as the realities of Toscanini's work than when Thomson first published them. And what I add this time is that the outsider is astonished to find these inventions and schematizations repeated as though the facts that contradicted them had never been pointed out, and is similarly astonished by the repetition of other such pieces of idea-spinning whose contradiction by fact was pointed out. It appears that Thomson—whose method of demonstration is mere pronouncement—deals with disproof by mere repetition of the pronouncement (though on one occasion[1] it caused him to lose

---

[1] (1973) In his *Herald Tribune* review of my book, *Conversations With Toscanini*, presumably because of my evaluation of his writing about Toscanini.

his temper in print in a manner anyone else would recall with embarrassment).

The "rave reviews" of *The State of Music* and *The Musical Scene* are only the first of the many items requiring correction in Thomson's account of his operation as a music critic. It wasn't all as good as he sees it; and the reason appears—without his realizing it—in his reply to Mrs. Ogden Reid, owner of *The Herald Tribune*, when she asked him what he thought of the idea of becoming its music critic: "I replied that the general standard of music reviewing in New York had sunk so far that almost any change might bring improvement. Also I thought perhaps my presence in a post so prominent might stimulate performance of my works." As it turned out, he did bring improvement to the reviewing of music: when he was content to do the reviewer's job of describing and evaluating what was placed before him he produced the only newspaper reports worth reading. But his second statement to Mrs. Reid reveals that he saw the *Herald Tribune* post as an opportunity to achieve other ends besides improved reviewing; and when his eye was on those ends, rather than on the object before him, he often produced what was not worth the paper's space and his readers' time and attention.

Thomson sees his *Herald Tribune* operation as that of a "species of knight-errant attacking dragons single-handedly and rescuing musical virtue in distress". More specifically, he felt

> engaged . . . to expose the philanthropic persons in control of our musical institutions for the amateurs they are, to reveal the manipulators of our musical distribution for the culturally retarded profit makers that indeed they are, and to support with all the power of my praise every artist, composer, group, or impresario whose relation to music was straightforward, by which I mean based only on music and the sound it makes. The businessmen and the amateurs . . . became enemies right off.

As I recall the operation, and see it in the pieces collected in the books, it was in addition that of someone himself a public performer, at all times conscious of his audience and concerned with the effect—and on occasion the shock effect—of his performance on that audience. Or rather, not in addition but primarily: his own performance, and his impressiveness in that performance, took precedence over all other

objectives, sometimes without damage to the proper objective of reviewing, sometimes with such damage.

The performances Thomson set out to impress his audience with
included the pieces of fancy idea-spinning about things made up in
his head,[2] some of which he evidently still admires, since he has
reprinted them again in *Music Reviewed*. A typical example was *The
Personality of Three Orchestras*, in which he contended that the differences
between the Boston Symphony, Philadelphia and New York Philharmonic Orchestras reflected only slightly the differences between their
conductors, and mostly the differences between "the cities that created
them and forged them slowly into the image of each city's intellectual
ideals", and specifically that the orchestra of "Boston, the intellectually
elegant and urbane . . . makes thin sounds, like the Paris orchestras,
thin and utterly precise, like golden wire and bright enamel"—concerning which it was pointed out that these thin sounds like golden
wire were what was produced by the Boston Symphony of 1943 conducted by Koussevitzky, but not what was produced by the Boston
Symphony conducted by Karl Muck that I heard in 1917, or even
by the post-1920 Boston Symphony created and conducted by Monteux.
And shock effect was achieved in addition by *The Toscanini Case*, with
its several pages of inventions and schematizations that would need
an entire issue of this magazine to deal with—exemplified by the
"streamlining" to achieve "purely auditory excitement" that was
Thomson's description of the Toscanini style which, for other listeners,
imparted expressiveness to plastically coherent shape.[3] In Thomson's
head it was extraordinary "how little musicians discuss among themselves Toscanini's rightness or wrongness about matters of speed and
rhythm and the tonal amenities"; but in Studio 8H Toscanini's rightness
in these matters was one of the things I heard NBC Symphony musicians
discuss at rehearsals at the time Thomson first made the statement;
and it is one of the things they talk about in *The Toscanini Musicians*

---

[2] (1973) As against what Leontyne Price can be heard to do in her recorded performances
on RCA LSC-3218, there is what Thomson imagines her doing in his notes for the
record—for example, in *Abscheulicher!* from *Fidelio*, her "grant[ing] full expressivity
to the melodic line itself, carefully not placing this expression inside the melody as
a personalized dramatic intensity but rather on top of it as a continued outpouring
in the bel canto manner."

[3] See pages 71-3.

Knew. In Thomson's imagined world "Toscanini's influence lies, so far, chiefly in America. Europe follows Furtwängler and Beecham and great French conductors like Monteux and Münch. It has no need of exchanging their interpretations or their working methods for anything so oversimplified as Toscanini's." But the fact of the real world was what Hugo Burghauser reported about the Vienna Philharmonic—that after its years with the great conductors it had played under, "the orchestra, with Toscanini, realized that this was the climax of every musician's experience."

An example of a good objective vitiated for shock effect was the extension of range in what to review, which led to Thomson's reviewing a number of events that deserved his and his readers' attention—among them Klemperer's concert with a W.P.A. orchestra, an opera at the Juilliard School, the High School of Music and Art, a Bach oratorio in a church, Disney's *Fantasia*, a Broadway musical of Kurt Weill, a swing concert at the Museum of Modern Art. But he was willing to review anything out-of-the-way if he "[got] a lively piece out of it"; and his choice of occasions to review that he was aware were "by the conventions of the time wildly capricious" resulted in reports to New York music-lovers on things like "a Negro preacher in New Jersey who wore frilled white-paper wings over his blue suit and played swing music on an electric guitar . . . a W.P.A. orchestra in Newark, three other suburban and regional orchestras, a *Southern Harmony* sing in Benton, Kentucky, the Boston 'Pops' in Boston, and the Goldman Band in Central Park". Moreover, some instances of excessively extended range turned out to be related to what he had, in his reply to Mrs. Reid, foreseen as the way the *Herald Tribune* post might further his career as a composer. He doesn't quote any reply by her; he writes that his editors "found nothing suspect" when conductors who previously had left his music unperformed now suddenly began to perform it; and he thinks, incorrectly, that he adequately disposes of the question of propriety when he says the conductors "knew that if they played it in New York, I obviously could not review that concert" (they knew also that he would be reviewing their other concerts). What he says nothing about is the occasional Sunday article that began with an evaluation of the chorus of a little college in some remote place, of no interest to anyone in New York, which was not explained until the statement one learned to expect in a later paragraph: "In a performance of this

writer's cantata . . . " Here the college music department that put
on the performance of Thomson's piece did get an article by him about
the chorus; and these articles were a shameless abuse of *The Herald
Tribune* and its readers, which Thomson will never get me to believe
the paper's owner and editors didn't dislike, though they put up with
it.

The concern for his own effective performance won out, on occasion,
over his "support . . . [of] every artist" against the "culturally retarded
profit makers" who were "the manipulators of our musical dis-
tribution"—by whom he meant the two large concert managements
whose at that time almost total monopoly of concert-giving in this
country made it extremely difficult for an artist not on their lists to
get engagements. Thomson warred chiefly with the Columbia Concerts
Corporation headed by Arthur Judson, which, among other things,
compelled its artists to perform only a limited number of familiar and
popular pieces throughout the country. And one of the artists Judson
had dropped was the distinguished pianist Webster Aitken, who had
insisted on playing the greater works of Bach, Mozart, Beethoven and
Schubert and modern works by Copland and Carter. Today this is
standard recital repertory; and today independent managers can secure
numerous engagements for a distinguished pianist who plays it. But
not in the forties; and Aitken had an additional formidable obstacle:
then as now a performer's engagements outside of New York depended
on the reviews of his New York appearances, and most of all on
the review in *The Times;* and in the ten years since his debut Aitken's
every appearance had been covered by the same *Times* reviewer, Noel
Straus, who had attacked his playing in his review each time. Indeed,
at a recital in 1945 at which Aitken played a superb program to a
warmly appreciative audience, Straus couldn't wait to write his disapproval, but proclaimed it during the concert loudly enough for people
in the vicinity to hear. This recital was covered by Thomson; and
as someone professedly anti-management and pro-artist, aware of the
hard time an artist had who was not on a big-management list, and
of the importance for such an artist of his New York reviews in obtaining
engagements outside of New York, Thomson could be expected to
say nothing less than what he thought about Aitken's recital, but to
choose his words with care, in order to give him as much support
as he could, and avoid doing him harm. That is, after a first paragraph

in which he elaborated on his opening statement, "Webster Aitken is a master pianist and a master musician," Thomson could have reported that after "a Bach toccata and a Mozart rondo . . . executed with admirable clarity and with an amazingly straightforward loveliness", Aitken had performed Beethoven's *Diabelli Variations*, which Thomson realized was a highly regarded monument of the piano literature that evidently had interested the large audience in Town Hall, but which he found "laborious, cumbersome, and long", though it "was far from boresome as read by Mr. Aitken." What Thomson did instead was to title his review *Young Man, Why So Serious?*, and to develop this idea in the review, writing that he had been bothered by "what seemed to him an excessive seriousness about . . . both program and playing"; that after the Bach and Mozart pieces, instead of "something lighter to follow up these substantial matters"—as though these two small pieces so taxed the listener's mind that nothing more could be asked of it—Aitken had played the *Diabelli Variations*, which "was far from boresome as read by Mr. Aitken . . . but was tiring nevertheless," and "brought out all the rather heavy seriousness of this pianist's temperament." The impression of program and playing that Thomson gave was one to scare off any concert manager outside of New York; and the performance which achieved Thomson's objective of being interesting and amusing to his readers, had the effect of an additional torpedo into the Aitken career.

On the other hand, Thomson could on occasion refrain from exposing the amateurishness of a philanthropic sponsor of a concert series. It was astonishing once to read a Sunday article on The New Friends of Music in which Thomson quoted its statement of aims and commented: "One cannot deny that the aims . . . are excellent and that the New Friends have pursued them assiduously." For it was impossible to believe he didn't perceive the triviality of some of the aims and the failure to live up to others that were important. At the very least, with his attachment to French music, one would have expected him to point out that the professed aim of offering "complete cycles of composers' works" and "as complete a representation of the literature of the individual composers" had not been lived up to in the "comprehensive survey" of French chamber music "from Rameau to Ravel" that had offered instead a mere work or two by each composer. Thomson's unusual forbearance was impossible to understand. But it is

explained at last: in his memoirs he relates how—when Columbia Concerts Corporation threatened to withdraw its advertising from *The Herald
Tribune* until he was fired—the head of The New Friends, who was
the advertising manager of a department store, informed the *Herald
Tribune* advertising manager that he would match the withdrawn advertising line for line.

Thomson's image of the *Herald Tribune* music department he joined
and what he made of it also requires correction. The assistant reviewers
he found there when he began were Francis D. Perkins, who was
also executive editor of the department, Jerome D. Bohm, who also
wrote the record column, and Robert Lawrence. With them he "ran
a surprisingly efficient department"; and when the war removed two
of them temporarily, he brought in the composers Paul Bowles and
Arthur Berger; when it removed the paper's dance critic, he brought
in Edwin Denby; and later he got me to write a guest column on
radio music, and Rudi Blesh to write one on jazz. In addition he had
a number of outside writers whom he used when they were needed
for complete coverage; "and this pool of 'stringers' constituted a training
corps that comprised my future music editor, Jay Harrison, and the
present *New York Times* staff writers Theodore Strongin and Allen
Hughes." As Thomson tells it, he gives the impression of seeing it
all as justifying his satisfaction and pride; but actually most of it justified
the opposite. For some of it he wasn't responsible: he could do nothing
about the assistants he found in the department, who produced some
of the reviewing whose low standard he had spoken of to Mrs. Reid.
Actually he did make one partial attempt which failed: when he asked
me to write the radio music column he went on to ask whether I
would be willing also to write the record column; and when, taken
aback, I said, "But what about Bohm?," he barked, "That's my affair.
And besides Bohm doesn't care about it." But evidently he discovered
that Bohm did care about it; for I heard nothing more about it from
Thomson. Some years later, with Bohm gone, but with *The Herald
Tribune* unwilling to pay anyone to write the record column, Thomson
had to let it be filled with the rubbish that a member of the editorial
department, Herbert Kupferberg, was willing to write for nothing.
But the appointment of Jay Harrison to the staff was Thomson's, made
with full knowledge of the phrase-slinging that was the Harrison contribution to New York music reviewing—e.g. this about Menotti's

Amahl: "Once again Mr. Menotti has demonstrated that the lyric stage is his destiny. It is a destiny which becomes him as golden robes do a prince." Nor is the Strongin contribution anything for Thomson to pat himself on the back for. Being a composer didn't make Berger a good reviewer; and Blesh's pretentious schematizations about jazz were something *The Herald Tribune* and its readers would have been better off without. That leaves Denby as someone Thomson is entitled to feel proud of having brought to the paper; and Bowles—of whom my recollection is dim—may be another.

This must be added about Bohm. Not only did he lack accurate critical perception and write badly, but he wrote with his personal unpleasantness and he was unscrupulous: even bad singers could get good reviews from him by coaching with him and having their recital gowns designed by his apartment-mate. And in the spring of 1946 there occurred the sensational incident in which Bohm—covering the first recital of a completely unknown pianist, Maryla Jonas, which was attended by a handful of the public and a few second-string reviewers expecting to be bored—reported having instead been electrified by the playing of the "finest woman pianist since Teresa Carreño". The result was a packed Carnegie Hall for Jonas's second recital, concerning which Olin Downes wrote that he had heard "a poet and master of her instrument", but I reported having found the total sum of Jonas's interpretive resources to be an exaggeratedly dramatic alternation between the utmost extremes of soft and loud produced with ludicrously exaggerated visual theatricalisms. This led Thomson to attend her next recital and to write that Jonas "is everything the reviewers said of her last spring. . . . Straightforwardness . . . is the quality of her work that . . . puts it among that of the great. . . . When the musical texture is . . . complex . . . she organizes her melody, her accompanying figures, her bass, her countermelody, and her interjected melodic comments at different levels of loudness, using also different kinds of tone, orchestrating the piece, so to speak, for clarity." And more of same. As it happened, within a couple of years the public had learned better. And the true reason for Bohm's having been electrified by Jonas's first recital became known: on her manager's advice she had had her recital gown designed by Bohm's apartment-mate.

Thomson mentions as an additional achievement that he "organized a Music Critics' Circle (still in existence)." But one wonders what could have caused someone aware of how far the standard of music reviewing had sunk to organize the critics responsible for that low standard in such a group and to associate himself with them in its public acts (I declined his invitation to join it). And the reason seems to me to have been his strong impulse to be a mover and shaker, for which his *Herald Tribune* post now provided increased leverage. The last part of his book is largely an account of his further moving and shaking, which continues to need correction of his image of what it achieved.

Thus, in 1943 he and a French refugee musician put on a series of concerts at the Museum of Modern Art, "all involving rare music, much of it presented by artists so remarkable and so new . . . that our evenings offered a refreshing and particular splendor"—one of the works being Paul Bowles's setting of part of a Lorca play, which Thomson calls "quite beautiful". But concerning the promised "rare music ancient and modern" I wrote in *The Nation* that the rare ancient music turned out to be Mozart's best-known G-minor Quintet and familiar Symphony K.183, Bach's well-known Concerto in D minor, "with the solo part played on the harpsichord by Ralph Kirkpatrick with an ostentatious lack of feeling for either the music or the instrument", and a Little Suite by Handel-Beecham, "too big and with too much Beecham in the arrangement"; and that the rare modern music included "a new Piano Quintet by Martinu, which provided another example of this composer's ability to spin out nothing much to nothing much more," Revueltas's *Homage to Garcia Lorca*, which I found "atrocious", and Bowles's *The Wind Remains*, "described as a 'zarzuela in one act, after García Lorca,' which, as it was staged with painfully amateurish actors, carried incoherence to the point of sheer lunacy."

And when Flagstad, planning to return to this country in 1947, was threatened with picketing,

> looking into the matter to decide my attitude, I learned from the Norwegian Embassy that although this artist had been no patriot, neither was there any juridical hindrance to her traveling in freedom and practicing her profession. I even received from the chief justice of the Norwegian Supreme Court a letter stating this. So I covered in Boston her first concert, incorporating this information in my review. There were minor demonstrations there and a few at her first New York recital. But by the next year she was singing again at the Metropolitan . . .

Actually the demonstrations in New York and elsewhere, which were major—in Philadelphia a disturbance and a stink bomb inside the Academy of Music—continued for almost two years; and it was not until three years later, after Edward Johnson's departure from the Metropolitan, that Flagstad sang there again at Rudolf Bing's invitation.

The self-deluding self-importance attains, in this last section, a fatuous extreme, leaving one, at the end, with continuing respect for the man who produced *Four Saints* and other stage works, and for the man who wrote some of the criticism in *Music Reviewed*, but with no respect for the man who wrote *Virgil Thomson*. (*The Hudson Review*, Winter 1968)

A Plea for
Musorgsky's *Boris Godunov*

Suppose that Mrs. De Witt Wallace had given the Metropolitan Museum of Art several hundred thousands for the acquisition of a painting by El Greco or Van Gogh, and that the museum had exhibited it repainted by Norman Rockwell. This could never happen at the Metropolitan Museum; but the equivalent is on the way to happening at the Metropolitan Opera: Mrs. Wallace has given several hundred thousands for a new production of Musorgsky's *Boris Godunov*, and the Metropolitan's present announced intention is to produce the work with its substance—melody, rhythm, phrase shape and length, harmony—recomposed, and this recomposed substance reorchestrated, by Rimsky-Korsakov.

Nor is this anything new: it is only the latest instance of what opera companies have been doing with Musorgsky's opera for more than seventy years. There is not a museum anywhere that would knowingly exhibit a painter's work altered by another painter; but everywhere opera companies have knowingly exhibited Rimsky's recomposition and reorchestration of Musorgsky's *Boris*. In fact, one reason with which Rudolf Bing—who produced the Musorgsky original in 1953, saying correctly that if one was going to give Musorgsky's *Boris* one should give the *Boris* Musorgsky wrote—now justifies producing instead the *Boris* Rimsky rewrote, is that it is the standard version everywhere, including Russia. This is faulty reasoning: if other museums were to disgrace themselves by exhibiting known fakes, the Metropolitan Museum would not be justified in doing likewise; and even if all the European opera companies dishonor themselves by performing the fake *Boris* of Rimsky, the Metropolitan should act honorably by performing the genuine work of Musorgsky.

54

But such faulty reasoning has always been part of the history of *Boris*. It isn't only what has been done, and is still being done, to Musorgsky's work that is extraordinary; it is also the way people's minds have operated, and still operate, in relation to what has been done. What has made possible a sequence of events in this case that one cannot imagine occurring in any other art, is not only "the generally lower intellectual integrity of men of music" that W.J. Turner once pointed out in this connection, but the lower intellectual understanding and sophistication of the public where music is concerned. Painters, poets, novelists have found fault with other men's work; but I can't imagine one of them carrying this to the point of repainting or rewriting what he considered faulty and issuing this version to the public in place of the original. And if he did do this I can't imagine any argument whether the work was more effective with his changes or without them: it would be taken as a matter of course that they had no validity or legitimacy and could not be permitted, and that the original work must be restored. But Rimsky-Korsakov felt free to make—for performance and publication in 1896—a version of Musorgsky's *Boris* which "corrected" what for him were "the fragmentary character of the musical phrases, the harshness of the harmonies and modulations, the faulty counterpoint, the poverty of the instrumentation". And only a few who knew the Musorgsky original from the 1874-82 performances or the 1874 published score could say what Liadov said: "It is easy enough to correct Musorgsky's irregularities. The only trouble is that when this is done, the character and originality of the music are done away with, and the composer's individuality vanishes." But even Liadov didn't say what demanded to be said further: that such corrections of another man's work were impermissible. Nor did he add that Rimsky's justification of them—that they were needed for the "practical artistic purposes" of effective and successful performance—was belied by the fact that without them Musorgsky's own work had been sufficiently practical and sufficiently interesting to the public to be performed in St. Petersburg from 1874 to 1882.

So again in Western Europe, to which Diaghilev brought the Rimsky *Boris* in 1908, and in this country, to which it was brought in 1912. Until 1924 this was the only *Boris* the public knew from performances and published score; and without knowledge of the original Musorgsky work no one was in a position even to say what Liadov had said, or to question Rimsky's contention that he had made his version to achieve effectiveness and success for a work whose inept crudities had caused it to fail when it was first produced. Nor did it occur to anyone to say what could be said without knowledge of the Musorgsky original—that what Rimsky had done was impermissible, no matter how effective. And the situation did not change, as one might have expected it to change, after 1924. In that year the English edition of Rimsky's *My Musical Life* appeared, with his own contradiction of his contention that Musorgsky's own *Boris* had failed when first produced—the passage in which he wrote that it was produced in 1874 "with great success" and continued to be performed "with uninterrupted success" until 1882, and in which, discussing possible reasons for the cessation of performances, he mentioned "rumors that the opera had displeased the imperial family . . . gossip that its subject was unpleasant to the censors", but said nothing about inept crudities that had created practical difficulties. In 1924 also the famous article of Jean Marnold denied that there had been any inept crudities requiring correction, and revealed the actual nature of what Rimsky had done to make the work conform to his taste: "Rimsky-Korsakov cuts . . . one, two or three measures as serenely as he cuts fifteen or twenty. At will he transposes a tone, or a half-tone, makes sharps or flats natural, alters modulations. . . . From one end of the work to the other he planes, files, polishes, retouches, embellishes, makes insipid, corrupts . . ." And in 1924 Musorgsky's own piano-and-voice arrangement of *Boris*, published in 1874 and out of print for many years, was published again, making it possible to confirm what Marnold had written; to discover that nothing in Musorgsky's writing called for correction; to hear instead that every detail was right, powerfully effective, achieved with complete assurance and mastery, and that in the moment-to-moment invention extraordinary powers operated with an incandescent adequacy for every expressive point they were required to deal with—the powers which, for example, transformed the brutal four-note *ostinato* figure accompanying the bailiff's entrance in the opening scene into the lamenting *ostinato* figure of the introduction to the St. Basil's Scene. If in 1924 it had been revealed that a painter or poet had done to another man's work what Marnold revealed Rimsky had done to Musorgsky's *Boris*, there would, as I said earlier, have been no argument whether the work was more effective with the changes, but instead an immediate understanding that they constituted an outrageous and impermissible vandalism, and a demand that the original work be restored. But there was no such understanding in the case of Rimsky and *Boris*. True, W. J. Turner did point out that what Rimsky had done illustrated "the generally lower intellectual integrity of men of music"; and Donald Tovey did comment that Rimsky's brilliant mastery was that of a "conceited little mind" incapable of "telling a blunder from a stroke of genius or feature of style". But to the rest—opera directors, musicians, critics—Musorgsky's original *Boris*, wherever it was produced in Europe in the early thirties, demonstrated how much the work had gained by Rimsky's revisions; and after a year or two the Rimsky version was reinstated in place of the Musorgsky.

And so again, finally, here. In 1953 it seemed as though the battle for Musorgsky's own work had been won at last. Bing's statement at that time implied an understanding of the principle embodied in an observation attributed to Hindemith: "Music has a face; leave it alone. If you don't like it, don't play it; but don't change it." And his action anticipated Stravinsky's statement to Robert Craft in one of their published conversations ten years later—that "Rimsky's Meyer-beerization of Musorgsky's 'technically imperfect' music could no longer be tolerated": the Rimsky Meyerbeerization performed at the Metropolitan since 1912 was replaced with Musorgsky's own work exactly as he had written it, except for the strengthening of his orchestration to give it the carrying power that Fritz Stiedry, who was to conduct the work, feared it would not have in a theater as large as the Metropolitan. Karol Rathaus, who did this strengthening, was quoted in *The Times* as saying that Musorgsky, in writing for the orchestra, had a "definite tonal vision—'Klangvorstellung' ", and that his invention for the orchestra, "bold, orchestrally conceived and powerful", was "in conception and ideas . . . fifty years ahead of Rimsky-Korsakov"; but that his realization of his ideas suffered from his lack of practical experience in writing for the instruments of the orchestra. And Rathaus claimed that he had everywhere preserved the character and style of Musorgsky's own scoring embodying his tonal image, and had done only what would make it realize this image more fully and effectively. It is now known that when Rathaus delivered the result of his scrupulous work to the Metropolitan, he was pressured by Stiedry into making certain passages more effective in ways similar to Rimsky's—for example, by adding rich string sonorities to the wonderfully imagined sound of Musorgsky's writing for winds alone. But how little these occasional Rimskyisms counted for in the total work and its effect can be inferred from Virgil Thomson's statement in his review of the first performance —that "one knows at all times that one is listening to the composer's own musical thought." For Thomson the quiet passages were "delicious", but there was "no question about the louder ones being all a little ineffective in a big house", and the Coronation Scene lost, he thought, by the absence of Rimsky's grand climax. But others, including myself, were aware only of the unfailing rightness of Musorgsky's lean and sober orchestral coloring for his musical thought, and conversely of the wrongness of Rimsky's orchestral brightness, luxuriance and splendor; and Musorgsky's somber Coronation Scene was an example of this rightness: it was the correct embodiment of a commenting, evaluating image of the scene different from the image embodied in Rimsky's spectacular version.

There were still some in 1953 to whom a hearing of Musorgsky's original—"Musorgsky's so-called original", as *The New Yorker's* Winthrop Sargeant put it—demonstrated how much the work had gained from the revisions of a composer properly schooled in his craft. But the majority opinion showed itself in the audiences that filled the Metropolitan for the five performances in 1953, the nine in 1953-54, the six in 1955-56, the eight in 1958-59—audiences that not only stayed until midnight for the end of the Kromy Scene, but stood applauding and cheering for several minutes afterwards. One would have expected this to settle the matter; but in 1960-61 Bing replaced the Musorgsky original with Shostakovitch's reorchestration and partial recomposition of the work, which falsified Musorgsky's writing no less than Rimsky's, giving it the impress of Shostakovitch's vulgar mind. And now Bing intends to reinstate the Rimsky falsification.

The thinking behind this that is reported to me—in addition to the argument that the Rimsky version is performed by most of the world's opera companies—is that this version must be used because Musorgsky's own orchestration is too thin to carry in a large theater, and the Musorgsky orchestration as strengthened by Rathaus itself includes the occasional Rimskyisms that Stiedry pressured Rathaus into adding—from which the correct decision would seem to me to be instead that the Musorgsky orchestration as strengthened by Rathaus be used *without* the Rimskyisms insisted on by Stiedry. But the initial error in the thinking is its dealing with the matter as involving only alternative orchestrations—its failure to recognize that the Rimsky version is his reorchestration of his rewriting of Musorgsky's melody, harmony, rhythm and phrase structure; and that the Metropolitan can legitimately perform only the melody, harmony, rhythm and phrase structure that Musorgsky wrote, which Rathaus left untouched. It is this genuine *Boris* that the Metropolitan must perform, no matter how many companies perform the Rimsky fake. (*The New York Times*, 19 May 1968)

Postscript 1973 Unaccountably I didn't dispute the statement that Musorgsky's own orchestration wouldn't carry in a large theater, though I could have done so, since I had had no difficulty in hearing it in the Academy of Music when Stokowski had performed the original *Boris* in Philadelphia in 1929. (The Rathaus revision had been clearly audible even in the acoustically deficient old Metropolitan Opera House.) And I forbore to say that what Bing had said in justification of his producing the Musorgsky original in 1953 had turned out later to have represented not *his* correct understanding but that of Stiedry and Max Rudolf, his musical advisers at that time: with these two gone and Erich Leinsdorf in their place, in 1960, he had replaced the Musorgsky original with the Shostakovitch falsification.

The article dealt with only part of what I had been told by George Schick, the Metropolitan's official musical consultant, who in 1965 had expressed to me his whole-hearted agreement that both the Rimsky and Shostakovitch versions were not satisfactory, and to whom I had therefore written in December 1967 to ask why the Rimsky was being reinstated. He had suggested a meeting at the Metropolitan, where, in January 1968, he had shown me in the score of the original *Boris* the revisions written in by Rathaus—among them the additions, at Stiedry's insistence, of richly sonorous strings in passages Musorgsky had scored for winds alone—and had reported to me the thinking at the Metropolitan on this subject. And in March I had written to him the comment on this that I was putting into my article.

I did not discuss in the article another part of what Schick had told me. In further explanation of the decision to perform the Rimsky

Boris, in our talk, he had said it represented the preference of Claudio Abbado, who was to conduct the new production; and when Abbado had had to withdraw and had been replaced by Zubin Mehta, Schick had told me, in March, that the decision which version to use would be made in discussions with Mehta, in preparation for which Mehta was to examine the Musorgsky original and Schick would send him my March letter. Thus I was led to believe, at the time I was writing my article, that the matter was to be reconsidered and there was a possibility of a new decision to produce the Musorgsky original. But because of Mehta's successive cancellations of his scheduled appearances, the discussions had not yet been held by the time I had completed the article; and for that reason the matter remained unmentioned in it. However Mehta did conduct at the Metropolitan in the fall of 1968; and I wrote then to ask Schick whether *Boris* had been discussed with him. Schick replied that the problems of the *Boris* orchestration had indeed been discussed with everybody, and in particular with Mehta, and the unanimous decision had been to perform the Rimsky version.

But subsequently I discovered that Schick—speaking of course for Bing—had told me about everything except the real reason for Bing's reinstatement of the Rimsky *Boris*. And I reported what I had discovered in a letter which, as it happened, appeared in *The Times* on the same Sunday in March 1969 as a letter from Bing stating that "the Metropolitan Opera has never done 'the original' [*Boris*]. In 1953 we did a version by Karol Rathaus. For the new production next season, in consultation with the conductor, Zubin Mehta, we have decided to do the Rimsky-Korsakov version . . ."

Last spring [I wrote] I was informed that the matter of which version of Musorgsky's "Boris Godunov" to produce was being reconsidered by the Metropolitan Opera, and the final decision would be made after the conductor Zubin Mehta had examined the score of the Musorgsky original. It was the conductors Fritz Stiedry and Max Rudolf who had made the decision to use the original in 1953; and apparently Mr. Mehta was to make the decision whether to use it or the Rimsky-Korsakov version now. And in October I was informed that the decision had been to produce the Rimsky. But someone has just reported to me that Mr. Mehta, a few days ago, told him he had had nothing to do with that decision: the singer Nicolai Ghiaurov had made it a condition of his singing in the production that the Rimsky version be used, and Mr. Bing had accepted this condition. This is interesting and even amusing in view of the public image Mr. Bing has established of himself as the disciplinarian who tolerates no nonsense from star singers, and whom one certainly would expect not to tolerate this dictation by Ghiaurov. In the properly administered company Mr. Bing claims to be running, management decides which version of "Boris" to produce, and if one singer is unwilling to sing in it another is substituted . . .

My letter caused Bing to arrange to be interviewed during an intermission of the Metropolitan broadcast the following Saturday afternoon, and to be asked the question which enabled him to repeat that the Metropolitan had never performed Musorgsky's original *Boris*, but, after performing the Rimsky version for many years, had performed the version of Karol Rathaus, then the one of Shostakovitch, and now was going to perform the Rimsky again; after which he went on to say that neither Ghiaurov nor Siepi had been consulted in the matter, and that the decision had been made solely by him after consultation with the Metropolitan's musical staff. In this he contradicted not only Mehta's statement that Ghiaurov had dictated the choice of the Rimsky version, but his own statement in his *Times* letter that the decision had been made by the Metropolitan in consultation with Mehta.

And Bing's letter caused me to write this reply in *The Times*:

Mr. Bing's blatant misstatement of fact in his March 23 letter—"The Metropolitan Opera has never done 'the original' ["Boris"]. In 1953 we did a version by Karol Rathaus"—should be corrected. The "Boris" produced in 1953 Mr. Bing himself then referred to as the Musorgsky original, adding that if one was going to give "Boris" one should give the "Boris" Musorgsky wrote—a statement as true today as it was then. . . . In his review of the performance Virgil Thomson described the version as "Musorgsky's own, revised in a minimal way by Karol Rathaus"—"minimal" being a correct characterization of the Rathaus revisions I saw in the original 1872 Musorgsky score at the Metropolitan a year ago, which were analogous to Toscanini's doubling of winds to balance today's greater number of strings in Beethoven's tuttis. When Mr. Bing today equates this Rathaus "version" with the Rimsky and Shostakovitch "versions" he reveals once again his lack of the understanding he pretends to, which makes him incapable of perceiving the enormous difference between Rimsky's *recomposition* of the *essential musical substance* of melody, harmony, rhythm and phrase structure, and his bright recoloring of this changed substance, and Rathaus's truly minimal revisions, which do not touch Musorgsky's melody, harmony, rhythm and phrase structure, and scrupulously preserve the somber orchestral coloring that they strengthen in the manner of Toscanini with Beethoven's tuttis (except for the occasional Rimskyism that Stiedry pressured Rathaus into inserting).

But if Mr. Bing is without musical and artistic understanding, he is not without the gift of pejorative language in debate, which produces the "extremely vocal groups who, whenever 'Boris Godunov' is performed, start a hue and cry about which version should be used"—Mr. Bing's way of disposing of those with the understanding he lacks, who realize, as he does not, that for the Metropolitan Opera to produce Rimsky's recomposition of "Boris" is the equivalent of the Metropolitan Museum's exhibiting an El Greco repainted by some academician, and is to perpetrate an act of artistic scandal . . .

These exchanges provided confirmation of what I had been told about Bing by people connected with the Metropolitan—that he operated with a regard for truth and decency very much like Richard Nixon's.

The New Higher
Music Criticism

Part of my chronicle in the Winter 1964 issue of The Hudson Review:

I mentioned last winter my reading of a few articles in *The Nation* by Benjamin Boretz, and the fact that even when he wrote about such familiar matters as Schubert's C-major Symphony or Beethoven's Eighth I couldn't recognize what he discussed or find it in the score. Later someone showed me a *Nation* article in which Boretz wrote that Beethoven's Piano Concerto No. 5 "explores a remarkably wide range of associations derived from the opening sequence of proclamatory chords," and that Mozart's Piano Concerto K.491 "is [a] profound and extensive exploration of the entire range of associations that can be generated from a single idea (two notes, actually, first heard as the third and fourth notes of the opening melodic line, and later expanded to full sections side by side). . . ." My friend had been unable to find in the scores the passages in the Beethoven concerto derived from the opening sequence of proclamatory chords and the ones in the Mozart concerto derived from the third and fourth notes of the opening statement; and I couldn't find them either; so he wrote to ask Boretz to identify them, but received no reply. By now it looks to me as though the things discussed by Boretz . . . exist only in the highly elaborated and impressive-sounding Boretz prose in which he uses words for the same effect, and with as little exact meaning, as Father Divine.

Part of a Communication from Mr. Boretz in the Summer 1964 issue:

Mr. B. H. Haggin . . . refers to some observations that appeared in my music columns in *The Nation*, notes his inability to verify these by examining the scores of the works involved, and draws from this the inference that "the things discussed by Boretz that I couldn't find in the scores of (various works) exist only in the highly elaborated and impressive-sounding Boretz prose." Now while I am prepared to accept on faith Mr. Haggin's self-professed score-reading difficulties, I am also obliged to point out that these hardly provide a sufficient condition for his conclusion; and while I am indeed flattered by the remarkable suggestion that my own imaginative capacities are such as to have been capable of inventing all the extraordinary things I am able to hear and describe in the compositions of Beethoven, Mendelssohn, Mozart, and Schubert, I am reluctantly forced to point out, for conscience's sake, that such a supposition is completely, and demonstrably, unfounded. . . .

. . . Let me take just one statement that Mr. Haggin finds unverifiable, in relation to a single work, the Mozart K. 491 piano concerto, and indicate a few places in the score that correspond precisely to the terms of the quoted segment, which speaks of a "range of associations that can be generated from a single idea (two notes, actually, first heard as the third and fourth notes of the opening melodic line, and later expanded to full sections side by side)." The "two notes," to begin with, are the A-flat and G in the strings and bassoons in m. 3; the "associations" are the events that explicitly include the assertion of these pitches or of the interval they determine; and their "range" is from such a simple correspondence as their immediate restatements in m. 5, and in the first oboe at its first entrance in mm. 8-9, to the larger events (elaborations as triads, contour extrema of linear configurations, harmonic determinants, etc.) observable in mm. 10-28, at the cadence in mm. 33-34, in the passage between m. 35 and m. 62, the "deceptive cadence" at mm. 72-73, and the entire large succession thereafter, notably including the cross-rhythmed chromatic line between upper and lower woodwinds, and the unaccompanied opening notes of each of the piano's first two phrases at its entrance in m. 100, as well as the middle voice in mm. 102-3, and the upper voice at the end of the second phrase (mm. 106-7), to name only the most obvious and earliest occurring instances. . . .

If these few examples still leave questions in Mr. Haggin's mind about the reality of the events . . . referred to by the words he quotes,

I am prepared to indicate in Mr. Haggin's own scores all the occurrences relevant to my statements, as well as to supply any other educational deficiencies for Mr. Haggin or any other interested reader on request, for an appropriate professional consideration. But if he then still persists in maintaining the non-existence and non-specifiability of these events, I would most urgently insist that he name the events he *does* find occurring at the places I designate . . .

Beyond this, I leave it entirely to Mr. Haggin's own conscience whether the high moral indignation he so often hurls at the incompetence of others will now be directed at his own, and whether he will now feel impelled to make a consistent judgment regarding the appropriateness of further critical activity on the part of the one culpable individual over whose actions he can at last exert significant influence.

Part of my reply to the Communication:

. . . When Mr. Boretz wrote about the associations "generated from a single idea (two notes, actually, first heard as the third and fourth notes of the opening melodic line . . .)" in Mozart's K. 491, it was because of his contention that an awareness of these associations (the "unmistakable plot lines" of the work) was "a minimum requirement if the music is to hold any interest for either performer or listener"—which is to say that the performer, himself aware of those generated details, must play them in such a way that as they occur in the course of the performance the listener's ear will be caught by them as something he associates with the two notes in the third bar of K. 491—"associates" meaning that the detail presented to the listener's ear at a later point in the work has the recognizable identity which the generating two notes established in the third bar—an identity of physical shape given them by their rhythmic characteristics, and of the musical effect they have in the context of what they follow and are followed by.

Specifically, the A-flat and G in bar 3 are given a particular shape by being the stressed initial half-note and unstressed final quarter-note in the three-four bar; and they are heard with the effect not of something isolated and complete in itself, but of something inconclusive moving on for completion by the F-sharp leaping up to E-flat (two quarter-notes) in the next bar. And specifically, the A-flat and G in bars 106-7 that

Mr. Boretz cites have a totally different shape as the unstressed final A-flat of three (all quarter-notes) in 106, followed by a stressed G at the beginning of 107; and they have a different effect as the concluding notes of a melodic phrase beginning in bar 104. As a result, neither in my actual hearing of the work in the Glenn Gould performance nor in my imagined hearing of it when I looked through the score did the A-flat and G as presented to the ear in bars 106-7 "associate" themselves with—i.e. have or suggest the identity of—the A-flat and G as presented in bar 3; nor do they now after Mr. Boretz has pointed to them. The same is true for me of the A-flat and G that began this melodic phrase in bars 104-5 (another instance cited by Mr. Boretz —the A-flat a dotted half-note, the G the first eighth-note in a scale passage that falls away from the long A-flat. It is true for me of the two analogous successions at the beginning (G and F) and end (C and B-natural) of the preceding melodic phrase in bars 100-3 (also cited by Mr. Boretz). It is true for me of the oboe's A-flat and G in bars 8-9 (also cited by Mr. Boretz), which are the first two in a sequence of three half-notes: A-flat, G and F-sharp. It is true for me of the other details that Mr. Boretz identifies adequately in numbered bars; and I assume I would find it true of the details he doesn't identify adequately even in such bars, or in the swirling Boretz prose about the events in long passages like bars 10-28 and 35-62. For the instances I have dealt with suffice to establish that what he calls associations are any and all instances the eye can detect of an A-flat followed by a G—or any other note followed by a note at an interval of a second —with no regard for the particularities of relation in time, consequent shape, or context which create in each instance not the similarities that would strike the listening ear as associating the pitch succession with the A-flat and G in bar 3, but the dissimilarities that cause the ear to hear it as something which does *not* associate itself with the A-flat and G in bar 3, and in some instances not to hear it at all.

Actually, that is, the pitch succession Mr. Boretz points to in the accompaniment chords in bars 102-3 is one which the ear—with its attention on the melodic statement of bars 100-3—will not notice, unless the performer emphasizes it sufficiently to draw attention away from the melody, and in so doing to distort the passage. And actually, even when the ear does hear the pitch successions Mr. Boretz points to at the beginning and end of the melodic statement in bars 100-3, it hears them—because of their shape and context—merely as part of that melodic statement; and the emphasis in performance that would be required to get the listener to give special attention to them and perhaps to associate them with the A-flat and G of bar 3, would produce a distortion of the shape and expressive meaning of the melodic state-ment. Not only that, but the distorting emphasis which claimed the listener's attention for those pitch successions in bars 100-3 would be taking that attention away from the important dramatic happening in the "plot line" of the movement that it should be concentrated on—namely, the first entrance of the solo piano with a new melodic statement with which it establishes its identity as against the orchestra's. And so with other details of this kind.

I find Mr. Boretz's way of dealing with K. 491 not just amazing but ludicrous; nor is it of course the only thing that is ludicrous in his Communication. . . . A composer whom I encountered in the street last December brought up what I had written about Mr. Boretz and assured me that he was a good musician. I replied that I had been concerned with—and had expressed my opinion of—only what Mr. Boretz had written in *The Nation;* whereupon the composer said plain-tively: "Yes, but they're *all* writing like that [in the magazine *Perspectives of New Music*]. It's the influence of Babbitt at Princeton."

Postscript 1973 Shortly after this exchange in *Hudson* someone told me Boretz was "taking it very hard"; but a few years later, when I was to talk with John Simon about music criticism in a series of his at the Y.M.H.A. Poetry Center, he mentioned Richard Kostelanetz's having told him of Boretz's reference to me as "Haggin—the music critic who can't read score"; and in the course of our public dialogue at the Y.M.H.A. Simon asked me about this alleged deficiency in my equipment. I recounted the exchange in *Hudson*, and said in conclusion: "If he did take it very hard then, it's evident now from what you've told me that he has recovered."

Toscanini and His Critics

The English critic W. J. Turner, who is known here solely as the author of *Mozart: The Man and His Works*, wrote other excellent books on Beethoven and Wagner, and one on Berlioz which in 1934 established the truth about this man and his works that Jacques Barzun sixteen years later claimed to establish, and actually did not establish, with his pretentious *Berlioz and the Romantic Century*. Also, for twenty-five years Turner reviewed musical events regularly in *The New Statesman* and occasionally elsewhere; and a reader recently sent me an article in *The Illustrated London News* of 20 May 1939 which has great interest today.

The occasion for the article was a series of Beethoven concerts conducted by Toscanini; and Turner began by pointing out the supremacy of Italy in European music until "the astounding flowering of German music in the eighteenth and early nineteenth centuries", which made it possible to believe Germany now "had the monopoly of the great and sublime musical thinkers, while the music of Italy was altogether of a lighter character." It also came to be believed "that only in Germany and by German musicians could the profundities of the great German classical masters be understood and interpreted"—in support of which could be cited the many musical performers, including the great conductors from Hans von Bülow on, who were German. But "then, suddenly, there appeared an astonishing phenomenon—Toscanini. The idea that an Italian musician who had studied exclusively in Italy could understand and interpret German masters such as Beethoven and Wagner seemed ludicrous to the average German musician and music-lover." Turner recalled a letter from an Austrian friend about Toscanini's

first appearances in Vienna and the bewildered astonishment of the
Viennese at "an Italian conductor who shows us things in Beethoven
and Wagner that we Germans never heard before". It was inexplicable,
said Turner, only for those who believed in essential national differences
in musical genius, not for those who realized that genius was not
national, and that "it is just this universality, this passing beyond
national frontiers, which marks an outstanding genius." For Turner
there was no doubt that Toscanini was such an outstanding genius
among interpretive musicians: without detracting from the merits and
qualities of fine conductors like Nikisch, Weingartner, Richard Strauss,
Bruno Walter, Furtwängler, Klemperer, he would say Toscanini was
a unique phenomenon.

This view, it must be pointed out, was Turner's response not merely
to Toscanini's Beethoven performances of 1939: it was what he had
been led to by all the Toscanini performances he had heard in the
years since Toscanini's first concerts in London with the New York
Philharmonic in 1930—years in which Turner had developed his
remarkably accurate perceptions on those first occasions. In December
1929 Turner had written of a Furtwängler performance of Beethoven's
Fifth with the Berlin Philharmonic:

> These extraordinary pianissimos, these marvellously manipulated acceleran-
> dos, ritardandos and crescendos can absolutely get in the way of the music
> when they are all produced for the sake of effect, as a piece of showmanship.
> . . . On this occasion [Furtwängler and his orchestra] were quite obviously
> displaying their virtuosity to the disadvantage of the music.

And a few months later, after Toscanini's first concert with the New
York Philharmonic, Turner had written:

> What distinguished this performance of the Haydn symphony [No. 101,
> *Clock*] from a performance of a Haydn symphony by Furtwängler and the
> Berlin Philharmonic . . . not long ago was its absolute directness. . . .
> No conductor I have heard has succeeded in achieving such virtuosity and
> in keeping it always subservient to a purely musical intention. There is in
> Toscanini's conducting no trace whatever . . . of display or showmanship
> or self-consciousness. It is absolutely direct.

And with this directness, said Turner, there was a profound musical
sense. "The basis of music is rhythm . . . and what a beautiful, clear
and vital rhythmic structure Toscanini made of Haydn's symphony!"
Here already was a perception of what Turner continued to be struck

by in subsequent performances, and what—in his article on the Beethoven performances of 1939—he described in the statement that Toscanini's "intellectual grasp of the musical structure of the work he
is conducting is unique," and in this concluding statement:

> It is also a great mistake to think that Toscanini keeps strictly to metronomic
> time. One of his greatest virtues is his subtle variation of tempo; but always
> in the service of shape, and the shape is derived from the rightful expression
> of the music. It is in discovering this rightful expression and hence the
> perfect shape that Toscanini is supreme among living conductors.

Thus Turner, thirty years ago, discussed and clarified an important
issue which has come up again recently: whether the music of, say,
Beethoven has a specifically German character which requires a specifically German style of performance for its realization, and whether
therefore the music is best understood and performed by a German
conductor; and he did this with remarkably perceptive statements about
the work of the two conductors with whom the recent discussion of
the issue has been concerned—Furtwängler and Toscanini.

What Turner discovered after hearing Toscanini in Europe in the
thirties—that among the great conductors of the century he was
unique—had been recognized in this country when Toscanini had conducted at the Metropolitan Opera from 1908 to 1915; and it continued
to be generally believed in the years from 1926 to 1954 in which he
conducted the New York Philharmonic and the NBC Symphony. And
it was discovered by the other Europeans who heard first his concerts
with the New York Philharmonic in 1930 and then his performances
with European orchestras until the outbreak of war in 1939. Turner's
friend reported in his letter the effect on the Viennese of Toscanini's
work with the Vienna Philharmonic in Vienna and Salzburg from
1933 to 1937; and I can add the recollection of the orchestra's chairman,
Hugo Burghauser, that after its years with Weingartner, Strauss, Bruno
Walter, Furtwängler, Klemperer, "the orchestra, with Toscanini,
realized that this was the climax of every musician's experience."

The first authoritative voice of dissent in this country was that of
Virgil Thomson, when he became music critic of *The New York Herald
Tribune* in 1940. It was made authoritative by the equipment of perception and judgment which—on the occasions when Thomson was content
to apply it to what was actually presented to his ears—produced accurate
reports and evaluations that were the only newspaper writing on music

worth reading. But on many occasions Thomson found it more interesting to spin fancy ideas about things made up in his head—not only
more interesting to himself but more impressive to his readers, which
was important to a writer conscious of his own performance in a review
and concerned with its effect—on occasion its shock effect—on his
audience. On the one hand, then, he achieved the shock effect with
reviews of recitals by Heifetz and Horowitz in which he evaluated
correctly the performances he described accurately (by which I mean
that he described what one recognized as the playing of Heifetz or
Horowitz). But what Thomson described as Toscanini's performances,
on the other hand—the performances in which Toscanini, "like Mendelssohn, . . . quite shamelessly whip[ped] up the tempo and sacrifice[d]
clarity and ignore[d] basic rhythm"—had no resemblance to the actual
performances conducted by Toscanini that one had heard: they existed
only in Thomson's imagination. And this was true also of what he
said about them. As against "the marriage of historical and literary
with musical culture" in performance which Thomson said had been
transmitted from Wagner through "von Bülow, Nikisch and Beecham",
Toscanini offered "disembodied music and disembodied theater" without "personal poetry" or "historical evocation"—music reduced by
"streamlining" to "essential outline" for the purpose of "purely auditory
excitement". One of Thomson's explanations for this way of dealing
with music was the poor eyesight that he said compelled Toscanini
to memorize the scores he couldn't read at the concert.

> When one memorizes everything, one acquires a great awareness of music's
> run-through. One runs it through in the mind constantly; and one finds
> in that way a streamlined rendering that is wholly independent of detail
> and even of specific significance, a disembodied version that is all shape
> and no texture. Later, in rehearsal, one returns to the texture; and one
> takes care that it serve always as neutral surfacing for the shape. For shape
> is what any piece is always about that one has memorized through the
> eye and the inner ear. Playing a piece for shape and run-through gives
> . . . the most exciting effect that can ever be produced.

And in conversation once Thomson gave me another explanation: that
having been a conductor of opera until the age of fifty, and having
at that age had to conduct the symphonic repertory with no knowledge
of its traditions, Toscanini had solved the problem by "streamlining"
the music.

What Thomson was doing in all this was using impressive-sounding language to put across imagined points about imagined facts. This I can demonstrate even though after thirty years I still don't know what some of the impressive-sounding words refer to and cannot discover coherent sense in some of the impressive-sounding statements. "The marriage of historical and literary with musical culture" is an idea that I cannot relate to a performance of a symphony of Mozart or Beethoven; an idea that Thomson didn't derive from the actual performances of Wagner, von Bülow and Nikisch, which he didn't hear; and an idea that I didn't find demonstrated in the actual performances of Beecham, which Thomson did hear. What a Beecham performance presented to my ears was a pacing and shaping of the symphony in accordance with his general sense for musical shape embodying expressiveness, and his sense for the particular shape embodying the particular expressiveness of the particular symphony. And that was what I heard also in Toscanini's performance. The shape he gave the symphony was different from Beecham's; but it was a shape embodying the work's expressiveness, not the streamlined reduction to essential outline without texture, detail and specific significance that Thomson described. After thirty years I still don't see why running through a piece of music in one's mind must produce the result Thomson said it must; and I still cannot get any precise idea of "a streamlined rendering . . . wholly independent of detail and even of specific significance", or "a disembodied version that is all shape and no texture", or a texture which is "neutral surfacing for the shape". But apart from this the fact is that Toscanini away from the podium did *not* constantly run through a piece of music in his mind: he constantly read it in the score, and in this unending study of the score was concerned largely with clarity of texture. "I try everything," he said once, shaking his head dejectedly as he pointed to the bassoon part at one point in the score of Beethoven's *Consecration of the House* Overture, "but I am afraid I will never hear these bassoons." And an NBC Symphony musician recalled how, back on the podium, Toscanini would have "just, let's say, the second clarinet and third horn and violas—inner voices— . . . play alone", and make them "sing as if they were thematic, and then incorporate them with the rest of the orchestral texture", and "how beautiful the whole thing became." This clarity of texture he gave to a shape filled with significant detail that was, in Turner's words, "derived from the rightful expression of the music".

It was in Thomson's imagination, again, that Toscanini began to conduct symphonic music at fifty with no knowledge of its traditions. In fact, exactly like his Central European contemporaries, he began to conduct it a few years after he had begun to conduct opera, when he was twenty-eight; and like them he continued to conduct both thereafter. At his first concert in Turin in March 1896 his program included Schubert's great C-major; at later concerts that spring he conducted Haydn, Beethoven, Brahms and Tchaikovsky. He began, then, exactly like his Central European contemporaries, with knowledge of the symphonic literature—knowledge which he had acquired in the same way as they: from the performances he had heard and his study of the scores. Moreover the performances had included those of German conductors: talking in 1944 about the details he had changed in his performance of Beethoven's *Eroica* a few days earlier, he said, "Forty years ago when I play *Eroica* the first time I hear German conductors—I hear Richter—and I think I must play this German music as they play it. . . . But when I play this symphony later I play more and more as I feel; and now I have courage at last to take right tempo."

And so when Toscanini conducted Beethoven's Ninth at the Metropolitan in 1913 Richard Aldrich did not write in *The Times* that it had been the performance of an opera conductor with no knowledge of the traditions of the symphonic repertory who had solved his problem by streamlining the work. Instead he wrote:

> He revealed in the fullest measure the qualities of the great symphonic conductor. . . . Mr. Toscanini met in an unusual degree Wagner's criterion of the *melos*, of keeping unbroken the essential melodic line. . . . In all the nuances of the performance the melodic line was not interrupted; nor in all the plastic shaping of the phrase was the symmetry of the larger proportion of the organic unit of the whole lost sight of. It was rhythmically of extraordinary vitality. . . . There were subtle and significant modulations of tempo, but never of a disturbing sort.

And these words described the later performances of the Ninth with the New York Philharmonic and NBC Symphony that I heard.

Thomson was not the only one who dealt in inventions. In him it was the aberration of a critic capable of accurate perception; but for most writers, who cannot hear correctly what is presented to their ears, such inventions are normal practice enabling them to impress their readers with demonstrations of the perception they lack. Thus, in an article, *The Meaning of Toscanini*, in *The Saturday Review of Literature* of 25 March 1950, imagined distinctions between imagined Toscanini performances provided Irving Kolodin with material for the pretensions to profundity of mind and keenness of musical perception in such pronouncements as "He has lived, it seems to me, by a credo in which the explicit yields the implicit. This may be satisfactory in Wagner, a very explicit composer, or Strauss, an even more explicit one; it leaves considerable areas of doubt in Mozart and Haydn"; or "At best, this seems to me a reassurance that Toscanini, superior as he is to the common mold, is yet within it. For a stiff 'Magic Flute' Overture there is a superbly flexible 'Freischütz', for an overwrought 'Leonore No. 3' a wonderfully proclamatory 'Meistersinger'."

I don't recall any other dissenting voices during the last years of Toscanini's activity; and as long as his performances continued to be heard not even the attacks of an authoritative figure like Thomson produced any change in the public's long-held belief that Toscanini towered above all other conductors. It was not until some years after his disappearance from the public scene, when his greatness was no longer an immediate reality but only a legend, that doubt and attack could be effective. And in this the first authoritative voice to take note of is that of the late George Szell, who provided confirmation of what an NBC Symphony musician wrote me a few years ago: "It is a sad truth that many of the conductors who were adumbrated by Toscanini's brilliance have never forgiven him his greatness." Szell, speaking of Toscanini, clearly thought of himself as being now, with Toscanini dead, the Olympian figure Toscanini had been when alive—an Olympian who could point out inadequacies and defects and failures of his predecessor.

Thus, in a published conversation with Paul Henry Lang in the January 1965 issue of *High Fidelity*, when Lang complimented Szell for his not excessive attention to detail, as against a performance "by a very distinguished conductor of advanced years who brought out every little detail with the utmost clarity—to the point where eventually it seemed mere meaningless precision", Szell replied in agreement: "Because probably the big general line was lost"—which, if it had been true of the performance Lang and Szell referred to, would have made it unique among Toscanini performances. And when Lang asked about the great conductors of the past, Szell spoke with warm admiration about Nikisch and Strauss, adding that there were many others he could mention, of course, and only then citing Toscanini as a man whom "no one could leave unmentioned", but even then with the explanation that "whatever you may think about his interpretation of a specific work"—the implication being that Toscanini's interpretations offered much to men of superior taste like Lang and Szell to shake their heads over in pained disapproval—"that he changed the whole concept of conducting and that he rectified many, many arbitrary proce- dures of a generation of conductors before him is now already authentic history." In the Bell Telephone telecast commemorating the Toscanini centenary, two years later, Szell again expressed this view that Tos- canini's main achievement had been his correction of the excesses of earlier conductors. But in one of the commemorative articles in *The Saturday Review* he was able to say a great deal more. Describing the impact of Toscanini's concerts with the New York Philharmonic in Europe in 1930, he wrote:

> This was orchestral performance of a kind new to all of us. The clarity of texture; the precision of ensemble; the rightness of balances; the virtuosity of every section, every solo-player of the orchestra . . . in the service of an interpretative concept of evident, self-effacing integrity, enforced with irresistible will power and unflagging ardor, set new, undreamed-of standards literally overnight.

With this accurate statement about the brilliance of the orchestral execu- tion and the integrity of Toscanini's musical operation, Szell created confidence in the accuracy of his perception, the correctness of his judgment, the honesty of his purpose in the further comment on the musical quality of Toscanini's performances, his conducting technique, his method of rehearsal. But this comment, actually, revealed at the very least his deficiencies of taste, understanding and perception, and his factual inaccuracy.

It turned out that, although overwhelmed by the orchestral execution in those 1930 New York Philharmonic performances, "we were baffled by certain aspects of interpretation, especially what seemed some relent- lessly over-driven tempi," of which Szell's examples included the sec- ond movement of Beethoven's Seventh, the Scherzo from Mendels-

sohn's *Midsummer Night's Dream* music, and No. 5 of Brahms's Haydn
Variations. As it happened, Szell, in the Bell Telephone telecast,
demonstrated at the piano Toscanini's tempo for the second movement
of Beethoven's Seventh—or rather, what he said was Toscanini's tempo,
which would have baffled, or more probably enraged, Toscanini, since
it was much faster than Toscanini's actual tempo; and if one listens
to the performance he recorded with the Philharmonic one hears that
the tempo is the *allegretto* Beethoven prescribes, which, though understandably surprising to the ears that were accustomed to the traditional
slow tempo, is not in the least over-driven. And on other records
one can discover the same thing about the Philharmonic performances
of the Mendelssohn Scherzo and Brahms variation, and why, though
baffling to Szell, they were considered to be two of Toscanini's most
marvelous musical achievements. And not just in this country: recalling
the Toscanini rehearsal with the Vienna Philharmonic he managed
to sneak into in 1933, the violinist Felix Galimir said:

> Then there were the Brahms Haydn Variations; and THAT—WAS—PHE-
> NOMENAL! It always was probably Toscanini's best piece; there was that
> variation with the winds—the fifth variation—so fantastic; that we'll never
> hear again.

That fifth variation was indeed fantastic, not only technically but
musically; and what made it so was not just the speed of the woodwind
passages but their seemingly effortless lightness. Galimir, a student at
the conservatory, couldn't afford a ticket for the concert; but Burghauser reported that after the fifth variation the usually sedate audience
in the *Musikvereinsaal* burst into applause which interrupted the course
of the performance.

Moreover, though Szell, in his article, again credited Toscanini with
providing "a heaven-sent corrective" for the "mannerism and excess"
into which the style inaugurated by Wagner had degenerated in the
subjective interpretations of his successors, he now added that "the
cure seemed sometimes a little drastic for the ailment," since it ruled
out "spontaneous deviation from the pre-established plan [i.e. of the
rehearsals] . . . the 'spur of the moment', and with it the grace of
the moment." But Toscanini, in eliminating the "mannerism and
excess", was not ruling out what actually could not be ruled out—the
slight deviations at the concert from what had been established at the

rehearsal; and if, again, one listened to his performances on records, one heard the characteristic grace of the moment which no phrase conducted by Toscanini was without. Moreover, this talk of grace and the lack of it was ludicrous coming from a man whose own performances of Mozart, Haydn, Beethoven and Schubert were wholly graceless.

Szell also pointed out inadequacies and defects in Toscanini's technical operation as a conductor. His baton technique, said Szell, was fully adequate for his every purpose; and since he could expect "everything in his meticulously prepared performances [to go] the way he wanted", he didn't need what he didn't have—"the rapier-like readiness for emergencies" that Central European conductors schooled in the repertory system acquired through having to conduct poorly rehearsed or even unrehearsed performances. Szell cited the anxious moments during a performance of *The Magic Flute* in Salzburg in 1937, "when the Queen of the Night slowed down during one of her runs in her first aria" and "Toscanini did not give a millimeter," so that "they remained apart for fully five bars," whereas "any *routinier* could have fixed the matter in a bar and a half." Actually, as that *Magic Flute* demonstrated, emergencies arise even in well-rehearsed performances, and in his many years of conducting repertory in the opera houses of Italy and North and South America Toscanini must have had to conduct an occasional insufficiently rehearsed performance; but in whatever performances he conducted in those years he evidently acquired the "rapier-like readiness" for situations like the one in the performance of Mendelssohn's Violin Concerto described to me by the violist Nicolas Moldavan, when in the excitement of the concert Heifetz began the Allegro of the finale in a much faster tempo than at the rehearsal, and Toscanini at once adapted himself to it. He acquired also the readiness for the crisis of a different kind in the Salzburg *Magic Flute*, concerning which I can correct Szell's incorrect statements, since I was there too that night. The Queen of the Night didn't merely slow down one of her runs; in the ones that followed she became completely erratic; and not only did I for years afterwards remember how, when this happened, Toscanini managed within seconds to get into gear with her erratically changing tempo, but I had this recollection confirmed some years ago by a recording of the broadcast of the performance that I heard at the Library of Congress. A recent rehearing

of this recording revealed why he didn't slow down with the singer
in her first long run: his decision was to wait for her at its conclusion
and then adopt her slower tempo for what followed.

Toscanini's method of rehearsal was for Szell "not very efficient
or methodical", by which he meant that Toscanini wasn't "very articulate intellectually, and I rarely witnessed an analytical, verbalized
instruction." Instead "he would sing a phrase, berate the dullminded
or insensitive, ask angrily for the repeat of a whole section or movement
(not always with improvement), and thereafter whip the orchestra into
such a state of tension and fear that all of a sudden, magically, perhaps
hypnotically, they did exactly his bidding without knowing how and
why." For reasons I will come to in a moment, I doubt that Szell
observed many of Toscanini's rehearsals in this country; and his deri-
sively disdainful description—which left out much that I observed,
and specifically the superb efficiency that can be heard in Toscanini's
rehearsal of *Dite alla giovine* on the Musicians Foundation record
—revealed his lack of understanding of what he did observe, and
what the musicians who rehearsed with Toscanini understood. The
correct instrument, said Moldavan, for a conductor to use to communicate his wishes to an orchestra was not his tongue but his stick.
Verbalized instruction was something orchestra musicians hated and
didn't listen to; and the conductors who talked did so because they
didn't have the rehearsal technique Toscanini had—his knowledge of
how to get and keep an orchestra's attention, how to give it what
he had in him, by which Moldavan meant that Toscanini told the
orchestra what he wanted, even in phrasing of detail, not with words
but with the movement of his stick, which the musicians were used
to and understood and wanted a conductor to use. In this way, said
Moldavan, he achieved in two and a half hours what the other conductors
with all their talking didn't achieve in five; and sometimes he finished
in two. And another NBC violist, William Carboni, explained the
method that Szell considered to be no method and described with
derisive disdain. Because Toscanini was interested in the line of the
music there were many times when "we went through a slow movement,
and he wasn't satisfied with it and said, '*Da capo*,' and we did the
whole thing again, and this time we began to get a feeling of line,
of continuity—instead of stopping every two bars, with some conductors." It was after he had achieved this feeling for the whole that

Toscanini stopped "for little things—to get them exactly the way he wanted them".

Now Carboni's "stopping every two bars, with some conductors" was a reference to what Szell had done at his first rehearsal of Beethoven's *Eroica* with the NBC Symphony in 1941 for the broadcast that was to be his first major appearance in this country. Szell was dealing with an orchestra of virtuoso caliber which had had four seasons of work with Toscanini and, as it happened, had studied and performed the *Eroica* with him the year before. It was expected that Szell would acquaint the orchestra with the differences in tempo, dynamics and phrasing of his own conception of the symphony; what was not expected was his constant stopping for endless repetitions of short passages "in such a way," said Jack Berv of the horn section in a letter to *The Saturday Review*, "that we would never know what a number would sound like until the performance." The musicians began to amuse themselves by keeping count of the number of times Szell stopped and the number of times he repeated a passage; but Toscanini was outraged by a method of rehearsal that he considered mistreatment of the orchestra; and in the twenty-five years in which he had risen to his eminence in 1967 Szell could not possibly have forgotten his humiliating experience in the greenroom after the rehearsal, when Toscanini had berated him indignantly and Szell had apologized abjectly. Though his eminence would have been enough to produce his published condescension to Toscanini in 1967, he had an additional reason: the ineradicable recollection of his humiliation in 1941.[1]

What fortified Szell's inflated estimate of himself in 1967 was the undiscriminating writing about him in the press, which credited him not only with the impressive technical powers that were evident in the marvelous playing of his Cleveland Orchestra, but with the equally

[1] This 1941 experience produced also Szell's contemptuous dismissal of the NBC Symphony—that it was "not an orchestra in the sense of an integrated organism" but "rather the finest collection of virtuosic players money could assemble", which "left more than a little to be desired." This suggested an operation very different from the actual disciplined and precise playing, breathtaking in its energy and fire, in the first years; and it omitted mention of the "integrated organism" which the years of working with Toscanini made of the orchestra. I still remember the rehearsal in 1951 at which Toscanini began the first run-through of the Prelude to Act 3 of *Die Meistersinger* and, arriving at the chorale-like passage for the brass, got from the players, the very first time, chords whose blended sound was like that of one instrument.

impressive musical powers that were not evident in the boring performances of Mozart, Haydn, Beethoven and Schubert he produced with
that orchestra. Especially authoritative were the statements of Winthrop
Sargeant in *The New Yorker*—not only that Szell was "the Old Master,
the guardian of tradition, the vehicle of its communication to the present
generation of conductors," but that "his performances resemble[d] those
of the late Arturo Toscanini more closely than those of any living
conductor"—since Sargeant was a professional musician who had played
in the New York Philharmonic with Toscanini a couple of seasons.
One would have expected someone who had had a player's intimate
experience with the plastic shaping of structure, the sensitive inflection
of phrase, the rhythmic subtlety, the grace characteristic of Toscanini's
performances, to recognize that nothing was less like them than the
steely, hard-driven, graceless performances of Szell. (Nor was there
any resemblance to these Szell performances in the work of the outstanding conductors of today—Giulini, Kempe, Solti, Colin Davis,
Boulez—or even any similarities in their work, that would have constituted evidence of a tradition transmitted to them by Szell.) But
it turned out that Sargeant's two years with Toscanini had left him
with a strange idea of Toscanini's "adherence to rigid and speedy tempos". And in the spring of 1971 Sargeant amazed one by sol-
emnly proclaiming what had been disproved when Virgil Thomson
had said it thirty years earlier—that Toscanini's conducting of
symphonic music was that of a man who had not learned the tradition
of its performance. But before I discuss this contention I must go
back to an article which appeared in *The New York Times* in 1954.

It was an article by Henry Pleasants which began: "With the passing
of Wilhelm Furtwängler . . . the German-speaking world has lost . . .
its most dynamically eloquent representative of the German musical
tradition." Furtwängler, according to Pleasants, had revealed
inadequacies in his performances of Verdi, of French music, even of
Mozart's music with its Italian and French influences; but nineteenth-
century German music, "music of philosophic conception", he had
understood as few others have, and had played "more eloquently, more
movingly, more compellingly" than anyone else, accomplishing this
with his "supreme sense of form". Among the examples Pleasants cited
was the performance of Beethoven's Ninth, which, as it happened,
I had heard several times. In April 1929, after a performance of the

Ninth by Karl Muck with his Hamburg Philharmonic in Copenhagen, I got back to Vienna in time for Furtwängler's performance with the Vienna Philharmonic; and after the steadiness and control with which Muck achieved impressive power it was a shock to hear Furtwängler's constant alternation of slowed-down *diminuendos* to barely audible *pianissimos* with rushed *crescendos* to climaxes, which excited the audience to sheer hysteria at the end. In August 1937 I heard the Ninth that Furtwängler conducted in Salzburg, which—as a result of his preoccupation with now this, now that effect of the moment—emerged without continuity or shape. And in the fifties I heard on records the Furtwängler performance of the Ninth that had opened the Bayreuth Festival of 1951, in which I noted, in addition to the discontinuities produced by the slowing down of *diminuendos* and rushing of *crescendos*, the ponderously slow tempos that were Furtwängler's way of achieving profundity in this "music of philosophic conception". This undisciplined, self-indulgent operation and the shapeless performances of Beethoven and Schubert it produced have come to be preferred, and Toscanini's unfailingly disciplined operation and the perfectly shaped performances it achieved have been rejected, by an increasing number of people, including a group of musicians headed by Daniel Barenboim, whose enormous verbal pretensions have won him the eminence he would never have attained with his meager gifts as a musician, pianist and conductor.[2]

[2] In a *New York Times* interview Barenboim talked about Toscanini's reputation for "playing only what was written in the score. If it said *piano*, he played *piano*. If it said *crescendo*, he played *crescendo*"; and pointed out that Furtwängler too "studied every possible edition of the score . . . to see where every *crescendo* started. . . . But that was only the beginning for Furtwängler"—implying that it was the end for Toscanini. "Unless you can see the importance of the position of that *crescendo* in the architecture of the whole movement, unless you can make the proportion right . . . no amount of study [of the score] will help," said Barenboim—the implication being that this was something Toscanini could not do. In all this Barenboim sounded as if he knew only Toscanini's reputation, not his actual performances, in which one hears confirmation of what NBC Symphony musicians said: that "the printed score didn't tell you everything, but Toscanini believed it was what you had to start with"; so that although "the opening phrase of Mozart's G-minor was marked only *p* . . . this didn't mean one played it in an anemically unmodified *p*: one made the modifications in the *p* that were necessary to give the phrase a singing quality"; and that Toscanini's "sense for proportion . . . was really incredible". And Barenboim sounded also as if he hadn't listened as carefully to Furtwängler's performances as the London critics who had, he said, attacked them as exaggerated, wayward, exhibitionistic—which is to say, *not* rightly proportioned.

Winthrop Sargeant is one of those whom Barenboim has persuaded that his appallingly bad performances are those of "one of the world's important artists of the keyboard" and "the most promising conductor of his generation"; and in one orchestral performance Sargeant noted approvingly evidence of Barenboim's interest in reviving what he called the Furtwängler style. This, he went on to explain, included Furt-wängler's "adherence to the standard nineteenth-century attitude toward rhythm and tempo", which "permitted ritardandos and accelerandos every few bars." A paragraph later the changes in tempo that Sargeant recalled in Mengelberg's and Furtwängler's performances of Beethoven's *Eroica* were "part of the great Central European tradition of performance"; and "the change of fashion" in performance from this freedom to rigidity, he said, was brought about in the mid-twenties by Toscanini. "His performances were masterpieces of clarity, beautiful tone, fine intonation, and dramatic form. . . . But the fact remains that he came to symphony-conducting late in life," without having "served an apprenticeship in Central Europe, where most great symphonic music came from", and therefore without knowledge of "the tradition of interpretation practiced by men like Mengelberg and Furtwängler"; and making "a virtue of necessity . . . he claimed that tradition was unimportant and that he would go back to the notes as the composer wrote them"—which meant that "he gave more literal performances, held stricter tempos, and generally avoided any liberties of expression." But "the notes a composer writes down on paper convey little and leave much to the imagination of the performer or to perform-ing tradition." And whereas Toscanini's genius, said Sargeant, enabled him to succeed in spite of his repudiation of tradition, the conductors who imitated his repudiation but lacked his genius produced an age not only of "literal, unimaginative interpretation" but of monotony: every conductor today gave the one standard performance of Beethoven's Fifth.

Though Sargeant said "the fact remains" about Toscanini's having begun to conduct symphonic music late in life without knowledge of the tradition of its performance, the actual facts of this matter (as I pointed out earlier) were not what Sargeant (and Thomson) said they were; and the same must be said of the rest of what Sargeant stated as fact about Toscanini. Thus, the statement on p. 374 of Carse's *The Orchestra from Beethoven to Berlioz* about two great nineteenth-century conductors—that Berlioz "believed in maintaining an exact and steady *tempo*, without *rubato* or any of the flexibility and variability which characterized Wagner's conducting"—establishes that there was not "the standard nineteenth-century attitude" in this matter that Sargeant alleged, but even then the attitudes of those who believed in steady tempo and those who believed in the opposite. And the two performances of Beethoven's Ninth conducted by Muck and Furtwängler that I heard in April 1929 established that there was not the one "great Central European tradition" exemplified by Furtwängler's performance that Sargeant alleged, but again the different ways of the Central European conductors—not only Muck but Weingartner—who conducted in steady tempo and those who did not. Moreover, just as there were unmistakable differences in the performances that Muck and Weingartner produced in their steady tempos, there were differences in the performances that Nikisch, Strauss, Furtwängler and Mengelberg produced with their variability in tempo: what was controlled by taste in Nikisch's and Strauss's performances was allowed to degenerate into "mannerism and excess" (Szell's words) in Furtwängler's and Mengelberg's. It was not, then, "the great Central European tradition" that Toscanini repudiated, but the excesses and distortions like Furtwängler's and Mengelberg's (he spoke well of Nikisch, and glowingly of Schuch in reply to my question on one occasion). And the repudiation did not lead Toscanini into the rigidity alleged by Sargeant; it led him into "the subtle . . . modulations of tempo" which Richard Aldrich reported hearing in the performance of the Ninth in 1913, which Turner reported hearing in the Beethoven performances in 1939, which I can report having heard in the performances from the mid-twenties to the mid-fifties, and which can still be heard in the performances on records. Aldrich's review acquired additional significance in relation to Sargeant's contentions from the fact that he wrote in 1913 as one who had been hearing Beethoven performed in New York by Nikisch and Muck with the Boston Symphony, and therefore, when he credited Toscanini with the qualities of a great symphonic conductor, must have meant the qualities of conductors like Nikisch and Muck; and that he did not qualify this by reporting any defects in Toscanini's performance caused by ignorance of the tradition Nikisch and Muck knew, but wrote, on the contrary, that in this performance with all its subtle modulations of tempo Toscanini had kept the essential melodic line unbroken in accordance with the criterion of *melos* enunciated by Wagner (in the writing that became the ideational basis of German orchestral performance). As for the rest of what Sargeant said, some conductors followed Toscanini in respecting the composer's text, but others did not; and the untalented among those who followed him produced boring performances, as did the untalented among those who did not follow him; but the outstandingly gifted Guido Cantelli, who was as fanatical as Toscanini in his respect for the composer's text, produced performances, including one of Beethoven's Fifth, that were not only marvelous but fascinatingly different from Toscanini's—something that went unrecognized by Sargeant, who can be impressed by the pretentions of a Barenboim but wrote once that Cantelli's "claims to distinction as a symphonic maestro have always seemed to me rather dim".

What Turner perceived as a listener—that there was "in Toscanini's conducting no trace whatever . . . of display or showmanship or self-consciousness"—was attested to by the orchestral musicians who experienced it directly in their work with Toscanini, and who spoke of having been moved, awed, inspired to exceed their capacities by a way of employing his extraordinary powers that was unique in their experience. To perform a piece of music was, for him, to produce in sound the truth that was on the printed page; to produce this truth was a moral obligation to the composer; in his work with the orchestra he was concerned with nothing but the fulfillment of that obligation; in the performances he produced one heard nothing but that fulfillment. And so it is saddening and disheartening that those unique performances which embodied such purity of intention should have been misused and misrepresented by the shoddy writing—much of it impurely motivated, some of it representing mere pretentious stupidity. (*The Sewanee Review*, Spring 1972, with material from *The Hudson Review*, Winter 1970)

Stravinsky and Robert Craft

Part of the Stravinsky story of recent years has illustrated a statement of Goethe which Randall Jarrell quoted once: "In the face of the great superiority of another person there is no means of safety but love." But another part has shown that some, when faced by that superiority, find their safety in hate—the hate, someone remarked to me, of the untalented for the talented.

The love was seen first in the relation of Stravinsky and Robert Craft that began in 1948. As it happened, I heard Craft's first concerts at that time, and reported the remarkable performances of difficult works of Stravinsky that he produced with only two or three rehearsals of his small pick-up orchestra, chorus and soloists—performances in which he demonstrated his impressive gifts as a musician and conductor in his knowledge of every detail of the works that was evident in what he asked of the performers and was able to get them to achieve. And I heard the concert in which Stravinsky participated, conducting his Symphonies of Wind Instruments and *Danses Concertantes*. It became known that Craft had written to Stravinsky about the Symphonies in connection with the performance he was planning, and that the letter had so impressed Stravinsky that he had offered to conduct the piece himself, and had done so without fee when Craft had told him he had no money.

The understanding and feeling about Stravinsky's music that Craft had revealed in the letter, the gifts he revealed at the rehearsals and concert, made understandable the continuing and close professional relation of Stravinsky and Craft in the years that followed, and also the extraordinary personal intimacy of Craft with Stravinsky and his wife. There come to mind an NBC Symphony musician's recollection of Toscanini sitting in Studio 8H at the rehearsals of young Guido Cantelli in 1949 and "beaming like a proud father", and my own recollection of Toscanini exclaiming "I love this young conductor! I think is like me when I was young." After so many years of loneliness in his idiosyncratic dealing with the music that was his obsession in life, Toscanini was experiencing the happiness provided by one in whom he found a continuation of his musical self, the son in his musical life with whom he had bonds of understanding, and inevitably of feeling, that he did not have with his musically ungifted actual son.[1] And at that very time, as it happened, Stravinsky—grim, prickly, suspicious after his many battles as a ceaselessly innovative composer—also was establishing bonds of mutual understanding, devotion and love in a relation with a young musician that went even further than Toscanini's with Cantelli—to the point where Craft shared the personal life of the Stravinskys as, in effect, an adopted son.

One could understand that this might disturb, and be resented by, Stravinsky's children of his first marriage, and others close to him; but it was hard to understand the disapproval and hostility of people not personally connected with him, among them critics whose proper concern was solely with what he presented to their ears in public. Thus, Paul Henry Lang—a professor of musicology at Columbia University who demonstrated in *The New York Herald Tribune*, for more years than it required, that a scholar's knowledge did not give him a critic's perception and judgment or even the ability to think clearly—wrote repeatedly about the Stravinsky-Craft association as one in which Craft exercised a deplorable ascendancy over Stravinsky; and he was one of those who attributed to Craft's influence what he described as Stravinsky's "surrender of his essential musical personality to an alien faith" in the works he wrote after 1948. It was one thing to

---

[1] Walter Toscanini's resentment of these bonds of his father with Cantelli caused him to assert falsely that it had been Cantelli's dedication, not his musical gifts and achievements, that Toscanini had admired; to write to an English biographer of Cantelli the false statement (published in *The Gramophone*), "You should not in any way state that Guido Cantelli was my father's protégé"; and to obtain from NBC and CBS the tapes of Cantelli's broadcasts with the NBC Symphony and New York Philharmonic and bury them in Yale University Library to insure that they would forever be unheard by the public.

recognize, and regret, that his becoming acquainted with Schönberg's and Webern's music through Craft had resulted in Stravinsky's writing works like *Movements, Variations* and *Requiem Canticles,* which many music-lovers, including me, found as meaningless and unattractive as the works of Schönberg and Webern. But it was another thing to attribute Stravinsky's writing them to an ascendancy of Craft over him which I, for one, found it impossible to believe anyone could exercise over so strong-minded a person as Stravinsky. And shortly before the concert in January 1960 at which Stravinsky conducted the première of *Movements,* an interview in *The Herald Tribune* had given Craft himself an opportunity to say:

> No one influences Stravinsky; he chooses his own . . . absorbs what he thinks is best for his own music. When I met him he knew very little of Schönberg, apart from "Pierrot Lunaire", and the only Berg he knew was the Violin Concerto, which he didn't like. He'd never heard anything by Webern. Understand, I didn't take this music and slip it on his desk. I simply played it at all my concerts and he was there listening. . . . You can't go to Stravinsky and say, "Look, here is some music you should be interested in." He must find out about it on his own. No one *tells* Stravinsky anything.

Craft could have said the same thing to those who were sure he must have written what Stravinsky said in their first volumes of published conversations, and in particular to Lang, who added offensiveness to improbability with his contention that Stravinsky, in those three volumes, was a mere puppet speaking what Craft, "the ventriloquist of God", got him to speak with his "questions, some straight, some leading, some loaded", and that "by now the collaboration has reached a stage where Mr. Stravinsky should use the business designation 'A Division of Craft Products Inc.' " Craft, that is, could have answered that it was no more possible for anyone to tell Stravinsky what to think and say than for anyone to tell him what to compose. Nor did the actual questions and answers support Lang's contention (he did not cite a single example of what he claimed to be describing). "The musical idea: when do you recognize it as an idea?" Craft asked, to make it possible for Stravinsky to say:

> When something in my nature is satisfied by some aspect of an auditive shape. But long before ideas are born I begin to work by relating intervals rhythmically. This exploration of possibilities is always conducted at the

piano. Only after I have established my melodic or harmonic relationships
do I pass to composition . . .

And so with the further questions: they clearly were devised to enable
Stravinsky to say what he wanted to say about himself as a composer;
what he recalled of his life, his musical education, his composing of
particular works, the now historic events he had observed or had
himself been involved in, the famous persons who had been involved
in them with him; what he thought about the music of other composers,
about jazz, about singing music in translation, and about other matters
that interested him. The substance of what he said could be only
his; what was known of him disposed one to believe that the powerful
mind, the sharp eye for human character and behavior, the grim sense
of humor, the gift of pungent statement exhibited in the saying were
also his; and strong evidence for the authenticity of the writing was
provided by the next two volumes in the Stravinsky-Craft series,
Dialogues and a Diary and *Themes and Episodes*, in which the concise,
powerful and grimly humorous writing attributed to Stravinsky in
the dialogues and the expansive, light and deft writing of Craft's diaries
and other solo pieces presented the operation of two strikingly different
minds. In addition, my own conjecture of the nature of the Stravinsky-
Craft collaboration was confirmed by this statement in a letter of Stravinsky reprinted in *Themes and Episodes:*

> . . . My written language is more elegant than my spoken, but I have
> noticed that I share this fault with Mr. Auden and Mr. Eliot as well as
> with most "public personalities" I have met. It is also true that my colleague
> and collaborator, who is co-author of my books of conversations, polishes
> my language when it is ungrammatical or ungraceful but, then, assistance
> of this kind is also common and has been celebrated in such examples as
> Pound's help to Eliot, or Perkins's to Thomas Wolfe, or Ted Sorensen's
> to the late President Kennedy.

When, therefore, the inevitable question about the authenticity of
Stravinsky's writing was asked, on one occasion early in 1968 at the
Poetry Center of the Y.M.H.A. in New York, my reply was that
Stravinsky was a strong-minded person who had shown himself inclined
and able to speak for himself in the past, and whom I would expect
to want to speak for himself now; that he would let someone else
help him to improve his saying of what he had to say, but would
not, I was sure, let his name be attached to the thinking of this other

person; and that, for me, to read his writing and that of Craft was to be struck by the evidently different operation of two unmistakably different minds. This continued to be my view on the subject; and it was not changed by the sensational interview in *The New York Times*, in March of last year, in which Lillian Libman, who as Stravinsky's business manager for a dozen years had come to know a great deal about his private life, talked to one of the *Times* music-reviewers, Donal Henahan, about the book with her recollections that was to appear in the fall, and claimed that what had been published as Stravinsky's writing in books and articles had actually been written by Craft. My view was not changed by this claim because of the statements of Mrs. Stravinsky and Craft that were reported in *The Times* the next day:

> Mrs. Stravinsky says that the authenticity of the Stravinsky-Craft books . . . is indisputable. She says that for years she saw the two men working together. . . . Mr. Craft went into further detail about the collaboration. ". . . Stravinsky would talk and I would write down exactly what he said. Later I would face him with his words, and he would throw out a lot. Finally we would decide on a finished version . . ."

Craft thus spelled out specifically the procedure of the collaboration that Stravinsky had described in the statement I have quoted from *Themes and Episodes*. It was the procedure that had produced "the earlier books in the series", which Craft, in *The Times*, went on to characterize as "practically all autobiographical". But even the ones "toward the end", in which "the words were more mine than [Stravinsky's]", were produced by the procedure Craft described in this statement in *The New York Review of Books* a month later:

> What Miss Libman appears not to have been aware of is that Stravinsky's and my joint journalism was the result of hundreds of hours of, above all, listening to music, and of the most painstaking piecing together, on my part, of his thoughts and reactions.

For me this was confirmed by what one actually read in the later and last Stravinsky writings—the articles on Gesualdo's music and Beethoven's last quartets reprinted in *Retrospectives and Conclusions*, the comments on Debussy's *Pelléas et Mélisande* and Boulez's recorded performance of it in Stravinsky's very last article in *The New York Review of Books*, early in 1971: the musical perceptions, the musical judgments could be only Stravinsky's; and Craft was merely the transcriber and

arranger of the words in which Stravinsky had expressed them as he
had listened with Craft to the music and talked with him about it.
It was Stravinsky who heard that the Boulez performance of *Pelléas*
"is stylistically questionable . . . it overaccents and overarticulates
(the dotted notes in the Interlude between the first two scenes of act
2 are too short and bouncy); substitutes *forte* for *pianissimo* (cf. the
winds at 35, act 2)"; Stravinsky who heard that "the singers are the
main problem"—that the diction of the non-French-speaking cast
"affects not only color but pitch and rhythm. . . . Of the two inexact-
nesses of the singers, in rhythm and intonation, the former is the more
surprising. Not that exactness is all; but suppleness comes after, not before, fidelity to the written rhythmic values, and each of Debussy's
distinctions does its bit. Yet the singers do not always observe them. For
example, more often than not the duration of the upbeat, or first note
of a phrase, is doubled. Thus, choosing at random, Pelléas's *'mais il
y a longtemps'* (beginning of scene 2, act 3) is set to five sixteenths
but sung to an eighth and four sixteenths." It was Stravinsky who
heard that the singers' "accents and mispronunciations . . . attract
too much attention to the words," adding, "And what words! How
could Debussy, the friend of Mallarmé, stomach Maeterlinck, let alone
underline some of his most irritating mannerisms?" And it was Stravinsky who, after all this, exclaimed, "But enough. What beautiful things
the score contains!"—only to have to add that "my impression of
the musical whole is of a decline in effectiveness after the *'Hair'* scene,"
and that the idiom of the work, "like a drug, wears off with time"—which
raised the question for him whether that idiom "is . . . a too confining
one for an opera of this length," in whose later scenes "simplicity
and restraint turn into limitation and constraint, beautiful monotony
into just plain monotony."

And Craft's explanation of Libman's attack on the authenticity of
the Stravinsky writing—that she appeared to be unaware of the actual
procedure that had produced it—was confirmed by a reading of her
book, *And Music at the Close*, when it was published last fall. Unlike
Henahan's interview and his later article in *The Times*, it was written
with obvious love—the love for Stravinsky himself and his wife which
they had reciprocated, and affectionate understanding for Craft, whose
personal problems and eccentricities had introduced burdensome com-

plications into her work for Stravinsky. Moreover it was written by a person with good will and intelligence, but without the subtlety of mind and feeling of the extraordinary people she had been involved with—so that there must have been much that went on among them that she had been, in Craft's words, "not . . . aware of". Thus—in the matter I have been concerned with in this article—she reported that in New York in August 1967 she informed Craft of the commission from Fratelli Fabbri Editori in Milan for the 2000-word article under Stravinsky's byline that would be the preface to Volume 9 of their *Storia della Musica*, and that later was included among the Stravinsky writings in the final Stravinsky-Craft volume under the title *Some Perspectives of a Contemporary;* and she added in parentheses that Craft, "in order to meet his [sic] deadline, dictated the text to me in two of the most expensive long-distance calls he ever made from Hollywood." For her this was an instance of Craft being the actual author of what appeared as Stravinsky's; and there appeared to be no awareness on her part that what Craft dictated to her from Hollywood was the accumulation of all he had heard Stravinsky say on the subject during the preceding twenty years, and that it probably included the very words of Stravinsky that by this time must have become fixed in Craft's mind. It wasn't necessary for Craft to invent a Stravinskyan style, as Libman contended he had done: he had in his mind, and could write down fluently, the actual words of Stravinsky and the actual way he had used them.

What was for me a convincing reply to Libman was contained in the novelist Paul Horgan's book, *Encounters with Stravinsky*, written, like hers, with love, but in addition with a sensitivity of mind and feeling which had enabled him to experience in person the sharpness of mind and wit that Libman claimed was invented for Stravinsky's published writing by Craft. The book contains Horgan's letter to *The New Yorker*, in January 1972, about the assertion of its music critic, Winthrop Sargeant, that "those who knew Stravinsky know that he was fluent only in Russian and French, and that his numerous writings in English in recent years were the work of his amanuensis, Robert Craft . . ."—a letter in which Horgan wrote that "Stravinsky in his recorded dialogues (not 'writings') with Mr. Craft always sounded like the Stravinsky I listened to time and again in direct English conversation," and said of this conversation that "I have never known conversational English more pungent than his, or more grammatically correct, precise (often devastatingly so) in vocabulary, and original in style, all within the frame of the natural syntax of the language."

And there was, after all, Stravinsky's statement in the letter that appeared in *The Los Angeles Times* in the summer of 1970, in reply to an article in which Boulez had been "charged with impugning the 'authenticity' of certain statements of my own" and had apparently " 'suggested' that my 'arch-disciple' [Craft] has put words into my mouth":

> . . . It would be strange indeed if we had *not* put words into, or helped to get them *out* of, each other's mouths: after all, we have been working together for 23 years . . . (*Encounter*, March 1973)

The Grand Manner of Charles Rosen

The pianist Charles Rosen is also a writer on music, who a year ago provided interesting notes for his recorded performances of Beethoven's last sonatas that proved to be disappointingly ineffective. In this he demonstrated his possession of the theoretician's knowledge and perception that enabled him to point out features of style and structure in the sonatas, but not the artist's ability to create the progressions of shaped piano sound in which the sonatas produced the effect as works of art that we know from other pianists' performances they are capable of producing.[1] And something similar can be said of his book *The Classical Style*, in which he examines the musical language of Haydn, Mozart and Beethoven, and demonstrates in particular works the use of its melodic, rhythmic and harmonic elements by each of these composers in the textures and structures of the sonata form they defined and developed. Though offered by Viking Press as a trade book, it is really a treatise for the special group of readers who have enough of Rosen's technical knowledge of music and his awesome familiarity with its entire literature to be able to follow his discussions of language, style and structure; it is not a book for the general reader with the mere music-lover's familiarity only with the music performed at concerts and on records, the music-lover's interest only in the effect of the shaped progression of sound as it reaches his ear, his sensitivity to that effect, and perhaps an ability to read music and play it on

---

[1] Rosen is nevertheless described as "one of the great keyboard performers of our day" by David Hamilton; but by the evidence of the Hamilton evaluations of Toscanini and Furtwängler, Flagstad and Ponselle, that I have encountered, he speaks as not one of the great critics of our day.

the piano. This was pointed out, in effect, by the dissenter in the
jury which selected the book for one of the National Book Awards
prizes: Stanley Burnshaw's contention was not that the book wasn't
good enough to receive the prize, but that as a juror in a competition
of books for the general reader, and as such a general reader himself,
he couldn't even judge the value of a book which he was "unable
to read and follow except in so vague and superficial a manner as
to be meaningless". And his statement interested me because it brought
up the important matter—apart from that of quality and value—of
what and how one writes about music if one wants the general reader
to be able to follow the writing with understanding.

This is a matter I have had occasion to discuss a number of times,
insisting each time on one basic fact about the "how": that a statement
about a passage of music, like a statement about a painting or a passage
in a poem or novel, can have real meaning only for someone in whose
mind it connects with knowledge of the music it refers to—the sound
of it that he either has heard and remembers, or hears when the statement
is made. In a lecture the speaker can, and in fact must, play what
he speaks of; and I pointed out concerning Glenn Gould's first lecture
at Hunter College a few years ago that his audience couldn't understand
most of what he said because his statements—representing his knowledge of the music they referred to—were made to people who didn't
have this knowledge that was needed for the statements to be meaningful
to them, and whom Gould didn't provide with the knowledge by playing
the music for them on the piano.[2] With a book there is the difficulty
I described when I reported on a volume of *The New Oxford History
of Music* a couple of years ago: that one can print in the book the
poem one is writing about, or insert in it a reproduction of the painting,
but cannot provide in it the sound of the passage of music. One can
give the passage in musical notation; but then there is still the difficulty

---

[2] In this report on Gould's lecture I cited Donald Tovey's practice in his writing—on
the one hand in the detailed description of the course of events in a particular piece
of music; on the other hand in the general statement about a composer's operation
that summarized the observed detail of particular works. In the first he quoted passages
in musical notation; in the second he referred to them in the expectation that the reader
would look them up in the printed scores; and in both he made possible the correlation
of statement with music that was essential for understanding of the statement.

that not everyone can read this notation and translate it into sound on the piano. *The New Oxford History's* solution was to persuade a record company to issue a set of LP records with performances of some of the pieces of music discussed in the book; and my solution in 1937, in *A Book of the Symphony*—a book devised, I said in the introduction, to "be read with understanding and profit by a person who had not studied music, as well as by one who had"—was to provide, next to the quotations and mentions of thematic details, measurements that enabled the reader to find these details on existing records with the ruler provided in the book—a method possible with the wide-groove records of that time, but not with the microgroove records of today.

My introduction also dealt with the questions "What does the person who has not studied music need to be told about a symphony?", "What can one tell him?"; and my decisions were fortified by a statement of Donald Tovey about the pleasure from a device of Mozart:

> It depends on a delicate sense of key, but has nothing to do with the technical knowledge which enables us to name it; indeed it is certain to be keenly enjoyed by any attentive listener whose knowledge of music is the result of relish for classical works, stimulated by frequent opportunities for hearing them under good conditions.

I decided, that is, not to say anything requiring the technical knowledge the reader was presumed not to have—in particular the knowledge of so important an element in the form of the symphony as key relations —in the belief, with Tovey, that when the reader's attention was directed to the sound on a record of details in the progression of a symphony movement, he would hear the harmonic shifts and appreciate their effect, and did not, for this, need in addition "the technical knowledge which enables us to name [them]".

With Rosen's book there is now need to say more about Tovey's statement. He made it in his famous essay on Mozart's Piano Concerto K.503 in C major, after describing something that happens in the exposition of the first movement: three times a striking rhythmic figure is carried to a point where it is proclaimed on the note G—the first time in the course of the opening orchestral tutti, where the G's, heard in the key of C major, are followed by a theme in C minor; the second time in the course of the first solo section, where the G's, heard in the key of C minor, are followed by the surprise of the piano's shift to E-flat major; the third time in the second orchestral tutti, where the G's, heard now in G major, are answered by the piano's startling reiteration of the figure on the note B, initiating a shift to E minor that is the first of a succession of such shifts of key in the development section. The essay in which Tovey describes this—like all the others in the volumes of *Essays in Musical Analysis*—was written for the audience that was to hear the concerto performed at a concert of the Reid Orchestra in Edinburgh; and he described details which he could expect "attentive listeners" to recognize and appreciate as they listened to the performance—even those listeners who couldn't play the passages in musical notation that he included in the essay. This was the way he wrote in these essays for the mere music-lovers at his concerts—at the same time as he taught the advanced students with technical knowledge at the University of Edinburgh the kind of things Rosen is concerned with in his book. I know nothing about these seminars of Tovey's, and merely allow myself to imagine that, as in the other seminars I have been told about, he sat at the piano with the small group of students seated around him, with a Mozart score, say, open before him, in which he pointed out how something on one page was transformed at its reappearance on a later page, with other Mozart scores at hand in which to point out Mozart's similar or dissimilar practice, and with other composers' scores available in which to point out *their* practice.

The right medium of communication for the contents of Rosen's book would, then, be a seminar in which he would operate in the way I have just described for people with the technical knowledge required to understand most of what he said. His use instead of the 460 pages of his book necessitates the substitution of passages in musical notation for the sound of these passages produced on the piano; and this requires the reader to be able to play the quoted passages whose details Rosen points out and comments on, or to hear them in a performance on a phonograph record. The general educated public includes people interested in music who *can* play the piano or read musical notation as they listen to a record. But even for these poeple the Rosen book presents two difficulties. One is that Rosen doesn't hold what he writes to the limits of what he quotes in musical notation: though the book has much more of such quotation than is usually provided, it is far from providing as much as the text requires. I can imagine the readers I have just described locating in the Haydn scores the passages in the Quartets Op. 20 No. 1 and Op. 64 No. 3 which Rosen doesn't quote but of which he gives the measure numbers, and managing to hear them by playing them on the piano or listening to them in a recorded performance. And I can imagine them using the score of Mozart's Concerto K.459 to follow the entire course of the finale that Rosen describes without providing even measure numbers of the passages he refers to. But I can't imagine these readers supplying for themselves from the Haydn scores the passages Rosen doesn't quote or specify with measure numbers that are needed to give meaning, for the reader, to the summary statements on pp.138-41 about the changes in the quartets of Op. 50 from those of Op. 33, in those of Op. 54 and Op. 55 from those of Op. 50, and so on; or to the preliminary statements on pp. 137-8 about the quartet form and its relation to tonality. Nor can I imagine these readers being able to supply for themselves the passages Rosen doesn't quote that are needed to give meaning to his statements on p. 221 about Mozart's Concerto K.451; his statements on p. 94 about the *ricercar* fugue; his statements on p. 79 about the differences in the handling of "the balanced relations between the main and subordinate tonalities in a work" that are exhibited by J. C. Bach, C. P. E. Bach, Mozart, Haydn; and in the introductory section the paragraph on tonalities at the bottom of p. 26, the discussion of the isolation of the elements of music on pp. 28-9, the discussion of the mistaken ideas about sonata form on pp. 30-3, and the chapter *The Origins of the Style.* I am not surprised by Burnshaw's inability to follow that introduction: with the specialized musical education he presumably doesn't have, and much longer experience as a listener, *I* can't follow some of it.

But even when it does provide in musical notation the passages of music Rosen refers to, the book presents a difficulty—and not just to the general reader but to someone like myself. I am speaking now of Rosen's demonstrations in particular sonata movements of the melodic, rhythmic and phraseological manipulation of thematic substance in the progression that is given structural coherence and symmetry, and resolution of its dramatic tensions, by the basic, essential harmonic progressions of the sonata movement: the shift in the first part, the exposition, from the initial tonic key to the dominant; and, after the development with its further shifts of key, the return to the tonic in the recapitulation. The description of the form and the demonstrations of its achievement in particular examples are the enlightening contribution of the book, which is valuable and useful, but only up to a point—only as long as it remains within the limits of what the reader can hear, or can be enabled to hear. And the difficulty presented by the Rosen book is that it goes beyond that point to what *he,* with his special capacities, may hear, but what *I* do not hear and can't imagine the general reader hearing. One can say, I think, that Rosen and the general reader listen in different ways, for different things. And not only Rosen: reporting on Gould's Hunter College lecture I said that he had characterized the opening statement of Beethoven's Sonata Op. 109 as a chorale, playing it as a series of chords embodying the essential harmony and remarking that the figuration wasn't important. This was what he heard, because the essential harmony was what he listened for. But Beethoven didn't write the series of chords; he wrote the figuration, which was the thematic idea he was concerned with and developed; and for most listeners the opening statement of Op. 109 is that figuration, because their listening, unlike Gould's, is directed primarily at the progression of thematic ideas and their developments, with concomitant awareness of the underlying harmony as one element involved in the developments. And I would say there is a similar difference in what Rosen and the general reader listen for and hear.

Thus, as obsessive in his hearing of descending thirds in the *Hammerklavier* Sonata as he says Beethoven is in his use of them, Rosen hears in the theme of the fugal development of the first movement:

his skeleton of it, in the uppermost stave, as a sequence of slowly descending thirds, which I—and I am sure most listeners—cannot hear in place of, or at the same time as, the rapidly and differently moving theme Beethoven actually wrote. Again, in a later passage of the fugal development:

I am sure it is the textural intensification of the thematic activity of both hands that holds most listeners' attention, as it does mine, not the skeletonized slowly decending thirds of the left hand that Rosen hears in measures 175-6, or the D of the right hand in 174 that he retains in his mind until it descends to B in 177. And at the climactic conclusion of the fugal development:

I am sure most listeners' minds are gripped, like mine, by the tremendous chords which subside (measure 198) into the bare D's in quiet rhythmed broken octaves that end with the wonderful rise (200-1) to the D-sharp beginning one of the movement's important melodic ideas; and that with their minds so gripped they don't hear what Rosen's mind is concentrated on: the long pedal point on D he hears beginning in measure 191; the D's descent of a third (200-1) to B, which "changes the key to B major"; "this modulation . . . as the last and inevitable step of the process; the pause before it [on the D's in broken octaves] only set[ting] it in relief, and signify[ing] that it is a descending third of a different nature, one which changes the tonal framework."

There is also the "long-range linear sense, overriding the immediate voice-leading", which causes Rosen to hear in a passage of the *Hammerklavier's* slow movement:

the melody's G at the beginning of measure 56 "hanging in the air, unresolved and unconnected" until it is resolved to the F-sharp in 58—which I am sure is not what most listeners hear: for them the G is connected immediately to the A in the section of the line of melody ending with the E in that measure. And there is the sense for unity that causes Rosen to hear in the piano's opening melodic statement in the slow movement of Mozart's Concerto K.488:

"a simple descending scale, accompanied by a parallel longer movement above it":

into which Mozart introduces "the irregularity of rhythm and variety of phrasing which reveal every expressive facet of the two descending lines"—which again I am sure is not what most listeners hear or can be persuaded to hear: for them the melody is, and implies nothing but, the series of notes Mozart actually wrote. This sense for unity also causes Rosen to hear the beginning of the piano's opening melody combined with the orchestra's subsequent phrase:

in the piano's second melody:

which once more I am sure is not what most listeners hear: the differences in note sequence, rhythm and shape of phrase produce what they hear as three different statements.[3] (Nor, for the same reason, can I imagine them hearing, as Rosen does, the later themes of the first movement of Beethoven's *Waldstein* Sonata as derived from the opening statement; "the 'second' theme of the *Appassionata* as a variant of the opening".)[4]

There are many more examples that should be dealt with; but for obvious reasons I must limit myself to only one more, concerned this time not with a brief passage but with the entire slow movement of Mozart's Concerto K.453. The reader who concentrates on following Rosen's difficult-to-follow demonstration, in the movement's progression, of the sequence of keys in the exposition, development and recapitulation of a sonata movement, may miss something else which doesn't emerge clearly in what Rosen writes—the lay-out of the thematic material presented to the listener's ear, which is unique in Mozart's writing and produces one of his most extraordinary and overwhelming utterances. This lay-out is the alternation of (1) the several occurrences of the meditative opening phrase that ends inconclusively in silence, like a question left unanswered, with (2) the several sequences of ideas, each beginning after the inconclusive meditative phrase and eventually leading to its next occurrence. The shifts of key startle one at the beginnings of the piano's increasingly impassioned sequences; and the last of these sequences builds up to the piano's quasi-

---

[3] I was correct in saying one hears nothing of the piano's opening melody in its later statement after the orchestra's phrase. But Tovey, I find, is correct in pointing out that in this later statement "the pianoforte takes up [the orchestra's phrase] in a chromatic variation." The sequence of five notes—C-sharp, D, C-sharp, B-sharp, C-sharp—with which the piano's later statement begins is not, as Rosen contends, the beginning of its opening melody—C-sharp, D, C-sharp—again, but instead an ornamental turn around an introductory C-sharp, as the additional B-sharp and the rhythm and shape make it unnecessary for Tovey to say.

[4] Only when I reread the article in *Sewanee* did I perceive my failure to add that even when Rosen speaks of something which *is* audible in the music he magnifies it enormously into what one does *not* hear. The "dramatic surprise at the moment" that Tovey rightly points out as "the essential character of Haydn's form" includes the strokes of harmonic daring in his developments; and in the development of the first movement of Haydn's E-major Trio the moment of silence followed by the main theme in the remote key of A-flat provides such a dramatic surprise; but it provides only that, not what Rosen inflates it into: one doesn't hear it as "electrifying" and as "the climax of the whole movement [which] everything before leads up to [and which] everything afterwards resolves."

improvisatory cadenza; after which the inconclusive meditative phrase is heard again from the woodwinds, this time with harmonic and melodic changes that give it a new poignancy, and this time, also, concluded at last by a statement of the piano with implications of summation, resignation and sublimity that are overwhelming. Part of what I have described is mentioned in the conclusion of Rosen's own demonstration:

> The recapitulation reserves the closing theme of the exposition for a coda, after the soloist's cadenza. But before this closing theme, the initial phrase is used once more with magnificent effect. The woodwinds play it immediately following the cadenza; until now, each time it appeared it was left unresolved on the dominant—not only unresolved, but almost isolated, with a silence that separated it from all that followed. This last time, it melts into the succeeding phrase and is resolved in one of the most expressive, and yet perhaps most conventional, phrases that Mozart could have written:

moving chromatically through the subdominant into the piano's cadence. This withholding of the main theme until the very end of the movement, together with the silence that sets off each one of its appearances except the last, are only the most salient points of a work that is an important step in Mozart's transformation of a genre, making it capable of bearing the greatest musical weight.

This brings to mind again what kept occurring to me as I read the Rosen book—Otis Ferguson's remark, in 1939, about Winthrop Sargeant's book *Jazz: Hot and Hybrid:* ". . . Mr. Sargeant is a sort of teetotaler chemist for a liquor concern—he sure is hell on analysis and charts of specific gravity, but as to what the stuff tastes like and will do to you, that rests with some other department." I may exaggerate a little—since Rosen does speak of the "magnificent effect" and the "most expressive phrase"—but only a little.

It is of course only the book that is important; but things like acknowledgments and bibliographical notes can have interest; and Rosen's have for me. One that does, is what he adds after saying he must have missed many essential articles and books in spite of all his efforts: "It seems prudent to draw a veil of silence over these matters and confound in one decent obscurity those secondary sources which I have not read, those which I read but which taught me nothing, and, finally, those which taught me a good deal and which I am ungratefully not listing." And as against this inordinately self-conscious, mannered and convoluted posturing there is what he says about the sources he does acknowledge his debt to—what he writes, for example, after his statement about Abert's unequalled discussion of Mozart's style: ". . . Alfred Einstein's *Mozart* (1945) is less satisfactory, but it has the inestimable merit of having been written by a man who loved Mozart and knew his music thoroughly, and it discusses almost everything that Mozart wrote." Having noted nothing myself, I am interested in anything specific that Rosen would say he owes to Einstein's book, and that demonstrates to him the "inestimable merit" of love and thorough knowledge operating with a complete lack of the musical perception I would expect Rosen to recognize as essential, and therefore producing only the worthless comment which he characterizes as "less satisfactory" than Abert's writing.

Interesting to me in the same way was the article on the problem of performing music of the past, in *The New York Times* last March, in which Rosen rightly ridiculed the idea of both the "innovationists" and the "conservationists"—that "the true tradition of the past was a total and capricious freedom and a complete disregard for the composer's text"—but misrepresented the issue between them with his statement that "Stokowski's lurid arrangements of Bach were answered by performances of Handel's 'Water Music' on real 18th-century instruments which had apparently been left untuned since then for greater authenticity." Actually Stokowski's lurid orchestral arrangement of Bach's Chaconne for unaccompanied violin was answered by Szigeti's and Grumiaux's performances of the work on the violin; and the Harnoncourt group plays old music on perfectly tuned old instruments. As for Rosen's contention that the playing of Chopin by Hofmann, Friedman and Rosen's teacher, Rosenthal, was "cooler, more elegant" than Rubinstein's "rich, passionate sweeping line", and was "in certain respects more like the style that younger pianists prefer today", the fact is that even the earlier flamboyance which Rubinstein no longer exhibits today was exceeded by the distortions of Friedman and the older Hofmann whom Rosen heard; and the straightforwardness and continence of Cliburn, Ashkenazy, Harasiewicz, Pollini and Rogers today are at the opposite pole not only from the styles of Friedman and Hofmann but from the mannered style of Rosenthal when I heard him in the twenties. (*The Sewanee Review*, Spring 1973)

Note This article was to have been part of my regular chronicle in the Winter 1973 issue of *The Hudson Review*, of which I was contributing editor for music and ballet. Impressed by the review of Rosen's book in *The Times Literary Supplement* when it was published in England, I asked *Hudson* to get the book for me when it was published here in April 1971, but, as in earlier instances of such formidable books, had to wait for a long enough stretch of clear time in which to read it and write about it. This would have been provided by the summer of 1971 if it hadn't been pre-empted by travel in Europe; and I didn't get to the book until the summer of 1972. The editor of *Hudson*, Frederick Morgan, hadn't objected previously to such long delays in my comments on books, and hadn't expressed impatience this time; so I was astonished in May 1972 to hear from a friend that Rosen's book was being reviewed for *Hudson* by William Youngren. I had several times in the past got Morgan to send a book on music to Youngren for review; but he had never before sent Youngren or anyone else a book which he knew I had asked for with, presumably, the intention of writing about it in my chronicle. The mere fact of his having done this now was therefore surprising; but what was additionally surprising was that Youngren had asked for the book without first inquiring whether I was intending to write about it, and that Morgan, on receiving Youngren's request, hadn't inquired whether I *was* writing about the book, and hadn't said anything to me about the request and his sending the book to Youngren for review.

When I inquired of *Hudson* and was informed that Youngren had asked for the book and *was* reviewing it, I was told also that this didn't affect my commenting on it in my chronicle—that it would in fact be interesting to have the two viewpoints. I had inquired to make absolutely sure there would be no difficulty; but actually there had been no need of the inquiry: from the start in 1958, without a word having to be said, it had been understood that the regular chronicle I was to write would be my platform for saying what I wanted to say about whatever I thought called for comment, which the magazine committed itself to publishing; and in the fifteen years since then Morgan had published whatever I sent him, without a word of objection even about what he occasionally had disapproved of in it. Nor did he, in August 1972, explicitly refuse to publish the chronicle with my comment on the Rosen book, which he said interested him very much. What he did instead was to write me first (August 14) that two long pieces he was committed to publishing in the Winter 1973 issue—a travel article by Joseph Bennett and a translation of work by the Hindi poet Nirala—would leave no space for my chronicle, which, therefore, he had to ask me not to write (though I felt sure he had by that date received the chronicle I had already written and sent in); then (August 18) that since I had already written the chronicle I would be paid for it even though, as he had written earlier, there would be no space in the Winter issue in which to print it.

Morgan wrote as though this were a case of an article designed specifically for a particular issue of a magazine, and one which, therefore, if for some reason it couldn't be used in that particular issue, had to be paid for and scrapped. But in fact this was not such a case: there was nothing special about the Winter 1973 issue of *Hudson*, or about the chronicle I had sent in for it, so if there was no space for it in that issue it could appear in the next. I had to conclude, therefore, that what Morgan had written me was a maneuver, a strategy to achieve —seemingly as a mere incidental consequence—what actually was his real objective: not to publish my chronicle with its comment on the Rosen book. The motivation in this, as I saw it, was that Morgan— having voted to give the book the National Book Awards prize—didn't want to publish my unfavorable comment on it, even though his vote would be backed by Youngren's favorable review; but this he could hardly say to me or anyone else, or expect me or anyone else to accept as a reason for not publishing my chronicle; therefore he adopted the

line, for his objective, that my chronicle was one specifically for the
Winter 1973 issue which, since it couldn't be used in that issue, had
to be scrapped.

In reply to Morgan I said (August 21) that having written what
I considered important to point out about the book I expected this
to be published in the Spring issue; and that if he now found he
didn't have space for the two viewpoints he could explain this to Youngren. On further thought I realized that if my comment on the book
appeared in my chronicle in the Spring issue it would leave no space
for reviews of performances of the preceding fall; and I hit on, and
suggested (September 7), a way of publishing both pieces that would
leave my chronicle in the Spring issue for the reviews of performances:
either my piece instead of Youngren's in the book-review section
of the Winter issue, with Youngren's piece as a Communication in
the Spring issue, or Youngren's review in the Winter issue, with my
comment as the Communication in the Spring issue. And concerning
my insistence that the comment must be published I added: "If I were
to print a card like Edmund Wilson's famous one it would state that
B. H. Haggin (1) does not write for the amounts of money his writing
earns, but only to say in print what he considers important to say;
(2) does not write what he submits to editors for their decision whether
or not to publish it, but writes only what an editor has committed
himself to publish; (3) does not, therefore, write what an editor may
pay for and not publish. These statements define my working relation
with *Hudson*." But Morgan, in his reply, now denied that our working relation included the commitment to publish I said it did, and chose
to take my assertion of this commitment and my suggestions about
publication of the two pieces as a usurpation of his authority as editor
that compelled him to end my connection with the magazine. Also,
ignoring my reminder of the long delays in some of my reporting on
books in the past and my explanation of the delay this time, he contended that I had decided to write about the Rosen book only after
I had learned that Youngren was reviewing it; and, not surprisingly
(in the light of his own tactics), accused me of what he characterized
as extraordinary duplicity in the matter.

Nor was I surprised, when the Winter 1973 issue appeared, to find
in it no poetry of Nirala, and Youngren's review not in the book-review
section in the back but in the space in the front which Morgan had

said wasn't available for my chronicle. What *was* surprising—to the point almost of being unbelievable—was Youngren's review titled "Better Than Tovey?", as a performance of the mind that had dealt so perceptively with Mellers's *Music in a New Found Land* and Kerman's *The Beethoven Quartets*. But though almost unbelievable, his dealing with the Rosen book was not inexplicable: it was that of someone with exceptional intellectual powers in, among other things, abstract, theoretic, conceptualizing, systematizing thinking; someone—not surprisingly, therefore—with an interest in such thinking as exceptionally powerful as his capacities for it;[5] someone, finally, so concentrated on his own interests and his own powers in satisfying them as to be incapable of awareness that they *were* exceptional, and that when he spoke to other people he had to take into account the fact that *their* interest in theoretic, systematizing thinking, and *their* capacity for it, were not of the magnitude of his. It was understandable, therefore, that he should not only write in a glow of appreciative enthusiasm about Rosen's theoretic discussion of the Viennese classical style, but insist that Rosen's book "is very definitely for the intelligent general reader, not for the specialist alone." Conceding that the book "is indeed intellectually difficult . . . and is specialized in the sense that Rosen . . . refers to and quotes more pieces of music than most non-specialists are likely to have at their fingertips," he proceeded to the seemingly inconsequent statement that "these are hardly defects, considering the benefits to be gained"—seemingly inconsequent, since for readers unacquainted with the many pieces of music that Rosen merely referred to without quotation there could not be the "benefit" of understanding the points he was making about, and with, the pieces. But it turned out that this wasn't the benefit Youngren had in mind: "The best way to read [the book] is to go straight through, skipping the analyses of pieces one is not familiar with, in order to get hold of Rosen's argument"; after which "the book can be returned to again and again, and the omitted analyses read and enjoyed, both in themselves and for their contribution to the argument." In this there was no awareness,

---

[5] This powerful interest impelled him, in a review of a collection of my critical writing, *Music Observed*, to say limitations of space prevented discussion of my particular judgments, and to devote his review instead to the theoretic basis of my work—what he thought were the ideas about music and criticism underlying the particular judgments—in disregard of one repeatedly expressed major idea underlying the writing: that the critic must keep his eye strictly on the particular object before him, which in this instance was the particular pieces of writing in the book.

no taking into account, of the fact that *he*, with his exceptional capacity for theoretic thinking, *could* get hold of Rosen's argument without what the mere references to, or analyses of, the unfamiliar pieces of music contributed to it, but this was something the intelligent general reader and non-specialist could *not* do.

But Youngren was also someone with an intense interest in particular pieces of music and an attentive and perceptive ear for what happened in them; and this made it hard to understand, first, the little attention he gave in his review to Rosen's analyses of particular works. (One could have thought Youngren had himself gone straight through the book not only without stopping for the analyses on the way, but also without going back for them afterwards—from the fact that he referred to so few of them and didn't go into detail even with these few.) But what it made impossible to understand was his estimate of the analyses: "It's hard to imagine a more sensitive and helpful guide to this music than Rosen." What *I* found hard to imagine was Youngren hearing—and expecting the general reader to hear—what Rosen said was to be heard in the passages I have cited in my comment on his book. Moreover, Youngren had, in his review of *Music Observed*, mentioned with relish my demonstration of the absurdity of Benjamin Boretz's dealing with the occurrences of A-flat followed by G in the first movement of Mozart's Concerto K.491; and I found it hard to imagine, therefore, how he could read what Rosen made of the numerous and various occurrences of the note E that his eye detected in the exposition of the first movement of Haydn's Quartet Op. 50 No. 6 (pp. 125-8 of his book) and not recognize the similarity to the Boretz performance.

And so I came to the question "Better than Tovey?" in the title of Youngren's review. This question he related to the uniqueness until now of the writing in which Tovey had dealt with the same subject as Rosen, and to the fact that "Tovey's catalyzing influence is . . . apparent on virtually every page of Rosen's book." Tovey's writing on the subject, I was surprised to learn, had left Youngren unsatisfied because of its failure to draw from the analyses of particular works the "generalization[s] about the ways in which phrasing or key relations or rhythm changed in the late eighteenth century"; and it was because Rosen "fill[s] out and consolidate[s] Tovey's view of the classical revolution" that *The Classical Style* was for Youngren "the book that I, and perhaps other readers of Tovey, have been waiting for." Moreover, citing Rosen's insistence that "the priorities of hearing must be respected," Youngren could "almost hear Tovey cheering from the grave" Rosen's adherence in his writing to Tovey's guiding principle that one "should never set down anything that his ear has not recognized apart from the appearance of the printed page." My interest in theory being less intense than Youngren's, I hadn't been left unsatisfied by Tovey's analyses of particular works: I had wanted no more than what they gave me—reports of what he had heard happening in the works, which I then could hear when I listened. But I *was* left unsatisfied by Rosen's analyses, with their evidence of the catalyzing effect not of Tovey but of whoever it was at Princeton that seemed to have influenced Rosen as well as Benjamin Boretz, and the effect in addition of Rosen's own pretentiousness. His professed objective in his book was identical with Tovey's in his essays: to show how the essential sonata-style operation as he had defined it produced the detail of particular sonata movements of Haydn, Mozart and Beethoven. But the important difference between them was that Tovey did exactly that and nothing but that, pointing out what any ear could then perceive happening in melody, rhythm and harmony in the moment-to-moment progression of the music; whereas Rosen pointed out in addition many things which seemed to be constructions of his mind, not perceptions of his ear. Thus, in the first movement of Haydn's Quartet Op. 50 No. 6, he pointed out the cello's four F-naturals in measures 26-9 (bottom of p. 126) as something to continue to hear, through all the activity of the following eight measures, as the preparation for the F-major chord in measure 38—which I couldn't do and couldn't imagine most other people being able to do. And not only was it hard to imagine anyone being able to hear as the "skeleton" of the opening melody of the second movement of Mozart's Piano Concerto K.488 the two parallel descending scale lines that Rosen said it was (top of p. 244), but it was impossible to imagine what anyone would gain, in listening to the melody, that justified his trying to hear the parallel descending scale lines as its skeleton. Much of what Rosen's analyses pointed out, then, didn't give the intelligent general reader the beneficial guidance that Tovey's provided, and therefore wasn't worth the enormous effort it cost. This made Rosen's book, in my opinion, definitely not one for the intelligent general reader; and made my answer to the question "Better than Tovey?" an emphatic no.

Music and Ballet Chronicle
1964-73 *

Winter 1964 Enterprise and adventurousness are admirable things in the operation of an opera company only if they are governed by a sense for value; and this sense for what is worth doing is something the director of the New York City Opera has repeatedly shown he doesn't have—most recently with last fall's opening production of two works that were not worth doing, Stravinsky's *The Nightingale* and a staging of Honegger's *Jeanne d'Arc au Bûcher*.

Stravinsky wrote the first act of *The Nightingale* in 1909, and the remaining two acts in 1913, when his musical language, as he says, "had been appreciably modified." It is the first act—with writing in the orchestral style of *The Firebird* and at times reminiscent of Rimsky-Korsakov, but bearing the impress of Stravinsky's mind even on what is derivative—that has what little attractive music there is in the work, principally the song of the Fisherman. But even in this act, what the Nightingale sings is arid artifice which creates no believable illusion of the singing of a living bird (nor did Patricia Brooks's labored delivery of the difficult high *tessitura* resemble a bird's spontaneous flow of song); and the writing in the later acts is thin and ineffective. As for *Jeanne d'Arc au Bûcher*, I would say the subject of Joan is one for the treatment—at once simple and monumental—it got in the great Dreyer film years ago, not for the inflated rhetoric of the Claudel text and Honegger's complementary mood and background music of the kind and quality one hears in films.

One further manifestation of managerial ineptitude: the Mozart

---

* In *The Hudson Review*, with two exceptions that are identified.

operas that the public knows well and enjoyed at City Center when they were sung in Italian—these the company has damaged in recent years by singing them in English; but Stravinsky's unfamiliar opera it presented in Russian; and on the other hand the Honegger work —though many in the audience understood French—it presented in English.

Summer 1964 Menotti's operas have provided some of the occasions to point out that what is of primary importance in an opera is not the play which is set to music but the music to which the play is set. For in his operas it has been the play that has engaged and held interest primarily, and for some in the audience so strongly as to mislead them into thinking the dramatic force was in the trashy music carrying the dialogue and action; though for others with a taste for the trashy—e.g. for Puccini—the music has added its own attractiveness to the interest of the play. The most recent such occasion was provided at the Metropolitan the past season by *The Last Savage*, which was unusual only in the feebleness of both the play and the music: one heard in the music the operation of the mind of the fool who wrote the libretto—the pretentious fool who would a satirist be, and in whose satire about a jungle savage's rejection of our civilization the savage actually was a native of India acting the part for pay, and the civilization he rejected was embodied in the familiar caricature of the big cocktail party of and for the intellectually and artistically fraudulent; and whereas Winthrop Sargeant heard rich evidence of the subtlety and sheer virtuosity of Menotti's musical workmanship, I was struck by his loss of the fluency he used to exhibit in his trashy invention, and the discrepancy at point after point between the evident attempt and the feeble achievement even in his own terms.

It says something about Bing's taste that he should have taken until 1964 to produce Verdi's *Falstaff*, presumably considering this masterpiece—which should never be out of the repertory of a company like the Metropolitan—less urgent than such matters as *Andrea Chénier*, *Turandot*, *Martha*, Barber's *Vanessa*, and the Offenbach and Johann Strauss operettas that should never be *in* the repertory of the Metropolitan (any more than should the works of Jerome Kern and Cole Porter). Bing may have thought he was serving Verdi as well as his publicity department by getting Leonard Bernstein to conduct the work; and in fact Bernstein the gifted musician paced and shaped much of *Falstaff* effectively; but Bernstein the overstimulated extrovert began the work with a whipping up of the tempo that made the opening scene frenetic; and such occasional bursts of excessive speed alternated with occasional excessive slowing down and lingering. As it happened, moreover, with the exaggerated speed of the opening scene there was the exaggerated buffoonery of Bardolfo and Pistola—which is to say that the work of Franco Zeffirelli, the director as well as the designer of the production, also exhibited occasional excesses. Though the sets were good and the costumes handsome, and the stage action included such felicitous inventions as the added silent characters in the inn scenes who created an enlivened context for the doings of the principals, or Ford's prolonged teasing of Falstaff with the purse of money in their interview, it included the exaggerated buffooneries I have mentioned, the exaggerated boyish rushing and stumbling about of Fenton, and a certain amount of hubbub that represented the mistaken idea that something must be going on at every moment. The italicizing by conductor and director was damaging to the delicate-textured work; and damaging also right from the opening scene were the sounds which Corena, the Falstaff in the performance I attended, produced in his struggle with a part he lacked the voice to sing.

I was reminded of the Metropolitan's productions of foreign operettas by the Jean-Louis Barrault company's performance of Offenbach's *La Vie Parisienne*. When this company was here the first time it gave a performance of *Hamlet* which struck me as the most impressive I had ever seen; and it seemed to me that its effectiveness came from a French style of stage speech and gesture which—like French conversational style—was much more rhetorically expansive and intensified than the English and American. In the performance of *La Vie Parisienne* one got this rhetorical heightening in the special style of a particular French theatrical genre using characters, situations and ways of thinking, behaving and joking from the French life of its period; and one got it done by actors completely familiar with the genre, the life it satirizes, and its style of performance. Or rather, one got this to start with, and in addition the work of the extraordinarily gifted actors of the Barrault company—including such superb comics in their different ways as Pierre Bertin and Jean Parédès—in a brilliantly contrived piece of theater craft. It should have taught Bing, who sat a few seats away from me, that the operettas of Offenbach and Johann Strauss exercise their charm only when performed in their original languages by companies at home in their styles, and lose all savor when given in English adaptations with people like Patrice Munsel and Theodor Uppman.

In Winthrop Sargeant's *New Yorker* reviews the works of Menotti, Carlisle Floyd and Douglas Moore have produced a dawn of American opera; in the columns of *The Herald Tribune*, where Alan Rich has succeeded Paul Henry Lang as music critic, "the banners of American opera were carried forward a considerable distance" by Hugo Weisgall's *Athaliah*, commissioned and performed this season by the Concert Opera Association. It is a work in the twelve-tone idiom which, according to Rich, causes one to "forget technique" and "hear a thoroughly modern opera in the great operatic tradition"—an opera, that is, in which "one senses the hand of an immensely gifted master of musical drama," whose "effects grow simply and logically out of intense dramatic tensions," who uses the twelve-tone technique in "strong, beautiful[ly?] shaped vocal phrases", and who thus "has set to rest—once and for all, I sincerely pray—the canard that atonality is incompatible with beauty." A notable and impressive achievement in Rich's prose, but not in Philharmonic Hall, where I heard only ugly sounds with no expressive relation to the text and not even mutually coherent relations in themselves.

A day later the American Opera Society gave New York its first hearing since 1895 of Rossini's *Semiramide*. And listening with expectations born of the beautiful writing Rossini showed himself to be capable of in *William Tell*, I was disappointed by vocal writing in *Semiramide* which struck my ear, this first time, as a mere competent exercise in the conventional style of the period, with an orchestral accompaniment that merely strummed along uninterestingly except for the one or two instances of a dramatically enlivening use of a powerful figure. But the vocal style was one that utilized the extraordinary capacities of the singers of the period; and the high-ranging florid writing in *Semiramide* provided the occasion for some of the most remarkable singing I have ever heard—not only by Joan Sutherland, whose breathtakingly accurate florid passages and fully rounded and secure high notes were produced in superbly shaped and styled phrases, but, unexpectedly, by Marilyn Horne, who exhibited a similar accurate agility and a similar impressive phrasing in her use of a voice far more beautiful than Sutherland's throughout the range from its rich dark contralto low notes to its bright and lovely soprano high notes.

Quite as remarkable singing, in its differnt way, had been done a couple of days before by Teresa Berganza at her Carnegie Hall recital. The difference was the delicacy and subtlety of her style in the effortlessly accurate delivery of the florid passages of *Nacqui all' affano* from Rossini's *La Cenerentola*—delicacy and subtlety which made her phrasing of the opening melodic section of the aria enchanting. And they operated as impressively in the songs of Schubert, Wolf and Brahms, producing details like the *"Mein Herz!"* in Schubert's *Die Post*, the *"Ach, nein"* in Wolf's *In dem Schatten meiner Locken*, that conveyed new and wonderfully effective insights.

31 October 1964 Bernard Shaw's statement about the refined and subtilized art of Verdi's last works—that it was something age gave in exchange for Verdi's early spontaneity and fertility and power —seemed so reasonable and acute that it took me a long time to realize that Verdi operates with the same spontaneity and fertility and power in the refined and subtilized vocal and orchestral writing of the *Requiem*, *Otello* and the *Te Deum* as in the cruder writing of the early works. What made Shaw's contention seem so reasonable was the fact that I knew it to be correct about performers. I had observed how the need of using an aging voice with care had brought a new continence and coherence in Lotte Lehmann's phrasing of songs. Flagstad had deployed her beautiful voice in flawlessly shaped phrases right from the start; and so her subtler inflection of phrase in later years could be taken to represent a maturing of her musicianship; but it too served the needs of an aging voice that had to be used with care and skill. And great as Schnabel's post-war recorded performances of Beethoven's concertos were, they revealed losses of some of the spontaneity, grace, continuity of tension and outline of the pre-war performances—age in this instance having brought a lessening of the powers of the musician as well as the pianist. All this has been brought to mind by Artur Rubinstein's performance of Beethoven's Piano Concerto No. 5 *(Emperor)* with the Boston Symphony under Leinsdorf, on RCA 2733. Rubinstein's case is like Verdi's: recently he has, in his seventies, amazed us not only with the tempering of his flamboyant style that has given his performances a new continence, repose, refinement and plastic coherence, but with the continuing technical powers that have produced the fine gradations of his beautiful tone, the clarity and accuracy of his rapid passage-work. All these, which we have heard in his recent performances of Chopin, we hear in the performance of the Beethoven concerto; and whereas his playing in Beethoven's Concerto No. 3 with Toscanini twenty years ago was made unsatisfying by its unsuitable Chopinesque elegance and melodic inflections, his playing this time—now powerful, now delicate and sensitive—adds up to a highly effective statement of the music. *(The New Republic)*

Spring 1965 After hearing the baritone Fischer-Dieskau only on records for several years I heard him at last in the concert hall—with the New York Philharmonic in performances of Wolf's *Harfenspieler Lieder* and Mahler's *Lieder eines fahrenden Gesellen,* in a recital of Schubert songs, and in the American Opera Society's presentation of Busoni's *Doktor Faust.* On records his extraordinary vocal and musical powers had produced performances that left one overwhelmed; in the concert hall not only did the singing itself have greater impact from being experienced directly, but it was reinforced by what one saw: the chubby, pleasant face which, as the song began, changed into a powerful and affecting dramatic mask that registered the singer's intense involvement in his performance.

Busoni's music has its cult, for reasons that were not discernible in *Doktor Faust*—to my ear the writing of someone technically equipped to make the gestures of saying the portentous things he didn't really say. It was a waste of Fischer-Dieskau's gifts; but their exercise even on nothing created interest in what otherwise would have been an unendurably boring three hours.

The New York City Opera presented still another dreary episode in the unending ballet it has performed in recent years with the Ford Foundation and some of the critics—in which each production of a worthless new American opera by the company as a result of a grant from the Foundation has elicited a statement by Winthrop Sargeant that the Foundation's support is bringing about a veritable explosion of exciting creative activity in American opera, whereupon the Foundation has made a further grant that has caused yet another worthless new work to be written, produced by the company, and praised by Sargeant. This time it was *Natalia Petrovna*, with a libretto by William Ball that was a shocking mutilation and coarsening of Turgenev's *A Month in the Country*, and music by Lee Hoiby, whose struggle to produce what he was incapable of—music worth listening to for its intrinsic quality and its expressive relevance to the dramatic situation—was painful to listen to. With the production of this work Julius Rudel demonstrated again that he has a gift for promotional ideas which bring in foundation money and publicity, but not the gift of artistic taste, values and standards that is more important in the director of an opera company. And a further demonstration of this was provided by his decision, when putting on Musorgsky's *Boris Godunov*, to use the Rimsky-Korsakov version.

A Carnegie Hall concert of the Boston Symphony gave me my first opportunity to observe Erich Leinsdorf as a symphonic conductor—this after a few recordings which had offered precise and beautiful playing by the orchestra in leaden performances of Beethoven's *Eroica*, Mozart's *Jupiter* and Mendelssohn's *Midsummer Night's Dream* music. In the Carnegie Hall performance of Dvořák's Symphony No. 3 it was clear that the enlivening effect of Leinsdorf's conducting on the progression—the effect of all his fancy stick-work and gestures—was zero. Note succeeded note—now in a *crescendo*, now in a *decrescendo*, now in an acceleration, now in a retardation; but there was no binding of the notes into phrases with cohesive tension and shape, no building up of tension and power in the *crescendo*, no release of tension in the *decrescendo*. Thinking back to his performances in the opera house, which had seemed more effective, I could see that the operation there had been a different one, because of the singers on the stage in addition to the orchestra in the pit. Even if Leinsdorf had done no more than set the traditional tempos and keep singers and orchestra together in them, there had been the life the singers imparted to the vocal parts to keep one from noticing the lack of life in the orchestral part. And as he fitted playing to singing he may have been impelled by the life in the vocal phrase to impart a similar life to the orchestral phrase.

Summer 1965 I doubt that Strauss was concerned, in *Salome*, with what Rudolph Heinrich and Günther Rennert were concerned with in the Metropolitan's new production—the "transition from a pagan to a Christian era", in the words of an interviewer; or that Strauss would have accepted their focusing this "world change upon the back yard of Herod's palace—'the only place a dangerous prisoner would be kept locked up in a cistern', the designer observes"—as embodied in the clutter of platforms and steps on the stage that impeded the action and made it obscure. But I am sure Strauss would have objected to their mishandling of important details of what he *was* concerned with. To consider only one: whether the banquet hall of Herod's palace faces the back yard or, as seems more probable, the terrace that Strauss specifies, to have Narraboth, as he looks through the doorway into the banquet hall, exclaim that Salome has risen, that she is leaving the banquet, that she is coming toward them, and then—while he is still looking at her through the doorway—to have her appear not in the doorway but on a ramp behind the palace, is to destroy dramatic tension with the sudden intrusion of sheer absurdity.

As for the New York City Opera, when Shostakovitch's opera *Lady Macbeth of Mtsensk* was first given in New York in 1935 I noted the contradiction between Russian esthetic theory and artistic fact. The theory expressed scorn for the distorted Western music that it considered to be the artistic manifestation of decay and disillusionment in Western capitalist society, and contended that only the new socialist society in Russia provided the possibilities of faith and affirmation that constituted the conditions of a healthy art; but the fact was the distorted, jeering, grimacing music of Shostakovitch, who had grown to maturity in that new society. But I noted also the stylistic contradictions in the work itself: first the contradiction between the drama, which though brutal was completely serious, and the sardonically jeering music to which much of it was set; and the further contradiction between this music and the occasional serious music—with the result that the work oscillated between taking the characters and their actions seriously and ridiculing them. And these stylistic contradictions remain in the somewhat revised version of the work, now called *Katerina Ismailovna*, presented by the New York City Opera. The undistorted lyricism of a lament by the unhappy Katerina takes her unhappiness seriously; but more often the music jeers at what it deals with. As for the quality of the music, in this early work, as in later ones, Shostakovitch operates with a resourceful fluency that for many people is enough to make him an important composer; but it is a resourceful fluency in writing that is not original—whether it is the undistorted lyricism of Katerina's lament, or the jeering and grimacing in which I hear a reworking of some of Prokofiev's writing by as low-grade and vulgar a mind and taste as has ever communicated itself to me through an artistic medium. Political pressures didn't turn a good composer into a bad one: the music was bad from the start, and political pressures merely made it worse with the required bombastic affirmations of the later works.

The new American opera this time, Jack Beeson's *Lizzie Borden*, turned out to be yet another in the succession of works produced by the company in which the audience's attention is held by an interesting play whose words, instead of being spoken, are sung to musical sounds that don't satisfy the first requirement of any musical writing, namely that it have intrinsic musical value, or the additional requirement of operatic writing, namely that it have expressive force which heightens the effect of the words—these vocal sounds, moreover, in a context of similarly valueless orchestral sounds.

25 September 1965 Reviewing a recital of Horowitz once, Virgil Thomson described the *affetuoso* "teasing" of melody that alternated with bravura in the playing that was "more often than not musically false", and regretted that a man who could play his own pyrotechnical elaborations of things like *Stars and Stripes Forever* and *Danse Macabre* so satisfyingly "should spend so much of the evening worrying standard repertory." I cite this to establish the fact that I am not alone in my low estimate of the musical value of the Horowitz operation, which I would describe as a manipulation of instrument and music for the purpose of exciting an audience, now with its mannered and sensationally fine-spun phrasing of melody, now with its bursts of sensationally supercharged virtuosity, and always with its febrile excitement—a manipulation in which Horowitz not only uses his own pyrotechnical elaborations of "pop" numbers but misuses standard repertory for his purpose. He and his public, of course, take a different view of the operation and what it does with standard repertory, as was demonstrated by the uproar last May over his return to the concert stage after twelve years' absence. The news stories with built-in critical estimates in the magazines—all about the marvels achieved by the matured musicianship operating with unimpaired technical powers—included a *New Yorker* Talk of the Town about a group assembled in the Horowitz living room to hear the Columbia recording of the recital; and in this one read that when Schumann's Fantasy in C came over the speakers, Goddard Lieberson of Columbia Records remarked that he had never seen an audience so quiet and spellbound for this piece, and found this "flabbergasting", since "it's such a profound and difficult piece for an audience. . . . It's not for the usual public. ['It's *against* the public,' Horowitz interposed.] It's like reading Goethe aloud to an audience, the way *you* played it." It was these comments that were "flabbergasting" to me: in my experience Josef Hofmann's performance of Schumann's Fantasy in 1915 or 1916 was the first of a number of performances of the work that held spellbound an audience which found it completely accessible—so accessible as to be one of the familiar works with which pianists demonstrated their powers at debut recitals. My most recent hearing of it, in fact, occurred at the debut of a young pianist named Michael Rogers, who amazed and delighted me with a technical mastery that operated in the service of first-rate musical intelligence and taste to produce a superb performance of the work. It had the spontaneous, natural, unaffected lyricism and warmth, the coherence that is so difficult to achieve in the episodic first movement, the mere tonal beauty—everything that the work calls for, and that turns out to be missing in the Horowitz performance on Columbia M2L-328 (mono). I have listened also to the performance of Chopin's G-minor Ballade, with its distortions that reach their climax in bars 206-7: the first three of the sequence of eighth-notes hammered out with immense slowness, the rest a sensational cascade. Horowitz is still doing the anti-musical playing he has always done, for those who want the excitement it provides. (*The New Republic*)

Fall 1965 Interested in Pierre Boulez's conducting, after Stravinsky's praise of it, I heard the concert in the BBC Symphony's Carnegie Hall series in which he conducted Webern's Six Pieces Op. 6, the three excerpts from Berg's *Wozzeck*, his own *Doubles*, and all three of Debussy's *Images*, of which *Rondes de Printemps*, though one of Debussy's most marvelous scores, is so rarely played that I had never heard it in a concert hall. Of the new works, Boulez's *Doubles* made no sense to me, but Webern's Six Pieces, since it is a still early transitional work, offered actual phrases, some of them stated with wonderfully calculated subtle orchestral coloring, and sometimes producing a moving expressive or atmospheric effect. In the production of these phrases Boulez operated with a complete grasp of the music and command of the magnificent orchestra, a complete adequacy, and never more than adequacy, of what he did for what it got the orchestra to do, that made this the most impressive conducting operation since Toscanini's and Cantelli's. It was an operation I could best appreciate in the Debussy pieces I was most familiar with—in particular *Ibéria*, which I knew almost entirely from Toscanini's performances: in Boulez's superb performance the first movement was brisker; the second, if I remember correctly, more languorous; the third astonishingly different from Toscanini's in its strict tempo, in complete disregard of Debussy's indicated modifications of the tempo.

Winter 1966 Reading about the newly formed Guarneri Quartet last spring, I was interested in whether it would prove to be a replacement for the regrettably short-lived New Music Quartet. And at one of its concerts last summer in Harvard's Sanders Theater I had an opportunity to hear that while it didn't achieve the sheer incandescence, technical and musical, of the New Music Quartet's operation, it was clearly superior to any string quartet I have heard recently. Understandably, it did not, in the opening Quartet K. 589 of Mozart, play with the relaxed ease and security, and therefore the effectiveness and impressiveness, that it attained later in Alban Berg's Quartet Op. 3 and Dvořák's Op. 105; however, even in the Mozart its playing was that of a first-class group which hadn't yet worked off its initial tenseness. But in *The Boston Globe* the next day I found this difference between the later and early playing enormously magnified in Michael Steinberg's statement that "depending on the repertory, the Guarneris can be a group of the most impressive expertness or one that is just the raw material of a good string quartet," and his further statement about the "style of playing [in the Mozart] wherein every phrase had one explosion while the rest was mumbled unintelligibly." Recalling the earlier instances of such strikingly immoderate statement in Steinberg's reviews, I now realized that it was habitual, and that it kept him from being as good a critic as he was equipped to be, and made one unable to read him with confidence that a good thing was as good as he said, or a bad thing as bad, or even, on occasion, that what he spoke of had happened at all.

Landowska on Music brings to mind someone's remark once about how much went into the making of an established poet besides the mere writing of poetry. For with the musical gifts that produced her best performances, Landowska had the gift for self-promotion that won her the status of a deity who commanded rapturous acceptance of her worst excesses of later years. Even newspaper gossips had learned to refer to her as the "high priestess of the harpsichord" in their columns, in which she gushed archly about her communion with "my Bach and the others" who told her they were happy to be alone with her in her Lakeville house, and about her dedication of herself to "my last will and testament"—her recording of the *Well-Tempered Clavier*, which the high priestess offered as divine revelation, but whose distortions of tempo and phrase had no discoverable basis other than the lifelong self-assertion that had grown to the point where musical intelligence and taste no longer exercised any restraint on what was asserted in the playing. The self-promotion included the way, at a concert, she glided mincingly toward the harpsichord, primly holding up her voluminous skirt, and sank into a prayerful pose on the chair. And it included a large amount of writing, some of which is reprinted as Holy Writ in *Landowska on Music*.

The early writing in the collection, represented by a condensed version of her 1908 book, *Music of the Past*, was part of her battle for a cause —for recognition of the value of eighteenth-century music in its original state, performed on the instruments it was written for by musicians who knew how to execute the ornaments, to vary the repetitions, and to do whatever else was required to bring the music to life from the written page in the style of its period. But the later writing, done long after that battle had been won, was part of her battle for herself —her attempt to win acceptance for whatever she chose to do, for which she claimed the sanction of authenticity if it justified her, but, when it did not, set above it the supreme law of her own interpretive insight. On the one hand (p. 307), on behalf of her playing of some

Mozart piano pieces, she claims knowledge of the "science of touch" that can achieve on the modern piano the various colors of the keyboard instruments of Mozart's time; but although some listeners no doubt are persuaded by this that they hear in the playing those sounds of the eighteenth-century clavichord, harpsichord and pianoforte, I could hear only the sounds of Landowska's twentieth-century Steinway; and— more important—I heard in her playing of those pieces the arbitrary distention of tempo and phrase, the thumping of bass, the graceless enunciation of melody, that even the eighteenth-century sounds wouldn't have justified. And on the other hand, one finds her writing about her harpsichord performances (p. 356): ". . . I am sure that what I am doing in regard to sonority, registration, etc., is very far from the historical truth. . . . At no time in the course of my work have I ever tried to reproduce exactly what the old masters did. Instead, I study, I scrutinize, I love, and I recreate. . . . With the Jesuits I say, 'The result sanctifies the means.' . . . I am aware that the disposition of the registers in the harpsichords of Bach's time differed somewhat from those of my Pleyel. But little do I care if, to attain the proper effect, I use means that were not exactly those available to Bach"—which is what Stokowski says in justification of *his* excesses. Or (p. 407) "If Rameau himself would rise from his grave to demand of me some changes in my interpretation of his *Dauphine*, I would answer, 'You gave birth to it; it is beautiful. But now leave me alone with it. You have nothing more to say; go away!' . . . I know that while playing *La Dauphine* I take incredible liberties. Rameau improvised this piece during wedding festivities. Why couldn't I do it too?" The answer to her "why" is that Rameau had the privileges of the composer of the piece and an extraordinary improviser, neither of which Landowska was. And her improvisation in *La Dauphine* amounts to less than the extravagances of pace, style and registration in the performances of this and the other pieces in her recorded *Treasury of Harpsichord Music*.

As against Landowska, Marc Blitzstein had a gift for self-promotion that won him his established position even without genuine creative musical gifts. The evidence of the gift for self-promotion was last year's obituary tributes and memorial concert; the evidence of the lack of creative gifts was his musical works. I made the acquaintance of the gift for self-promotion in 1926, when I had published my first occasional pieces of critical writing, and a Philadelphia friend wrote that Blitzstein was interested in meeting me. Not more than two minutes after his arrival he was seated at the piano, playing from an impressive many-staved and beautifully written manuscript the music for a projected ballet, *Cain*, and expounding the esthetic basis of this and that detail. And in 1931 I had barely arrived at Yaddo when I found myself in his studio, listening to him play from another impressive many-staved and beautifully written manuscript the inconsequential piano concerto he was writing for the League of Composers, while he expounded *its* esthetic basis. This was the last occasion of its kind for me, but not for other people; and the talk about the why and the how that didn't persuade me did persuade these others of the value and importance of the what—the actual music that in fact had no value or importance. The talk changed with the years: In the early thirties when Blitzstein was writing for the small League of Composers audience a string quartet with the novel feature of all three movements in *largo* tempo, the talk was about achieving differentiation of the movements through changes of texture instead of changes of tempo. Later, when he had obtained the attention of a larger audience with music about the class struggle, the talk was about other novel features—for example, the love duet of the working-class couple in *No For an Answer* in which the boy sang, "Fra-a-a-ancie, ta-ta-ta-ta-ta." And later still Blitzstein contributed to the talk about the American musical show as the basis of the American opera—this in connection with his setting of Lillian Hellman's *The Little Foxes* in his opera, *Regina*, and of O'Casey's *Juno and the Paycock* in his musical show, *Juno*.

As for the works themselves, I described once, in these pages, the destructive effect, in *Regina*, of Blitzstein's musical-show writing on certain of the serious dramatic situations of the Hellman play, and on the other hand the failure of his attempts at serious operatic writing for other situations; and, in *Juno*, the falsification of the situations of both pathos and comedy of the O'Casey play by the musical-show lyrics and tunes—more monstrous since it was inflicted on a great play. On another occasion I pointed out that even in 1937 the text of *The Cradle Will Rock*—which won for the work the attention the music would not have won—was a crude agit-prop caricature of the situation it dealt with, on the intellectual level of readers of the *Daily Worker*. And last year's production of the original Brecht-Weill *Dreigroschenoper* revealed how the work had been falsified by the English words and the scoring of Blitzstein's *Three Penny Opera*. We lost with his death not an important creator of American music, but only someone with the ability to persuade a lot of people, including some who should have known better, that he was the important creator he actually was not.

For a performance in the obituary style carried to sheer farce, I offer Harold C. Schonberg's *Times* piece on Galli-Curci. Titled *Galli-Curci the Stylist*, it contended that she was not a flamboyant or an extroverted coloratura singer but "primarily a musical one", and that "her recording of the 'Caro nome' from Verdi's *Rigoletto*, made around 1919, stands as probably the greatest performance ever put on a disk. . . . Musically it is of extreme elegance. . . . Every phrase is turned with extreme finesse and sensitivity, and with a delicate sense of rhythmic variation that lent all kinds of shadows to the performance." Schonberg knows all the right words, but not the right performance to apply them to. I couldn't say of any one performance that it was *the* greatest ever put on a disk; but there are coloratura performances I would say were *among* the greatest on records; and these include some of Hempel's and Ivogün's, but not Galli-Curci's and not her *Caro nome*—the difference being precisely Hempel's and Ivogün's possession of the musical style Calli-Curci lacked. One can say for her *Caro nome* that her fresh voice flows simply and prettily through most of it; but several times she holds on to the initial note of a phrase, not for the additional moment or two that would produce stylistic emphasis within the shape of the phrase, but for the many moments—in order to show off the prettiness of the voice—that each time pull the phrase out of shape. A more striking demonstration of her deficiency is provided by the 1928 recorded performance of *Parigi, o cara* from *La Traviata*, in which Schipa sings first with the delicate tonal and rhythmic inflections and accents of an enchantingly elegant musical style, and Galli-Curci answers with a spineless, characterless slithering around of her by now unattractive-timbred voice.

Some of the material in the Deutsch *Mozart: A Documentary Biography* is of no interest to the general reader; but some of it—the printed and written reports of where and what and for whom Mozart played this day and the next, what operas of his were performed where, what works publishers announced for sale, what was said about him in the announcements, in the press, in letters, in diaries—is enlightening, fascinating and moving. Enlightening, since it establishes the recognition of Mozart's pre-eminence in his lifetime, which didn't keep him from dying in wretched poverty; fascinating and moving, since it gives his day-to-day existence such immediacy.

Spring 1966 The New York City Opera's new production of Rossini's *The Barber of Seville* reminded me that in New York it was this company, not the Metropolitan, that started the business of directors and designers changing the face of an old opera with fancy new ideas. The company was set up in 1944 not—as recent writing would have it—with any idea that it was to provide the New York public with exciting novelty in repertory and production, but merely to make it possible for this public to hear the operatic repertory at low prices. Its small financial resources were enough to secure the numerous young singers with good voices who were available for modest fees, but not to provide first-class scenery and direction; and the 1944 *Carmen*, with shabby old scenery and absurdly inept staging, but conducted effectively by Laszlo Halasz and sung well by a cast headed by Jennie Tourel, was typical of the performances which the public considered sufficient value for the low prices. But while the public was content with this modest operation, Halasz was not; and his attempt at something more impressive took two forms: worthless new works, and new productions of old ones with the deplorable innovations of designers and directors. Even before the Metropolitan's 1954 *Don Giovanni* with the permanent circular ramp destructive to every scene, there was the New York City Opera's 1947 *Don Giovanni* with its tasteless set and the innovations in staging that included Don Giovanni's being seen stealing into Donna Anna's bedroom during the last part of the overture; and this was the first of a series that has continued to this day. In this tradition last fall's *Barber of Seville* had a hideous permanent construction designed by Lloyd Evans, which began as the exterior of Dr. Bartolo's house and later opened up to become an interior inadequate in size and in other respects for the needs of the action. And inadequate for those needs too was Riccardo Moresco's staging; but the production that dealt inadequately with essentials managed to offer unnecessary innovations—for example the front wall of the house that became transparent, allowing Rosina to be seen walking about inside, as the Count sang *Se il nomine*.

In repertory too the adventurousness that exceptionally gave the New York public its first stage productions of Rossini's *La Cenerentola*, Berg's *Wozzeck*, Britten's *A Midsummer Night's Dream*, Copland's *The Tender Land*, more often wasted the company's resources on what, for one reason or another, was not worth hearing—Flotow's *Martha*, Nicolai's *The Merry Wives of Windsor*, Massenet's *Werther*, Strauss's *Die schweigsame Frau*, Walton's *Troilus and Cressida*, Egk's *The Inspector General* and a long series of American works: Still's *Troubled Island*, Tamkin's *The Dybbuk*, the successive Menotti products, Blitzstein's *Regina* and *The Cradle Will Rock*, Weill's *Lost in the Stars* and *Street Scene*, and in recent years the operas of Douglas Moore, Carlisle Floyd, Hugo Weisgall and others subsidized by Ford Foundation grants. The latest of these, this season, was Ned Rorem's *Miss Julie*, which in the columns of *The Herald Tribune* offered "a score . . . of genuine quality" with "arias of compelling lyricism" that merely didn't work with the libretto, but which in the City Center offered a futile and boring two-hour-long attempt by a man of no talent to make like a composer.

These have been the realities of the New York City Opera's operation, as against the grandiose ideas of Julius Rudel about the "fantastic repertory . . . of 110 works", of which "fully one-half constitute perhaps the largest repertory of contemporary works available anywhere" (the many contemporary works dropped after only one season don't constitute "available repertory" or anything to point to with pride), and about the personnel that "moves from Mozart to Weisgall" with unfailing authenticity in every "essential style" (hardly an accurate statement about the recent *Carmen*, *La Traviata* and *The Barber of Seville*). Or as against Alan Rich's echoings of those grandiose fantasies, rising to his apocalyptic conclusion that "the presence of the New York City Opera at Lincoln Center stands as a justifiable inevitability. In its present state the company is an integral artistic unit, impossible to compare, and without need of comparison, to any other operatic venture in the world. Its triumphs are dazzling, and it hasn't ever even made a mistake that wasn't interesting."

It is convenient for Mr. Rudel that he has an unrigorous mind which makes it possible for him, among other things, to defend himself against the criticism that the American operas he has produced have not been masterpieces ("Consider the very small number of operatic masterpieces that exist, and that opera-writing has been going on for three and a half centuries"), when the actual criticism is that they haven't had the minimum of quality and interest that justified their being presented in City Center to a paying audience. He argues that they had to be produced so that American composers might learn and we might reap the fruits of their learning—presumably masterpieces—years from now. But it wasn't the company's producing Still's *Troubled Island*, Tamkin's *The Dybbuk* and Menotti's various pieces of trash that taught Copland how to write *The Tender Land;* and producing the worthless operas of Douglas Moore, Floyd, Beeson, Rorem, Weisgall and the rest is not what will enable someone to write a valuable opera years from now.

Summer 1966 An opera director with the sense for artistic values that Julius Rudel lacks, considering what unusual work to use for a splendid and costly production—paid for by Mrs. John D. Rockefeller, Jr.—to open the New York City Opera's first season in the New York State Theater, would have chosen, possibly, the second part of Berlioz's *The Trojans*, or the original Musorgsky *Boris Godunov*, or—if he wanted a distinguished American work—Virgil Thomson's *The Mother of Us All*. Rudel chose instead the Argentine composer Alberto Ginastera's *Don Rodrigo* as the work on which to lavish the rich and effective sets by Ming Cho Lee and costumes by Theoni V. Aldredge, the skillful stage direction of Tito Capobianco, and the excellent singing of Placido Domingo and Jeannine Crader and playing of the orchestra in the musical performance impressively conducted by Rudel himself. There comes to mind Ezra Pound's likening of Wagner's method to that of the Foire de Neuilly: "You confuse the spectator by smacking as many of his senses as possible at every possible moment" so that "you may slip over an emotion, or . . . sell him a rubber ball or a new cake of glassmender during the hurly-burly." For the dazzling production in the New York State Theater helped to slip over on the audience a mere simulacrum of what it thought of as opera. I say simulacrum because there was the dramatic action—about an eighth-century Visigoth king of Spain undone by passion—that the audience was accustomed to seeing in nineteenth-century romantic opera, but with this only a mere going through the external motions and appearances of the lyrical or impassioned arias, the grand or exalted ensembles which the audience was accustomed to hearing, since their contemporary discordant idiom was incapable of expressing lyricism, grandeur or exaltation.* A *Times* article on *Don Rodrigo* based on an interview with the composer included the statement "Berg's *Wozzeck* is its model"; and concerning this one can say that Berg's discordant music has an integral expressively intensifying relation with the nightmarish action of *Wozzeck* that Ginastera's discordant music does not have with the romantic action of *Don Rodrigo* (except in the one scene of Rodrigo's hallucinatory dream). The production was, then, still another and especially striking instance of the wasting of the company's resources on a work not worth producing. But this time there was not only Alan Rich to proclaim in *The Herald Tribune* the advent of "a magnificent new opera" and "one of the great, dazzling evenings in the history of the city's musical life"; there was the capacity audience that gave Rudel himself an ovation when he appeared to conduct the first act and that wildly applauded after each act, evidently persuaded of the value of the worthless contemporary operas the company produces.

This audience filled the theater and applauded wildly also at a performance of Poulenc's *Dialogues des Carmélites*, whose mellifluous writing had little musical interest for my ear and did very little for the dramatic action concerning the fear-ridden girl of the French nobility who seeks inner security in the Carmelite order, and, after wavering momentarily, finds the courage to ascend the scaffold with the rest. In this production—paid for by Mrs. Henry L. Moses—the stage action devised by Nikos Psacharopoulos was a continual climbing up and down and over the permanent construction of steps and platforms designed by John Conklin that didn't satisfy the imaginative requirements of the scenes.

But even the New York City Opera audience balked at von Einem's *Danton's Tod*, causing the cancellation of the performance I was supposed to attend.

The London Symphony, reappearing in Carnegie Hall's Festival

---

* (1973) Ginastera's *Bomarzo*, which the company produced two years later, was another example of this.

of Visiting Orchestras, with its new permanent conductor, Istvan Kertesz, opened its second concert with a symphony by a young British composer, Richard Rodney Bennett, seemingly expertly put together in an unattractive contemporary idiom which conveyed no musical meaning to me, but calling for the brilliant playing the orchestra did under Kertesz's direction. Prokofiev's Piano Concerto No. 2 provided a better opportunity to hear the beautiful tone of the strings, brass and woodwinds, the balance, beauty and refinement of their combined sonority, the precision and relaxed ease of their execution, and to observe not only the impressive competence and the straightforwardness of Kertesz's operation with the orchestra, but his gearing of its playing with that of Vladimir Ashkenazy in an admirably integrated joint performance of the concerto. One was prepared by all this for a straightforward and effective dealing with Schubert's C-major Symphony, only to be appalled by the personal show that Kertesz used the work for—the fussy inflection of this little detail, the distorting italicizing of that one, the lifting of the subordinate trumpet line into prominence over the oboe's melody, all done with a display of fancy movement of hand, arm and stick.

Ashkenazy, in the concerto, produced one of the most remarkable performances in my experience. Its basis was his mastery of his instrument, including the tone that kept its beauty throughout its dynamic range, from the lovely *piano* of the very first melodic statement to the utmost *fortissimo* of the crashing figurations at the climax of the first movement's cadenza-like development. And as in Cliburn's playing, this mastery served an equal musical mastery in the production of a statement of the work that was completely thought out and completely achieved to the last and the least note. It was a statement in which, as in a Cliburn performance, one heard the operation of an unfailing sense for note-to-note melodic continuity and for plastically coherent shape—in the crashing figurations at the climax no less than in the melodic opening statement. And so it was, like Cliburn's—but of course in its own style different from Cliburn's—the playing of one of the outstandingly, supremely great pianist-musicians of today, and not only of today.

At the last concert Kertesz conducted excellent performances of Berlioz's *Corsair* Overture and Vaughan Williams's Fantasia on a Theme of Thomas Tallis and another admirable context for Ashkenazy's playing, this time in Mozart's Concerto K.271, and ended with Beethoven's Symphony No. 7, which he was content to perform straightforwardly and effectively except for the introduction of an exaggerated accent on the first note of every bar in the Allegretto and an excessive retardation in the build-up to the restatement in the trio of the Scherzo. The high point of the concert was Ashkenazy's performance of the concerto: with the energy and wit in the Allegros, it offered the superb shaping of melody in the lyrical moments of the first movement, in the minuet that interrupts the finale, and above all in the slow movement, whose cantilena was enunciated with a clarity and power of articulation, a continuity of outline and tension, such as one heard in Schnabel's playing of Mozart slow movements.

Contrasting with this was Charles Rosen's performance of the Concerto K.453 with the Festival Orchestra under Thomas Dunn. I had heard Rosen only on records—in a superb performance of Debussy's Etudes and less successful performances of Schubert's posthumous A-major and Beethoven's *Hammerklavier* Sonatas which didn't prepare me for the dainty, mincing, tinkly playing in K.453 that I wouldn't expect from any pianist today, and least of all from one with the intellectual and musical sophistication Rosen has been described as possessing. Nor was I prepared to hear, from the co-winner with Ashkenazy of a Moscow competition, as undistinguished a perfomance of Beethoven's Sonata Op. 110 as John Ogdon's. I might add that his recital extended my acquaintance with Busoni's music by a transcription titled with characteristic pretentiousness *Sonatina super Carmen*, which was quite the most tasteless specimen of this genre that I can recall.

Alerted by a reader who reported a performance of Chopin's Sonata Op. 58 by Van Cliburn in Ann Arbor that was "the strongest Chopin we've heard—with no lingering, no melting, no rubato—with subtlety, firmness, tension and power—very beautiful," I went to Cliburn's recital at Hunter College and heard confirmation of my correspondent's every word except one: there *was* rubato in the performance of the sonata. It was, however, rubato controlled by the unfailing sense for continuity and plastic coherence in Cliburn's powerful shaping of the work. And he exhibited this power not only in the grand style of his delivery of sustained melody in the first movement and the Largo, but in an intensification of the left hand's running comment in the middle section of the Scherzo that was unprecedented. Its powerfully inflected sequences—like the powerfully shaped phrases of melody in Ashkenazy's performance of the slow movement of Mozart's Concerto K.271—clearly were the result of long thinking out and working out; and this was not the first instance of its kind—not the first performance of Cliburn's that was clearly something he had taken a long time to think out for himself to the last detail, and had thought out with the mind of one of the great musicians of today.

The extraordinary musical powers—and in particular the unfailing sense for continuity and coherence in shaping—that operated in Cliburn's Hunter performances have remained unperceived by the reviewers, who have treated him condescendingly as someone capable of dealing effectively with Tchaikovsky and Rachmaninov who had yet to learn how to deal with the music of greater composers. And in the *Times* review of the Hunter recital, what the reviewer had at last perceived was described as something Cliburn had at last learned: "His ability to hold large-scale movements together while investing them with rich details showed a vast increase in that complex composite called musicianship."

Winter 1967 The Guarneri Quartet, in its series of five concerts in Sanders Theater, Cambridge, last summer, played even more impressively than the summer before, and demonstrated that it was unquestionably the ranking string quartet in this country. The tonal beauty, the sensitive inflection, the integrated progression of the four strands of the texture, the musical understanding and taste operating in that progression—these produced realizations of Beethoven's last five quartets such as haven't been heard since the days of the New Music Quartet, and superb performances also of the unfamiliar little Quartet K. 168 of Mozart and the great Op. 20 No. 4 of Haydn. Each concert offered a modern or contemporary work: Webern's *Fünf Sätze* Op. 5 (1909), whose fragmentary sounds lost out in the competition with the noise that came through the open windows; Schönberg's Quartet No. 2 (1907), whose coarser writing could be heard, but conveyed nothing to me; Stravinsky's Concertino (1920), which I found as unattractive this time as when it was first played in New York by the Flonzaley Quartet; Leon Kirchner's Quartet No. 2 (1958), whose empty discordant ranting seemed as bad as anyone could contrive, until Roger Sessions's Second

Quartet (1950) demonstrated at interminable and excruciatingly hideous length to what extremes sheer will could drive lack of creative ability.

The youth of three of the Guarneri group made it inevitable that someone would use the immaturity ploy that is so plausible and so profitable; and the first to do so was the critic of *The Boston Globe*, Michael Steinberg, in his review of the group's first recording of two Mozart quartets. And for him, last summer, the evidence that the Guarneri's playing of late Beethoven was "not yet matured" included their missing—for his ears—"the implied 'attaca' between Cavatina and finale in Op. 130", and their similar missing of the transition between the first and second movements of Op. 131 and the transition from the Scherzo to the Adagio of that quartet. None of these were "missed" for my ears or for the ears of some other musically experienced listeners who heard the performances; but if we had thought they *had* been missed, we wouldn't have dreamed of taking such slight miscalculations of a particular occasion—in performances so impressively mature throughout—as indications of the Guarneri's playing of late Beethoven being "not yet matured".

My first opera of the fall was *La Traviata*—a performance by the Brooklyn Opera Company conducted by a young man named Vincent La Selva. I reported here a few years ago the remarkable technical and musical authority of his conducting of a small group of singers and players in Verdi operas in a parochial school in lower Manhattan; and he operated even more impressively with the more adequate forces of the performance in Brooklyn. It is clear that he has what Bernard Shaw described as the highest faculty of a conductor, namely the "magnetic influence under which an orchestra becomes as amenable to the *bâton* as a pianoforte to the fingers"—and not only an orchestra but singers. And he operates, in a performance of opera, very much as Toscanini did, creating first, with the movements of his stick, a basic orchestral shape, into which those movements of his stick further impel the singers to fit their phrases. Moreover, the molding of the shape is done, like Toscanini's, with the idiomatic *espansione* of the Verdi style within the limits of plastic coherence and good taste, and produced in *La Traviata* a third-act concluding ensemble of Toscanini-like power.

My next opera was the production of Mozart's *The Magic Flute* designed and directed by Beni Montresor for the New York City Opera.

Montresor's idiosyncratic style is as perfectly suited to the fantastic world of *The Magic Flute* as Eugene Berman's is to the grand one of *Don Giovanni;* and the scenery and costumes he designed (except for the pink costume of Pamina which clashes with the subtle colors of everything else) take their place with those of Berman's *Don Giovanni* as the most overwhelmingly beautiful and most effective I can recall seeing in opera—effective, moreover, like Berman's, not only in providing an enhancing context for the work, but in making possible the many changes of scene without the usual delays that destroy continuity. Perhaps in the years to come the company will acquire the singers and orchestra capable of the distinguished musical performance for which Montresor provided the visual context; but it hasn't them now.

Spring 1967 After Philharmonic Hall and the New York State Theater it was a relief to hear the natural, warm sound in the new Metropolitan Opera House, which is in this respect superior not only to the other two Lincoln Center theaters but to the old Metropolitan, whose acoustical deficiencies were reason enough not to preserve it. And after the curtain rose there was evidence of the new house's superior stage facilities—more evidence, in fact, than Verdi's *La Traviata* needed. In the parties in the first and third acts Cecil Beaton provided spectacular sets—the second with a double grand staircase—which seemed excessive for the salons of two Parisian *demi-mondaines*, even luxurious salons frequented by barons and marquises; and the bedroom of the last act was implausibly huge. But what Toscanini would have denounced was the transferring of Act 2 from the specified drawing room in a country house to an outdoor area between the house and the barn. What dramatic purpose and advantage this was intended to achieve I was unable to discover; but I did appreciate the absurdity of the elder Germont exclaiming "Such luxury!" as he glanced not at the rich furnishings of a drawing room but at some pieces of garden furniture, and of Violetta answering him by handing him a document that she didn't take from a drawer in her desk but picked up from the garden table. And I continued to feel the need of a room—for the intimate conversations, the writing of letters, the entrances and exits—instead of the outdoor space. Moreover, though Lunt's staging was skillful and effective, it included one piece of invention which I found open to strong objection: Violetta's beginning to dance with Baron Douphol, and the rest of the company joining them, as Alfredo sang his *Libiamo*. It made a fine stage effect, but contradicted the words introducing the song: Alfredo is asked for a toast, after Baron Douphol has refused; he asks Violetta if she would like it, and she says yes; the Marquis asks for everyone's attention; the chorus shouts, "Yes, attention to the singer!"—all of which requires Violetta and the others to listen to Alfredo's song, not to ignore it by beginning to dance. Much worse, however, were the consequences of the musical decisions that Bing reserved to himself—not only the choice of Prevedi for the role of Alfredo, in which he produced some unpleasant sounds, but, more important, the choice of Georges Prêtre for a work of Verdi, which he conducted with no feeling for the Verdian *espansione* needed to give it rhetorical effect and with nothing in its place that gave the work coherence and shape.

Summer 1967 Whereas the New York City Opera's *La Traviata* at the City Center three years ago anticipated the Metropolitan's of this year in transferring the second act from the drawing room to the garden, the new one at the New York State Theater last fall, designed by Robert Fletcher, left the second act in the drawing room, but had Flora, in the next act, give a *bal masqué* in the courtyard of her house instead of the salon specified in the score. This caused an important change in the action: instead of Violetta and Alfredo confronting each other alone in the deserted salon, and Alfredo then calling in the other guests from the adjoining rooms for his denunciation of her, the confrontation was witnessed by the others from the start. Moreover, the other acts were damaged by Frank Corsaro's innovations in direction. In the first act the girls running across the stage pursued by drunken amorous men grotesquely misrepresented the actual dramatic situation—a party in an elegant salon frequented by barons and marquises. In the second act the wheeling in of a tea table and Violetta's pouring tea for Germont and herself, distractingly incongruous in the tense dramatic situation, led to an even more damaging detail: during Violetta's anguished outburst a few moments later, Germont lifted his cup and took sips of tea. This was in accordance with the present-day idea of making opera into effective theater with the kind of action one sees on the dramatic stage, which, however, by drawing attention to itself and away from the music, makes the opera less effective as opera. That idea produced Patricia Brooks's performance as Violetta, with its profusion of novel movement and stage business not only between arias but during an aria, where it drew attention away from the music that was intended to be the medium of expressive communication. And it also led her to chew up the music in explosions of tremulous tone that made their dramatic effect with the impact of their intensity, instead of producing shaped phrases that made their dramatic effect by expressive inflection and coloring. However, there was excellent singing by Placido Domingo as Alfredo and good singing by Dominic Cossa as Germont, in a performance in which Franco Patane's conducting didn't exercise a control over the singers that fitted their singing into a musical shape it created with the orchestra (as Vincent La Selva's had done in the Brooklyn Opera performance), but was instead a mere beating of time that accommodated the orchestra's playing to whatever the singers did.

The production of Handel's *Julius Caesar* was another matter. Though I found Ming Cho Lee's permanent construction unattractive, its high platform with stairs leading down to the stage worked admirably in filling with action the enormous space framed by the proscenium arch. Excellent too were the costumes designed by José Varona in an eighteenth-century idea of ancient Roman and Egyptian styles; the choreographed movements of a stylized plastique that Tito Capobianco had the singers make; the singing of Norman Treigle, Beverly Sills, Maureen Forrester and Beverly Wolff; the conducting of Rudel. And it all added up to an outstanding achievement in opera production.

The new American opera commissioned with Ford Foundation money was Vittorio Giannini's *The Servant of Two Masters*, another appalling waste of the company's resources of talent and effort, and presumably not the last.

As for the Metropolitan, the new Wieland Wagner stage production of *Lohengrin* was another of those we are getting these days, which substitute the designer's and director's ideas for the composer's, sometimes with disregard of the meaning of the words that are being sung. Thus Wagner places the first act of *Lohengrin* on the bank of a river, and has Lohengrin make his entrance in a boat drawn by a swan, to which—after he has stepped onto the bank—he turns to sing his thanks and farewell. But his grandson chooses to place the act in a space enclosed by a vaulted and veined backdrop, with the chorus lined up on platforms in a large semi-circle at the back, and the principals spaced out in front; to have principals and chorus peer out into the Metropolitian's auditorium and sing their amazement at what is not there to amaze them—Lohengrin in the boat drawn by the swan—while Lohengrin actually makes his appearance behind them out of a backstage depth under a huge swan projected on the backdrop; and to have him step forward and address to the audience his thanks and farewell to the swan. Toscanini would have vehemently denied the right of anyone—even the composer's grandson—to change the scene and action in this way; as for me, I tried to discover what in the changed scene and action Wieland Wagner might have thought was better than the original, but could find nothing. And if the purpose was merely the elimination of the absurdity, for an audience today, of a knight arriving in a boat drawn by a swan, what was substituted was just as absurd.

I dispense with discussion of the other singularities of this kind that competed for attention with the largely excellent dramatic and musical performances by the principals—above all the Ortrud of Christa Ludwig, which revealed her as a singing actress of compelling power like that of Frida Leider and Kerstin Thorborg.

Whereas Beni Montresor's idiosyncratic style worked enchantingly for the fantastic world of Mozart's *The Magic Flute* in the New York City Opera's new production, Marc Chagall's by now tiresome clichés—in their irrelevance to Mozart's work, and on the gigantic scale of the many curtains and backdrops that overwhelmed it, in the Metropolitan's production—were an irritating obtrusion that one had to fight off all evening to see and hear the performance. The one I attended had the superbly sung and acted Tamino and Papageno of Nicolai Gedda and Hermann Prey, but the dumpt-figured and cold-voiced Pamina of Pilar Lorengar, a Queen of the Night whom Lucia Popp's tiny voice couldn't make the formidable personage she should be, and the hollow-voiced Sarastro of Jerome Hines. Krips gave it sufficient amination, but provided an excessively bland orchestral context for the singing.

Britten's *Peter Grimes* was given the benefit of the excellent sets and costumes of Tanya Moiseiwitsch and staging of Tyrone Guthrie, the musical performance superbly conducted by Colin Davis and made impressive—in spite of Lucine Amara's pallid- and tremulous-voiced

Ellen Orford—by the singing of Jon Vickers in the title role and Geraint Evans as Balstrode. But the music, with few exceptions—notably Peter's anguished phrases after his argument with Balstrode in Act 1, and the affecting orchestral introduction to Act 3—struck me again as resourcefully contrived to describe the scene and carry the words, but without the additional quality and power that would make those words eloquent and moving.

As for Marvin David Levy's *Mourning Becomes Electra*, it offered arbitrary vocal arioso with no expressiveness or relevance to the words, over dissonant orchestral hubbub with no relevance to the arioso. And it constituted the beginning of Rudolf Bing's participation in the Ford Foundation-American opera ballet originated by the New York City Opera's Julius Rudel, but on the Metropolitan's Tiffany—as against the New York City Opera's dime-store—scale. Which is to say that Bing wasted on the worthless Levy opera commissioned with Ford Foundation money a far more costly production (designed by Boris Aronson) and more costly singers (principally the superb Marie Collier and Evelyn Lear), orchestra and conductor (Zubin Mehta) than Rudel did on *The Servant of Two Masters*.

The mezzo-soprano Janet Baker, last fall, deserved the enthusiastic applause at her concert with the Melos Ensemble at Hunter College Assembly Hall and her solo recital in Town Hall for her singing in pieces by Handel, Spohr and Chausson at the first, and in songs of Berlioz, Duparc and Fauré at the second—the beauty of her voice, the security in its production that enabled it to do whatever was required of it, and the unfailing musical intelligence and taste revealed in what it was required to do. Playing with her in the Spohr songs were the extraordinary clarinettist Gervase de Peyer and a superb pianist, Lamar Crowson.

Of Fischer-Dieskau's three recitals in Carnegie Hall the greatest was the one at which he employed his remarkable voice and affecting art in the succession of marvels of expressive vocal writing in contexts of imaginative piano writing that Schubert produces in *Die Winterreise*. Thinking about certain characteristics of the performances, and groping for a description of the singer's operation that would include them, I received unexpected help. Harold Schonberg is forever placing performers in non-existent "styles", "traditions" and "schools"; and so "where other singers use their voice in an instrumental-like manner (this was especially true of some of the previous generation of lieder singers)," according to Schonberg, "Mr. Fischer-Dieskau is more of the Elena Gerhardt school." I don't recall any earlier *Lieder*-singers who used their voices "in an instrumental-like manner"; but one way to describe Fischer-Dieskau's operation is to say it is the opposite of Gerhardt's. With her—since the meaning of the words was embodied in the musical phrase—the correctly proportioned shape of that phrase established limits which the expressive inflection of vocal tone might not exceed; whereas Fischer-Dieskau allows the meaning of the words to impel him to vocal inflection which exceeds those limits. (The singer of the past who did this was Lotte Lehmann.)

Nonsense in *The Times* cannot hurt a foreign celebrity, but it can gravely damage the career of an uncelebrated young American, since managers all over the country make their decision to engage or not to engage a performer on the basis of the *Times* review, in the mistaken belief that a reviewer of *The Times* has the authoritative competence the paper's prestige would lead one to expect. A few years ago, at the request of friends, I attended the first recital of a twenty-two-year-old pianist named Michael Rogers, expecting to hear the talent they had told me about, but unprepared for his actual astounding mastery of instrument and music. This didn't keep *The Times's* Ross Parmenter from writing the customary report on a debut recital, in which he described what one might expect to hear at such a recital, and in so doing demonstrated his possession of the discernment that enabled him to recognize that Rogers had "an inborn flair for the keyboard" but was not "as yet a finished artist", that his playing "sometimes had moving quality" but "was often superficial," and so on. It wasn't a review that would bring a performer overwhelming demands for appearances; and there was no opportunity to hear Rogers again until his recital this year in the Metropolitan Museum's Young Artists Series. In the very first phrase of Schumann's Intermezzi Op. 4 I heard again the assured mastery of instrument and music that had astounded me the first time. Beethoven's *Appassionata* Sonata, which followed, was hardly a work in which to expect surprises; but Rogers did offer the surprise of playing more powerfully impassioned than I could recall ever hearing in the work—and this not only in the fast movements but in the Andante, which is usually rattled off as a mere interlude before the stormy finale, but which Rogers related to the impassioned fast movements by making it slower than usual and more intensely expressive. But readers of *The Times* were told by Robert Sherman of "a forceful keyboard personality [who] dives into his pieces with furious energy, seemingly more intrigued with their virtuoso potential than their emotional content", and who took the first movement of the *Appassionata* at "a breathless clip", and "after the slow movement, which seemed downright listless by comparison, took off again in the finale," which "went like the wind, with musical values trailing behind the sheer propulsive thrust of the playing." And that now became the official image.

Fall 1967 Opera continues to be written about in terms of ideas without regard for the facts that contradict them. The latest instance is the writing occasioned by the Hamburg State Opera's visit last June for a week of performances in the Lincoln Center Festival. The writing was concerned with the contrast between the opera presentations of a company like the Metropolitan which traffics in star singers —concerts in costume "with a bit of moving and posturing", in the words of Rolf Liebermann, director of the Hamburg Opera—and the presentations of a company like the Hamburg, which has no star singers but only the good singing actors who are required for the *realistisches Musiktheater* Liebermann believes in. An article by Paul Moor in the June issue of *High Fidelity* quoted this statement of Liebermann:

> Any opera of any real artistic merit deals with human emotions and conflicts which the performers *must* transmit to the audience, just as in a play. In the theatrical form which the word "opera" has for generations meant to most people, the musical notes in the score have ruled supreme and the text has come off a very poor second best. . . . Opera, in this sense, belongs to the last century. Realistic musical theatre, with neither music nor text subordinated to the other but both integrated into a new form, belongs to the twentieth century.

And Moor mentioned another feature of this new form—that "the performance also must make dramatic and psychological sense in all details." This required rehearsal; and Moor wrote that Hamburg put into rehearsals the money other companies paid for star singers. Hence, in place of concerts in costume by assemblages of such stars, Hamburg could offer the integrated dramatic performances of a well-rehearsed permanent ensemble of singing actors. And concerning these, Liebermann said:

> Musical theatre has of necessity developed a new breed, the singing actor, as demanded by a new art form. One reason you won't find the biggest operatic names in our house is that we demand of our people things you can't ask from the biggest stars—for one very simple reason: they can't do them. Our people even *look* different.

I disagree with Liebermann's contention that the opera performances in which the musical notes counted for more than the words were performances which didn't transmit the human emotions and conflicts the opera dealt with. The point of opera, as against the spoken play, is that it makes its effect through the music, and requires, to make that effect, first that the music be expressively convincing, and second that it be effectively sung. If, then, those performances in which the music counted for more than the words were performances of operas with expressive music and with singers who sang it effectively, they transmitted the essential dramatic values. And actually all of us have been moved by just such performances—i.e. by the dramatic values transmitted almost entirely by the music and the singing.

This doesn't mean I don't care about the words being pronounced clearly, and the staging of the performance making dramatic sense. I do care about them; but here I dispute Liebermann's contention that these are new things in opera production that can be achieved only by a new kind of opera singer, the singing actor, and not by the old kind, the star singer. It is my impression that some of the star singers—Fremstad, Chaliapin, Leider, Lehmann, Pinza—were remarkable singing actors. And from what Jan Peerce told me about Toscanini's care and work to obtain correct and expressive pronunciation of the words, confirmed by my observation of his NBC rehearsals of operas; from the reports testifying to his concern with scenery and staging—from all this I would feel certain that Toscanini's performances with star singers at La Scala and the Metropolitan were not mere concerts in costume "with a bit of moving and posturing". But having heard and seen the 1929 La Scala *Lucia* and *Falstaff*, I can say these *were* dramatically integrated and effective performances by sufficiently rehearsed assemblages of singers, some of them stars, and some of

them great singing actors; and I will risk the contention that their participation made them more effective, as *realistisches Musiktheater*, than
what Hamburg achieves with its singing actors of less magnitude. Nor
were Toscanini's the only productions of that kind. Mahler's legendary
productions in Vienna offered not only his distinguished performances
of the music with great singers like Slezak and Kurz, but carefully
planned and executed staging in which Mahler worked with designers
and regisseurs of his choice. His disciple Bruno Walter achieved similar
productions in Munich; even at the Metropolitan Walter and Herbert
Graf produced the *Figaro* of the early forties that was brilliantly sung
and acted by Pinza, Brownlee, Steber, Sayão and Novotna; and there
have been other productions there which have offered well-rehearsed
assemblages of star singers in impressive musical and dramatic ensemble
operations—e.g. the 1950 *Don Carlo*, the 1957 *Don Giovanni*, with its
great Eugene Berman scenery and costumes, the first *Wozzeck* with
Uhde—which were more effective, as *realistisches Musiktheater*, than
Hamburg's productions.

The Hamburg production of Berg's *Lulu* did offer a smooth-running
ensemble operation by a well-rehearsed group—certainly a satisfying
experience, but not one I had had to wait for the Hamburg Opera
to give me. Nor was it given an exciting new dimension as *realistisches
Musiktheater* by what the company claims as its innovations: the words
were not always audible through the orchestra, as they are not in
opera performances everywhere; the acting was not a new kind by
a new breed of singing actor, but for the most part the usual acting
of opera singers, directed by Günther Rennert as poorly for the work's
purposes as singers at the Metropolitan have been, by him among
others. Two exceptional achievements—through costume, make-up and
acting ability—were the ebullient Rodrigo of Gerd Feldhoff in the
Prologue, and the shifty old Schigolch of Kim Borg. But instead of
the *"Ungeheuer"* the work calls for, Anneliese Rothenberger's Lulu was
a pretty, capricious, immoral soubrette who now and then indulged
in a tantrum; and Erwin Wohlfahrt's Painter and Gerhard Unger's
Alwa, the writer son of Dr. Schön, were more like prosperous business-
men. Moreover, the needs of the work were subordinated to the idea
that Rennert and the designer, Teo Otto, considered more important
—the idea of the performance taking place in a circus arena before
the circus audience. One saw, then, throughout the performance,

beyond circus ropes and bars in the background, a backdrop with the circus audience that observed the happenings in the foreground on a permanent set on which changes of scene were effected by changes in a few pieces of furniture and props. As John Simon remarked, these changes didn't adequately convey Lulu's rise to luxury; but in addition the unenclosed unit set created difficulties with entrances and exits that were distracting and destructive to illusion. And worse still was the lowering of a movie screen—between the second act and what was presented of the uncompleted third act—and the projection on it of slides which told in words and drawings what happened to Lulu after the second act—certainly something that had never been done before in an opera production, but as certainly something not to do, and not to be expected in a production offered as *realistisches Musiktheater*.

As for *Lulu* itself, listening to it on records years ago I found that the music did not, for me, work effectively with the text as the music of *Wozzeck* had done. And now I found that it didn't work for me even with the text realized on the stage, as the music of *Wozzeck* had done. The reasons for this that occur to me begin with the difference between the texts: the words of *Wozzeck*, the predicaments of its characters, are themselves powerfully moving; the distorted vocal declamation heightens the effect of the words; the discordant orchestral writing provides a nightmarish context for the vocal declamation. On the other hand the situations and words of *Lulu* leave me uninvolved; and Berg carries the method of *Wozzeck* to extremes in which the exacerbated vocal writing has no relevance at all to the words, and the orchestral luxuriance no relevance to the vocal writing. To my ear, then—and as always I speak of what my ear heard, not of what my eye might see on the printed page—*Lulu* is not the masterpiece that others accept it as being.

Spring 1968 It was not surprising to read, in an interview with Vladimir Ashkenazy (in *The Gramophone* of August 1967), that Rachmaninov was one of the older pianists who had influenced him; but one was surprised that someone impressed by Rachmaninov's highly charged melodramatics should have been influenced also by playing so antithetical in its refinement, subtlety and elevation as Schnabel's. And one was dumbfounded that someone capable of appreciating these characteristics of Schnabel should be impressed by Serkin's violent belaboring of music and instrument, and should hear in it an "approach . . . so genuine and spiritual", and "interpretations [which carry] one to new regions of experience". But then one thought of Ashkenazy's own playing, and realized that it included nothing attributable to any of these older players: he had been impressed by what they did when he had listened to them; but when he sat down at the piano himself, his own remarkable musical intelligence and taste began to operate, and he did what they directed him to do.

Reading further, one was appalled to learn that a particular admiration for Serkin's performances of Beethoven's concertos was one of the reasons why Ashkenazy didn't record them—why, presumably, he hadn't recorded the superb performance of No. 3 two years ago, from which Serkin could have learned how to treat the piano and Beethoven's music. Equally appalling was the other reason: "With Beethoven and Mozart I feel at something of a disadvantage compared with someone like Daniel Barenboim who has been brought up in the classical Viennese tradition"—that Viennese tradition which has as much to do with Barenboim's playing as it had to do with the vastly different playing of Schnabel, or as the Texas tradition has with Cliburn's, the Toronto tradition with Gould's, the Moscow tradition with Ashkenazy's. The Viennese tradition is, I take it, a subject on which Barenboim has produced the kind of pretentious chatter he delivered at length about the concluding fugue of Beethoven's *Hammerklavier* Sonata on a National Education Television program a year ago; and on that program one got something worth listening to only in Ashkenazy's occasional sentence or two. And if one sets Barenboim's recorded performance of Beethoven's Concerto No. 3 against Ashkenazy's performance two years ago, or Barenboim's recent recorded performances of Mozart's Concerto K.491 and Sonata K.576 against Ashkenazy's of the Concerto K.271, it turns out that Barenboim's knowing all about the Viennese tradition doesn't enable him to produce anything like the superbly conceived and executed performances Ashkenazy produces with only his disciplined knowledge of how to play music on the piano—which Barenboim doesn't have.

Fortunately Ashkenazy's awe of his inferiors doesn't keep him from playing in the concert hall; and there he shames his equals, Cliburn and Gould, by fulfilling the obligation of his powers as they do not—which is to say, by playing major works of the piano literature they leave unlearned. The independence I spoke of earlier was most striking in this year's performances of Schubert's posthumous Sonata in B-flat and Beethoven's *Hammerklavier*, which were totally different from the authoritative Schnabel performances on records that I assume Ashkenazy must know. To begin with a small matter, he didn't follow Schnabel in the belief that the sacredness of the printed text extended even to the printer's errors, obliging one to play the clearly incorrect C-sharp in the fifth bar of the second movement of the Schubert: for Ashkenazy (as for Toscanini) errors in the text were something to correct, and he played the B that Schubert intended. More important, as against the occasional dramatic turbulence of Schnabel's performance of the first movement of the Schubert, Ashkenazy's maintained through-out the movement the retrospectively reflective character of the opening statement, which he evidently, and correctly, regarded as establishing the tone of the movement. A performance so quiet of a movement so long and episodic incurred a risk of failure—i.e. of loss of interest; but he made it succeed with the sustained tension that caused it to hold the mind from first note to last. Moreover, Ashkenazy carried over into the later movements something of the reflective character of the first; and this made his performance of the work, though different from Schnabel's—the second movement, for example, simpler, without Schnabel's prolonging of time values in an enlargement of the music's shape that enlarges its expressive dimensions—a unified statement of it that was an impressive interpretive achievement. (But Harold Schonberg heard that Ashkenazy "had given great thought to its architecture . . . and had pondered every dynamic relationship. . . . Every note was carefully weighted, every phrase tidy." As a result "spontaneity was lacking," and Ashkenazy was "a little boring in his determined perfection. After a while one longed for . . . a wrong note, even an error in taste. Anything. But nothing ever happened. And that was the trouble." At a later Ashkenazy recital a woman was heard to say: "Harold Schonberg thought his playing was too perfect, that it needed some wrong notes"; to which her companion answered: "Oh, but he is still young!")

In Beethoven's *Hammerklavier* too the sacredness of the printed text extends for Schnabel to the metronome marking that makes the first movement a frenetic rush which he cannot even execute clearly; but

Ashkenazy didn't follow him in this "mistaken form of piety", as Tovey characterized it, and instead found the tempo in which he could articulate and shape the movement in what emerged as the most effective statement of it in my experience. In the slow movement his simpler playing again did not achieve the expressive enlargement that Schnabel's achieves with its expansiveness in time, but it did give the long movement unfailing coherence and expressive eloquence. And I have never heard the concluding fugue given the clarity of texture and structure Ashkenazy gave it.

As unexpected as Haydn's extraordinary writing in the middle movements of his Piano Trios No. 11 in A-flat and No. 4 in E, at a New School concert, was the electrifying playing of the piano's variation in the one, and its florid aria in the other, by a young pianist named Murray Perahia. But his playing was impressive throughout the performances with Alexander Schneider, whose violin-playing had a little less than its former vitality, and the excellent cellist Robert Sylvester.

No one has contended that the paintings of Constable must be repainted in a contemporary style, or the novels of Jane Austen rewritten, to make them interesting to the public of today; but the designer-director teams who have in recent years inflicted on operas the monstrosities of staging that would make the works unrecognizable to their creators *have* contended that these were necessary to make the works valid for present-day audiences. The latest occasion for this contention is the Metropolitan Opera's new production of Wagner's *Die Walküre*, with scenery designed by Günther Schneider-Siemssen and costumes by George Wakhevitch for the staging by von Karajan. "Our work," said Schneider-Siemssen in the Metropolitan program, "and the work of *Neu-Bayreuth* have the same goal, which is to build a bridge into the future, in order that Wagner and his work be preserved for future audiences. . . . Because of the increased speed of living, contemporary man has lost his ability for endurance and patience. He tends to criticize Wagner . . . for the length of his operas." And "the public's interest . . . can be aroused again through the use of optical means of expression in the theatre." But actually "contemporary man" includes those who love Wagner's *Ring* operas and those who, like myself, dislike them; what the ones love, and the others dislike, is the music; those who love the music have done so when they have heard it with conventional stage productions and even, on records, with no stage productions at all, and do not need the drastic innovations of contemporary staging to persuade them to continue to do so; and those who dislike the music do not do so because of the conventional staging with which they have heard it, and will not be persuaded to like it by the "updated" staging Schneider-Siemssen advocates. In this actual situation the justification of such a staging—whether Wieland Wagner's at Bayreuth or the Schneider-Siemssen-Karajan *Walküre* at the Metropolitan—can be solely that it makes the opera work more effectively than a staging which executes Wagner's specifications.

In his superb little book on opera production, *The Ring at Bayreuth*, Victor Gollancz stated his general rule that the style of production must "help in realising the musical-dramatic intention of the work," and conversely that the producer "must never so obtrude his visualities (things seen on the stage) as deliberately to focus a preponderance of attention upon them"—which implied that some "visualities" *had* been intended to focus attention on themselves. In the Metropolitan program for *Die Walküre* the synopsis of scenes read "Act 1 Hunding's hut"—this in accordance with Wagner's text, which states further that in the center of the room there is a large tree, that the fire in the fireplace throws its light on the hilt of a sword thrust into the tree, that there is an adjoining room from which Sieglinde emerges and into which Hunding retires, and that there are doors at the back which, near the end of the act, spring open and reveal the moonlit spring night that Siegmund sings about. I cannot imagine what Schneider-Siemssen would contend the act gained by having the rising curtain reveal not the room Wagner specifies but only an enormous tree standing in dark space, and having the act performed in the hollowed-out base of this tree—specifically what it gained by there being no fireplace, no fire, no adjoining room, no doors at the back. What I do know is what the act lost by all this, and the damage inflicted by the "visuality" of the kind Gollancz described—the spectacular tree which at once drew the attention to itself that I think was its real purpose, and continued to distract one with thoughts of its evident deficiencies for the requirements of Wagner's work and the absurdities it asked one to accept.

The Metropolitan program placed Act 2 in "a wild, rocky pass"; but the rising curtain revealed a narrow platform curving around the front of the stage in the form of a ring—another distracting "visuality", to which was added the distracting absurdity of Wotan and Fricka berating each other from two widely separated points on the platform. Then the ring dissolved and was replaced by other constructions on the darkened and misty stage; and having Brünnhilde become visible to Siegmund in a circle of light high above him, from which she continued to address him, gave this confrontation in the *Todesverkündigung* an impressive effect it hadn't had when she had walked onto the stage. But at the end of the act, in Siegmund's combat with Hunding high at the back, Siegmund's sword was struck from his hand by a dazzling shaft of light, which was effective certainly, but no more so than what Wagner specifies here: the sudden appearance of Wotan, who breaks Siegmund's sword with his spear, to the words *"Zurück vor dem Speer; das Schwert in Stücken"*, which I don't think were sung at the Metropolitan. Moreover, Wagner's action continues effectively by having Wotan remain between the fallen Siegmund and the standing Hunding, whom he annihilates with a gesture of his hand, telling him to inform Fricka that she has been avenged by Wotan's spear; but at the Metropolitan Wotan, after the shaft of light had enabled Hunding to kill Siegmund, appeared ineffectively at one side of the stage, where he made the gesture that killed Hunding high at the back, and made the statement about his spear that was belied by what one had seen happen.

The new production also provided my first experience of von Karajan's conducting of opera in the opera house. At the incredible age of twenty Bernard Shaw was able to perceive the "highest faculty of a conductor" to be "the establishment of a magnetic influence under which an orchestra becomes as amenable to the *bâton* as a pianoforte to the fingers"; and von Karajan's magnetic influence over the Metropolitan orchestra was impressively evident in the extraordinary playing one heard. His conception of the work was criticized after the first performance for its understatement of the first act and parts of the second; but the understatement I heard at a later performance, though untraditional, worked convincingly; and where power was called for, von Karajan produced it. He had previously shown himself to be the possessor of remarkable powers that he used erratically and capriciously; but on this Saturday afternoon he operated with unfailing responsibility to his task, and achieved a performance that was an unforgettable demonstration of technical and musical mastery.

It remains to report that in his understated first act he had the benefit of the ear-ravishing *mezza-voce* singing of Jon Vickers; and in the second act Christa Ludwig's Fricka provided a briefer demonstration of the extraordinary powers as a singing actress than she revealed in last year's Ortrud. On the other hand, the unpleasant voice of Régine Crespin, the Sieglinde, was not one to enjoy hearing with Vickers's; Thomas Stewart was no more than an acceptable Wotan; and while the power and steadiness and accuracy of Birgit Nilsson's voice satisfied important requirements of Brünnhilde, its lack of warmth and luster and its basically unattractive timbre made her performance less than satisfying, especially to someone who remembered Flagstad's.

Summer 1968 The *Hamlet* of Jean-Louis Barrault and his company years ago impressed me as the greatest in my experience; their production of Offenbach's operetta *La Vie Parisienne* a few years ago was a delight; and so it is difficult to understand how a man who produced things as right as those could go so wrong in the *Faust* he created for the Metropolitan two years ago and the even worse *Carmen* this year. He was quoted as saying, "I was terrified at the idea of staging *Carmen*. What could I contribute?" What he contributed, we were told further, embodied an idea of Don José and Carmen as antagonists in Spain's erotic ritual of the bull fight. This could be a fascinating idea for a newly created ballet or opera; but applied to the actually existing Meilhac-Halévy-Bizet opera, it encountered the difficulty that it encompassed only part of that work—only Carmen's ensnaring of Don José in Act 1 and their final confrontation in Act 4, not the happenings involving them in Acts 2 and 3, and not the happenings involving others in the four acts. And a production of the entire work embodying an idea which encompassed only part of it worked badly with the rest. Thus, it meant that the bull ring whose exterior is part of the scene of the action of Act 4 of the opera appeared, in Barrault's production, also in the three earlier acts; and in Act 1 one saw its interior—in back the rising tiers of the amphitheater, on which members of the chorus were deployed as spectators of the happenings in the arena in the foreground. Now one could take the action involving Carmen and Don José figuratively, in accordance with Barrault's idea, as a happening in the arena of a bull ring; but not the soldiers watching passers-by, not Micaela's encounter with Morales, not the changing of the guard, not the factory girls flirting with the men of the town, not Micaela's duet with Don José. Perhaps for this reason—to make them happenings in an arena—Barrault converted the various activities of groups into choreographed dance; but one couldn't accept this stylization with the action of the principals that was left naturalistic; and in addition one objected to having the music obliterated by the noise of the stamping feet. Also, replacing the square in Seville with the bull ring meant that there was no factory for the factory girls to emerge from—which resulted in their emerging, improbably, from a passage under the amphitheater, and Carmen's entering at the top of the amphitheater, from which she worked her way down to the arena.

The bull-ring set had relevance to at least part of the action in Act 1; but it had no such relevance to justify its appearance in Lillas Pastias's tavern in Act 2, where in addition it created difficulties with entrances and exits. And the use of a few sections of the amphitheater topped by a few bare trees to provide the mountain scene of Act 3 was sheer absurdity. Moreover, someone reminds me that the smugglers' entrance at the beginning of this act was another choreographed dance. But I need no reminder of the appalling detail Barrault introduced at the end of the act: instead of being heard singing the Toreador Song in the distance, Escamillo returned to sing it standing spotlighted at the top of a section of the amphitheater.

Picking its way through the clutter of this production the cast headed by Grace Bumbry, Nicolai Gedda, Jeanette Pilou and Justino Diaz managed to give a performance of the opera that was quite good. Its chief point of interest was Bumbry's Carmen, which was excellently sung and acted, but created a difficulty for me I wouldn't have had if she had been the Amneris in a performance of *Aida*. It was the same difficulty I had had with Leontyne Price's Pamina in a televised *Magic Flute* and her Leonora in *Il Trovatore*—the difficulty of visual credibility that John Simon had with Diana Sands's performance in *Saint Joan*. One accepts a great deal in opera; but I am bothered by something so unbelievable as two proud Spaniards contending over a Leonora—or the gloating Moor Monostatos exclaiming over the white skin of a Pamina—who is a black. I believe that in law, medicine, the university, the symphony orchestra, direction of plays and films, and countless other fields, a black should be given any opportunity he or she is equipped for; but when I am looking at what is presented on a stage my imagination cannot accept a black actress in the role of, say, Irina in Chekhov's *The Three Sisters*, and wouldn't be able to accept a singer in the role if the play were to be made into an opera.

The writing about Daniel Barenboim brings to mind someone's remark years ago about how much went into the making of an established poet besides the mere writing of poetry. What goes into the reports in *The Times* of Barenboim's operating "with the maturity of a performer twice his age"—besides his actual undisciplined, which is to say immature, performing of music—is his gift for putting himself over as what he is not. And it is the gift not only of Barenboim the pianist but of Barenboim the conductor, as he demonstrated when he substituted for Kertesz at the four Carnegie Hall concerts of the London Symphony, with Ashkenazy in the four Rachmaninov concertos. His musical operation in Beethoven's *Eroica* and Fifth, Mozart's *Prague* and Schubert's Ninth turned out to be as undisciplined—as uncontained within the frame of the piece—as it had been in Beethoven's *Appassionata* Sonata at his Carnegie Hall recital, producing shapeless performances in which detail was distorted by tasteless italicizing. But these performances were put over, with audiences and reviewers, by the conducting operation that presented an appearance of assured, authoritative purposefulness and control.

For Schonberg in *The Times* "the 'Eroica' moved in a strong manner," and showed Barenboim to be an interpreter who "observes every note value, every nuance, and is scrupulous in following the composer's intentions." And it was clear that "Mr. Barenboim is a born conductor. . . . Technically [his work] was impeccable. Mr. Barenboim has a good ear, a fine feeling for balances, and the clearest, most incisive of beats. . . . His left hand is independent, busy but not fussy, supplementing and not echoing the right." As usual all the right words, wrongly applied. The poorer over-all sound of the orchestra this time testified to Barenboim's lack of the fine feeling for balance that produced its beautiful sound under Kertesz. And his lack of even a crude feeling for balance was evident in the performance of the Schubert that made it sound at times like a concerto for kettledrums, the similar thunderous performances of the Beethoven Fifth and the orchestral parts of the Rachmaninov concertos. Moreover, to get an expert's evaluation of Barenboim's technical operation, I had invited an experienced orchestral musician to the first concert; and I noticed out of the corner of my eye the occasional nervous movements of his hands, which he explained afterwards: they had expressed the anxiety he had felt vicariously at points where the windmill-like activity of Barenboim's arms had confronted a player with the difficulty of deciding which of their two contradictory indications to obey. "He is lucky that he conducts an experienced orchestra which knows itself what to do."

To someone who may say these are the failings of youth which should disappear with further experience, my answer is that I can't see ego and lack of discipline like Barenboim's correcting themselves, anymore than Bernstein's did; and I therefore can see the performances changing only for the worse, as Bernstein's did. Which amounts to saying that I see Barenboim continuing the debasement of our musical life begun by Bernstein.

Fall 1968 On the one hand there was the absurd overestimation of Daniel Barenboim; and on the other hand there was the latest instance of the condescending belittling, by the same critical pygmies, of one of the giants among pianist-musicians today. Having heard Cliburn's masterful performances of other works of Chopin, I was not deterred from going to hear him play the Concerto No. 1 with the New York Philharmonic by Harold Schonberg's statement, after the first performance, that it had revealed Cliburn's lack of understanding of how this work that was intended to show off the pianist's virtuosity had to be played. And I was not surprised by the great performance I heard—elegant in its grandly impassioned sculpturing of melody and also in the properly scaled execution of the interludes of brilliant passage-work that demonstrated Cliburn's understanding of what Schonberg didn't understand: that one doesn't play such passage-work in a concerto of Chopin as one plays the passage-work in a concerto of Liszt. But it wasn't only the *Times* critic who misinformed his readers about the performance: the critic of *The New Yorker* wrote that Cliburn's performance had been "a bit glib, with . . . no profound understanding of the Chopin style", and that "though Mr. Cliburn still has some of the attributes of a first-rate romantic pianist" and is technically brilliant, "he hasn't got the more refined nuances of his work within his grasp."

Schonberg's review of the Rome Opera's first performance of the Visconti production of *The Marriage of Figaro* in the Lincoln Center Festival did, however, cause me to consider not traveling back to New York for a later performance. One could, I thought, accept the purely factual details of the staging that Schonberg reported: that Visconti had had action going on at every moment; and in particular that Susanna, in the first act, had engaged in constant activity with an iron—a seventeenth-century rather than an eighteenth-century iron, incidentally, "for Visconti has set the action a century earlier than Mozart envisaged it"— which she had kept brandishing to cool and using to iron sheets during Cherubino's and Figaro's arias; and "when she was not ironing she was walking around, looking into the linen closet, doing this and that," distracting the audience's attention from the singing. I had reason to doubt Schonberg's statement that Giulini's conducting had produced awkward orchestral balances, ragged ensemble like that of a provincial company, questionable style of singing—all of which added up to an entire *Figaro* "unlike anything New York has been accustomed to" (not a bad thing if it was unlike the Metropolitan *Figaro* of recent years conducted by Rosenstock). But it was possible that "at the final curtain there was a rather cold reception . . . even a few boos". If, therefore, there had been only the *Figaro* I might have decided not to come back; but since there was also a production of Rossini's *Otello*, I decided to make the trip. And a good thing too; for if I hadn't I would have missed the most distinguished and effective staging of *Figaro* I have seen anywhere, and the best-conducted musical performance of it that New York has heard in years.

There were, first of all, the superbly imagined sets of Visconti and Filippo Sanjust—the most extraordinary in conception and in service to the action being the one for Act 3. Designer-director teams have transferred Act 2 of *La Traviata* to a garden, or Act 3 to a courtyard, not only without any imaginable gain, but with evident loss. But Visconti's transfer of Act 3 of *Figaro* from the specified drawing room to a spacious loggia worked advantageously for the action. With cloths shutting out the sun, the loggia was placed diagonally with a sharp bend at the left that created a set-off space where the Count could overhear Susanna and Figaro without being seen; and for the finale the cloths were drawn aside, revealing the late-afternoon scene outdoors, from which the peasant friends of the bride and groom came in to embrace them, to bow respectfully to their lord and lady, to dance a fandango. This was part of the intelligently conceived stage action throughout—action carefully thought out to individualize the characters, in addition to differentiating the earthy low-class from the aristocrats. And most of these characters were effectively realized: above all the Count by Tito Gobbi, with his extraordinary powers of presence and projection on the stage, and Susanna by Graziella Sciutti, but also Figaro by Rolando Panerai and the Countess by Ilva Ligabue. The one major exception was the Cherubino of Bianca Maria Casoni, who began with the handicap of her bulky figure and added to this an excessive amount of feminine rather than boyish pouting, flouncing and foot-stamping. This—whether it represented Visconti's direction or merely his tolerance—constituted one flaw in his great production; and the other was the one fact Schonberg reported correctly—that Marcellina did everything but listen to what Don Bartolo was singing to her, that Susanna did the same thing when Cherubino was singing to her and Figaro was singing to Cherubino, and that Susanna and the Countess kept whispering to each other during Cherubino's song. What Schonberg didn't add was that this happened only in these few instances, and therefore flawed only a small part of the production. And his long paragraph on his one major example turned out to be an enormous exaggeration of what Susanna actually did with the iron: I saw her iron a sheet for a few moments and change the iron once; and someone who had attended the opening performance said she had done no more that time. Incorrect also was Schonberg's statement that Visconti had set the action a century earlier than Mozart: the characters wore the late-eighteenth-century clothes of the Spaniards in Goya's paintings.

As for the musical performance, Giulini had a mediocre orchestra and the usual mixed bag of principals: two excellent singers, Sciutti and Casoni, and for the rest Panerai, with a once fine voice that had hardened and roughened, Gobbi, who managed to do a great deal with the little that remained of his voice, and Ligabue, whose voice was unattractive and explosive in the Countess's two arias, but agreeable and better-used in the ensembles. But he had the authority and musical feeling that got the orchestra to play with energy, precision and sensitive phrasing, and held orchestra and singers together in a progression which had liveliness, grace and expressive warmth. I heard no raggedness of a provincial company, no questionable style of singing; nor were these heard by the person who was at the opening performance. And at that performance he witnessed what I witnessed at the final perform- ance: increasingly enthusiastic applause after each act; a prolonged demonstration after the last act; no boos. I heard a woman in front of me exclaim to her neighbor: "There was not a single boo! Not one!"; and a friend who was at the second performance told me that as he got up at the first intermission, in a glow over the performance, he said to his companion: "Schonberg is an ass"; whereupon others pushing up the aisle turned to him in a chorus of agreement: "Yes! He is!"—evidence of the indignation and anger among musicians and music-lovers over Schonberg's review of this memorable presentation.

I could appreciate Giulini's powers because in the performance of Rossini's *Otello* the night before I had heard the lifeless playing the orchestra did when conducted by Carlo Franci (under whom, said Schonberg, "the orchestra sounded more alert and confident than it had at the opening 'Nozze di Figaro' "). The opera had astonished me at a performance by the American Opera Society years ago with its revelation of what Rossini was capable of when he wrote serious music (even for a travesty of Shakespeare's play)—the power of the slow introduction of the overture, the melodic beauty and the dramatic force of much of the vocal writing. This time I was surprised by the Allegro of the overture, which was in the absurdly unsuitable style of Rossini's overtures for his comedies—an example of Rossinian care- lessness that was the more incomprehensible for the care which was evident in the writing after the curtain rose, especially in what Rossini contrived for the orchestra in expressive support of the vocal writing—a notable example being the orchestra's powerful rhythmic figure in the final duet of Otello and Desdemona ("none of the material in 'Otello' is memorable," said Schonberg, contending that at "the big moment—the final confrontation of Otello and Desdemona" the music was "a reminis- cence of the 'Calunnia' patter-song aria from 'The Barber of Seville' "). The work suffered from the insensitive bawling of the two tenors and their insufficient agility in florid passages; but Virginia Zeani sang Desdemona's music impressively. And there was the pleasure of seeing this old-fashioned opera in a properly old-fashioned production whose scenery was given an acceptable modern look by De Chirico.

Winter 1969 A small instrumental group from Music S-259, a seminar in the performance of contemporary music, opened the final concert of the Harvard Summer School's series in Sanders Theater last summer with Schönberg's Serenade Op. 24, another of the works of his that communicate to me no expressive sense or mere internal coherence in the sounds my ear finds hideous. I was left deploring the musicians' waste of time and work required by a piece so difficult to perform and so little worth performing; deploring, therefore, a seminar for such waste of time and work on the performing of such music; deploring, further, the years of polemics that had succeeded in getting musicians to believe in the value of the music that justified the expenditure of time and work on the seminar and the performance; and reaching, in the end, a thought about Schönberg that I had reached earlier about Karl Marx. Twenty years ago Reinhold Niebuhr began a *Nation* review of a book on Soviet Russia with the statement "We are only beginning to appreciate that the real tragedy of our age lies in the fact that the Marxist alternative to the injustices of our society should have generated cruelties and injustices so much worse than those which Marxism challenged, and should nevertheless be able to gain the devotion of millions of desperate people in Europe and particularly in Asia upon the basis of the original dream, as if the dream had not turned into a nightmare." Considering these consequences of Marx's existence on earth, I thought this existence could be regarded as one of the great disasters in human history. And considering not so much Schönberg's own distorted and worthless music as the distortions in music and musical life that his existence resulted in, I think that existence can also be regarded as a major disaster in the history of music.

The program for the New York City Opera's production in October of Hugo Weisgall's new opera, *Nine Rivers from Jordan*, included an article by Mr. Weisgall in which he observed that

> the operatic form has not been too hospitable to complex subject matter. . . . It took Kierkegaard and Denis de Rougemont, not to mention Frazer and Freud, to tell us what *Don Giovanni* and *Tristan* are really all about. But even these works and the questions they raise are simple when compared

with imposing artistic form on such problems as collective guilt, or the responsibility for the concentration camps, or the human condition "after the bomb." Yet this is the subject matter that I feel cannot be avoided by the contemporary musical theater . . . if opera is to remain a valid 20th-century form.

My own view is that opera's remaining a valid twentieth-century form depends not at all on its dealing with this subject matter or any other, and entirely on its offering the music of high quality and expressive force that can impose heightening artistic form on whatever subject the text deals with. Mr. Weisgall's unpleasant-sounding and expressively pointless music imposed no such heightening artistic form on Pirandello's *Six Characters in Search of an Author*, some years ago; and now his endless pointlessly ugly music imposes none on Denis Johnston's text for *Nine Rivers*, which itself imposes no artistic form on the problems Mr. Weisgall's mind is obsessed by.

Not only did Berlioz command a superb prose style, but even his music criticism—for example, the essay on Rossini's *William Tell* in Strunk's *Source Readings in Music History*—conveys a personal intensity and passion, a greatness of spirit, that bring tears to my eyes when I read it. And these personal qualities are of course even more moving in his letters. For more than ten years the only collection in English was the one published by the ubiquitous Jacques Barzun, who did a poor job of selection and a worse one of translation. My examples of his mistranslation led him, in the introduction to his alleged new translation of Berlioz's *Evenings in the Orchestra*, to contend that real translation had to be the "recomposition" he had done to express in English the "atmosphere and continuity of thought, rhythm and emphasis" of Berlioz's French. This amounted to saying that if Berlioz wrote in English today he would write the prissy and fussy prose of Barzun—which I find impossible to believe. But it was believed by Barzun's fellow-academic, a professor of music named Homer Ulrich, who in a review of a new translation of *Evenings in the Orchestra* wrote:

Fortescue's [translation] is acceptable in spite of being somewhat literal; Barzun's, I imagine, more nearly captures the essence of Berlioz's style. A single comparison will make the point:
Fortesque: "Méhul had none of the prejudices of some of his contemporaries

against certain musical practices, which he used skilfully when he saw fit, and which the formalists wish to ban without exception."

Barzun: "Méhul had none of the preconceived ideas held by some of his comtemporaries with regard to artistic method. He made use of certain devices whenever he considered them useful, even though the professors of routine prohibit them in all cases."

Ulrich's "I imagine" seems to indicate that this scholar spoke without actually comparing the two translations with Berlioz's French. And when one does look at the French—"*Méhul n'etait imbu d'aucun des préjugés de quelques-uns de ses contemporains à l'égard de certains moyens d'art qu'il employait habilement lorsqu'il les jugeait convenables, et que les routiniers veulent proscrire en tout cas*"—it turns out that precisely because Fortescue adheres more closely to Berlioz's words, order of words and sentence structure, he more nearly captures in English the essential style of the French. And this is demonstrated again in Humphrey Searle's recent volume of Berlioz letters, which includes translations of some of the letters in the Barzun volume that stay closer to the Berlioz originals and as a result are not only accurate where Barzun's are inaccurate but produce an approximation in English of the Berlioz style in French where Barzun substitutes the Barzun style.

But Searle himself departs from his correct procedure occasionally, with damage to the result. This happens in the extraordinarily moving letter (not included in Barzun's volume) in which the twenty-one-year-old Berlioz tells his father of his unalterable decision to become a composer. I first encountered it in W. J. Turner's *Berlioz;* and surprised by the differences in Searle's version, I looked up the original, which revealed that both Turner and Searle depart from it, sometimes at different points, sometimes at the same points, and always with loss.

"*Je suis entrainé volontairement vers une carrière magnifique (on ne peut donner d'autre épithète à celle des arts) et non pas vers ma perte,*" Berlioz writes. Turner's translation is "I have voluntarily embarked upon a magnificent career (one can give no other epithet to that of the arts) and not upon my destruction"; Searle's is "I am driven voluntarily towards a magnificent career (no other epithet can be applied to the career of an artist) and I am not in the least heading for perdition." "I have voluntarily embarked" makes better sense than "I am driven voluntarily," but not the sense of Berlioz's French, which is "I am willingly swept away" toward the magnificent career; and the "*perte*" he is not being swept towards is not his perdition but his ruin. Where Berlioz writes: *"Si j'étais condamné sans remission à mourir de faim dans le cas de non-réussite (je n'en persisterais pas moins à la verité)"*—"If I were mercilessly condemned to die of hunger in the event of failure (this would not lessen my persistence, I assure you)"—Turner makes it "If I am mercilessly condemned to die of hunger in the event of failure (and in truth I would not stop sooner)" (Searle chooses to omit this moving passage). Where Berlioz writes: *"Tel est ma manière de penser, tel je suis, et rien au monde ne pourra me changer,"* Searle makes it "That is the way I think, the way I am, and nothing in the world will change me," which doesn't produce the effect of the repetition of *"tel"*: "That is the way I think, that is what I am." Similarly, when Berlioz asks his father not to attribute his letter to an excited impulse, and adds: *"Jamais peut-être je n'ai été plus calme,"* the English must be "Never perhaps have I been more calm," not Turner's "for I have never been more calm" or Searle's "I have perhaps never been so calm." But even with these occasional imperfections in Searle's translations the letters communicate the distinguished mind, personality and literary style that make them extraordinary and moving documents which no one should miss.

Opera companies everywhere persist in performing Rimsky-Korsakov's falsification of Musorgsky's *Boris Godunov;* but Sarah Caldwell, director of the Opera Company of Boston, rejects even Musorgsky's own 1872 revision of his work, and produced his first version of 1869. And in her prospectus for the present season she mentioned a possible production of Verdi's first version of *Macbeth,* instead of his revised version that has been produced and recorded until now. Does Miss Caldwell believe a composer's first idea of a work is an Original Sacred Truth concerning which he must not be allowed second thoughts? Or that his first idea is always better—or even that the first version of *Macbeth* is better? If she believes any of these, she is mistaken.

There are, certainly, instances where a composer's later changes are damaging in one way or another and should not be retained. The luxuriant later style of the Venusberg scene that Wagner inserted into *Tannhäuser* for the Paris production makes it incongruous with the rest of the work; the ballet music that Verdi introduced in the third act of *Otello* for the Paris production breaks dramatic continuity and tension; and both insertions should therefore be removed. But a year ago Erich Leinsdorf performed at Tanglewood Beethoven's first (1805) version of *Fidelio*, which caused one to marvel at how unerringly Beethoven had operated at every point in the revision of the diffuse, rambling and at times conventional and derivative writing, in the direction of the powerful conciseness and concentration in utterance and form of the 1814 masterpiece that we know. As for *Macbeth*, two of the pieces Verdi added in his revision—Lady Macbeth's second-act aria and her third-act duet with Macbeth—are, as Francis Toye remarks, among the best numbers in the opera; and he is correct in concluding that "the second version of 'Macbeth' is superior to the first and one would not willingly lose the admirable music it called forth." It is hard to imagine what other considerations make Miss Caldwell willing to lose this admirable music; but for that matter it is hard to understand her way of dealing with Musorgsky's *Boris*. Part of his 1872 revision was the addition of the new concluding scene in the forest of Kromy, in which the choral writing of the earlier scenes attains sheer incandescence; and this scene should be added even in a performance of the 1869 version; but Miss Caldwell sternly rejected it. Another major 1872 revision was his complete rewriting of the scene in the Tsar's apartments, which creates the difficulty of deciding which of the two superb but different versions to perform. One can understand Miss Caldwell's choosing the bleak and somber 1869 version; but what is beyond comprehension is that this purist who would have none of the superb 1872 Kromy scene replaced Boris's two monologues in the 1869 version with the ones in the 1872 version, whose richer writing is incongruous with its bleak, somber context.

This is an example of the mindlessness which pervades every part of the world of music, including one in which intellectual rigor would seem to be a *sine qua non*—that of the musical scholars. Not being a scholar, I was aware only of the muddleheadedness in the writing for the general public by Paul Henry Lang, Curt Sachs, Alfred Einstein and Hugo Leichtentritt that I began to report thirty years ago; but these reports caused readers to inform me of *their* discoveries; and one reader in particular, a student at the University of North Carolina, sent me examples of Lang's and Einstein's lack of scholarly rigor—notably Einstein's in arriving at his erroneous conclusion that Boccherini's quintets for two cellos were really for two violas, which by now is part of the body of what Bernard Shaw called the "stale rubbish of the musical book-makers" that writers of concert reviews and record-album notes traffic in. And only a couple of years ago a young reader in Texas wrote that he had listened with friends to a privately circulated recording of a performance of the 1905 *Fidelio*, which had left them glad that Beethoven had had second thoughts about it, because they had found it to be "full of conventionalities and over-written passages"; and that as a result he had been amazed by the statement in Lang's *Music in Western Civilization:* "In its first version *Fidelio* shows the guiding hand of the same great classicist who admired so much the disposition of tonalities in *The Magic Flute*, who like his revered model, Cherubini, used the leitmotif with discretion. . . . Despite the great advantages gained by the rewriting of the opera, the difference in time caused stylistic inequalities. . . . The opera should be restored to its original form." I am not aware of any "stylistic inequalities" in the 1814 *Fidelio*, but only of the "advantages" that make it a greater and more effective work of art than the 1805 version, and of Lang's unawareness of the primacy of esthetic values over historical interest in his insistence that despite the "advantages" of the 1814 version it is the 1805 version that should be performed: for him the version to hear is not the one that offers the experience of a great and effective work of art, but the one that enables us to observe certain facts of musical history—the operation of the "great classicist who admired so much the disposition of tonalities in *The Magic Flute*" and who, "like his revered model, Cherubini, used the leitmotif with discretion."

How was it, my Texas reader asked, that such remarks as Lang's "do not prevent [his book] from being given a revered place in the shelves of music libraries?"—a question which others have asked in connection with even worse statements in the book. And "what can I do when scholars are themselves apparently doing nothing about it?" One scholar's answer to this question was given by an English member of the fraternity, J. A. Westrup, who in *Music and Letters* a couple of years ago denounced my "exposing the errors of historians" on the ground that "such criticism is the province of historians, not journalists," and who denounced also my publishing the North Carolina student's exposure of Einstein's dealing with the Boccherini quintets on the ground that "people who are entitled to criticize a scholar like

Alfred Einstein do not need the assistance of students at the University of North Carolina. They criticize on the basis of their own knowledge and do not pad out their pages with second-hand opinions."*

Spring 1969 After years of Bernstein conducting the New York Philharmonic and Munch, Leinsdorf, Ormandy and Szell conducting the other great American orchestras, and with Lorin Maazel's mistreatment of Beethoven's *Eroica* and Daniel Barenboim's of this and other great classics last year still reverberating in my memory, it was refreshing and heartening to attend two of Colin Davis's concerts with the New York Philharmonic and hear what—except for Boulez's concert with the BBC Symphony a few years ago—one hadn't heard since the days of Toscanini and Cantelli: a conductor and musician of outstanding powers operating with complete unself-conscious absorption and impressive efficiency in his task of getting the orchestra to produce the realization he wanted of the work they were performing. I'm not saying that Davis's powers are of the awesome magnitude of Toscanini's and Cantelli's, and certainly not that his use of them produced perform-

---

*The way the reputation that Einstein earned with certain genuine scholarly achievements —his revision of Köchel's Mozart catalogue, his transcribing of the many sixteenth-century madrigals in his book on the madrigal—has commanded respect for shoddy performances like his book on Mozart (in which the episode of the Boccherini quintets occurs) and continuing respect for him in spite of these shoddy performances—this I find amazing. For example, the *Mozart Companion* published by Oxford University Press in 1956 is dedicated to him by its contributors, who quote numerous statements from his *Mozart* —statements, on the one hand, concerning which the impressively rigorous scholar Friedrich Blume writes that Einstein's argument "is unconvincing," or that "one must question the validity of his opinion," or that his assumption is "arbitrary" or "completely invalid", or that he "incomprehensibly tried to claim [a sketch for a concerto movement which belongs to K.459] for . . . K.466"; and on the other hand, statements, quoted by less impressive contributors, which say nothing worth quoting, including pure, and often silly, conjectures about Mozart's motivations (e.g., the conjecture that in the Scena and Rondo *Ch'io mi scordi di te / Non teme, amato bene* for soprano and piano obbligato ("for Mselle Storace and myself") Mozart "wanted to preserve the memory of this voice . . . and . . . wanted to leave with her in the piano part a souvenir of the taste and depth of his playing, and of the depth of his feeling for her"). Einstein once made a derisive reference to the writing he said was based not on music but on the writing of Tovey about music, not understanding that when writers like myself quoted a statement by Tovey it was because it stated so perceptively what we had experienced in the music, whereas Einstein's pretentious gabble of alleged profound insights revealed his lack of genuine musical perception.

ances which resembled theirs. Davis is a musician with a mind and taste of his own, who set a tempo for the first movement of the *Eroica* that was considerably less *con brio* than Toscanini's, but shaped the movement with unfailing continuity, coherence end cumulative power in that tempo; who also produced a *Love Scene* from Berlioz's *Romeo and Juliet* which moved slowly and with powerful expressive inflection, as against the animation and grace that Toscanini gave it, but which was effective and convincing in its own way; who, on the other hand, played the *Queen Mab* from *Romeo* faster than Toscanini and got the orchestra to execute the difficult piece with breathtaking perfection and brilliance. The movement beginning with *Romeo Alone* also was superbly performed, except that at the point in *Festivities at the Capulets'* where the brass proclaimed the earlier oboe melody of the Larghetto, the kettledrums, marked *mf* in the score, produced a thunder which obscured the festivities theme played by the violins and flute—something difficult to understand either as a miscalculation by a conductor with so excellent an ear for orchestral balance, or as the intention of so excellent a musician.

Davis's Berlioz program also included the early *Francs-Juges* Overture and *Cléopâtre*, the work that Berlioz, while still a student at the Conservatoire, submitted in his third unsuccessful attempt to win the Prix de Rome. In *Cléopâtre* the orchestra's very first measures established what is evident throughout, but most notably in Cleopatra's invocation *Grands Pharaons* over the orchestra's powerful bass *ostinato*—that this is not a fumbling of unmatured powers but an operation with absolute assurance in a style that is completely individual and already completely formed.

Another refreshing and heartening experience was young Claudio Abbado's conducting of *Don Carlo* at the Metropolitan. The precision of attack and inflection of the brass's opening statements demonstrated at once the control and authority one continued to hear in a performance which was disciplined in its impassioned shaping of the music—which, that is, kept the Verdi *espansione* within the limits of plastic continuity and coherence. And all this, again, with a complete unself-conscious concentration on his task that caused Abbado to whirl around with a gesture of furious protest when the audience's applause interrupted the musical progression at one point.

And after Abbado there was the considerably older Carlo Maria

Giulini, whom I heard with the New York Philharmonic. A Mozart
program began with a graceful performance of four movements of the
Divertimento K.251, which was followed by a suitably powerful performance of the Piano Concerto K.466; then, after the intermission, an
eloquent realization of the musical gestures of grief, solemnity and
resignation of the extraordinary Masonic Funeral Music K.477 was
the prelude to a performance of the G-minor Symphony which had
the impassioned character Toscanini's had had, but without Toscanini's
fierce intensity, and with other differences of detail that made it clearly
a product of Giulini's own distinguished musical intelligence and taste.
The pianist was Arturo Benedetti Michelangeli, who through efficient
press relations work at some point is always referred to as the
"legendary" Arturo Benedetti Michelangeli, and whose later performances on records didn't change the impression I got from a 1948
performance of the Schumann concerto—that his playing demonstrated
to what extremes wilful extravagance in tempo and dynamics and in
distortion of phrase could be carried. This time I heard from two
reliable listeners that at the Friday and Saturday concerts his playing
in the Mozart concerto had been mechanical and lifeless; and so at
the Monday concert I was unprepared for the forceful and disciplined
playing he did throughout the work.

Far from alerting the public to the extraordinary performances I
have described, Donal Henahan, for one, informed readers of *The Times*
that the *Don Carlo* I heard was "routine, flabby . . . conducted slackly
and without passion by Claudio Abbado", and that except in the scenes
involving Verrett and in Philip's monologue and confrontation with
the Grand Inquisitor "the night rarely rose to even decent mediocrity."
Harold Schonberg informed them that in Davis's performance of the
excerpts from *Romeo and Juliet* "somehow the music lacked tension and
bite. Rhythms were too inflexible; balances too one-sided. . . . There
were a few sloppy examples of metrics, too, accented upbeats and
the like." He also reported Giulini's unsuitably "elegant and classic"
conducting of the powerful orchestral part of Mozart's K.466; and
The New Yorker's Winthrop Sargeant wrote that Giulini's Mozart program was "of a sort that almost plays itself, and he presided over it
with a light, lyric approach," so that the concert was "an occasion
for only moderate enthusiasm". Moreover, both Schonberg and Sargeant reported unusual accentuations in the opening statement of the

G-minor that I didn't hear and that are not to be heard in Giulini's recorded performance.

The mezzo-soprano Teresa Berganza, in the Metropolitan's *Barber of Seville*, enchanted one with the style of her deployment of her delicate voice in melody, the ease and grace of her accurate delivery of florid passages. Her accuracy must have been embarrassing to Sherrill Milnes, the Figaro, who—required, in their second-act duet, to repeat a florid phrase of hers—each time produced a smear instead. Otherwise he used his fine baritone well, as did Luigi Alva his light tenor. Berganza's acting was as disciplined as her singing—in marked contrast to the excessive exuberance of Milnes and the coarsening of the other stage action originally devised by Cyril Ritchard. But the years hadn't made the Berman scenery less delightful; and Richard Bonynge conducted the musical performance well.

Frank Corsaro's new stage production of *Faust* for the New York City Opera was like his *Traviata*—another of the vandalisms which not only this company but the Metropolitan and European companies have been inflicting on operatic classics, and which Bing has described as "presenting masterpieces as seen through contemporary eyes". From a recent article entitled *Method Verdi*, in *Opera News*, I learned that the Corsaro *Traviata* represented the influence of an Actors Studio workshop production of a director named Witcover, which embodied "fresh ideas" that "translated the opera . . . into contemporary life" and in this way made it "more meaningful". One accompanying photograph showed a "swinging party" of today in the first act in place of Violetta's elegant nineteenth-century affair—from which Corsaro derived *his* first-act party with girls running about pursued by drunken amorous men. The idea that the nineteenth-century dramatic situations and action in *La Traviata* cannot be meaningful to an audience today and must be "translated into contemporary life" is as untrue of this opera as it would be of a novel of Turgenev or a painting of Degas; and the results of its application to the opera are as atrocious as they would be of its application to the novel or the painting, or as they are of its application to plays of Shakespeare and Euripides in the productions described by Alan Levitan of Brandeis University in a review in the magazine *Boston*. Witcover and Corsaro are not the inspired innovators breathing new life into a moribund art whom one reads about in *Opera News* and *The Times*; they are men without any understanding of the essential nature and requirements of that art. In an interview in the New York Philharmonic program Giulini—pointing out that he had fought to modernize scenery and production in opera and had collaborated with Visconti and Zeffirelli—contended that Zeffirelli and many others were now going too far. "These designers and directors don't have enough confidence in the music. They think . . . that Mozart and Verdi are not enough. They do things to support an aria, because they don't believe it stands alone. . . . The visual part has become so important that the music of *Traviata*, for example, becomes like movie music—a comment, not the central issue." And Balanchine, who has staged operas in Hamburg, showed the same understanding of the music being the central issue, and the aria not needing the help of action, in his statement in an interview in *Opera News*—that in opera "while a person sings . . . he should just stand and sing," and there should be "minimum of gesture and movement, maximum of music". Because they don't understand this, directors like Witcover and Corsaro think they must help the aria with visual action that achieves the opposite of help—action "translating the opera into contemporary life" that draws attention to itself, which is to say away from the music.

It was from Balanchine that I got my first information about the new Corsaro *Faust* the day after the first performance. When Marguerite, he said indignantly, sang her beautiful aria in her garden after her first meeting with Faust, one didn't hear it because one was distracted by her struggling to take off her dress (of which Balanchine gave a vivid imitation). This was as much as he told me; the rest I saw when I attended a later performance. One thing I learned was why Marguerite took off her dress in the garden while she sang the ballad *The King of Thule*. In Gounod's own version of this act there is, facing the garden, a house, at whose window Marguerite, still fully clothed, appears at the end of the act to sing of her love for Faust, who is listening in the garden and is impelled to rush into the house. In Corsaro's version the garden rose to a house with its front walls seemingly removed by a tornado, revealing the bedroom with its bed; and Marguerite's removal of her dress left her in a filmy white garment in which, at the end of the act, she was pushed by Faust into the bedroom and onto the bed. Gasp-provoking? Yes. Necessary to make the opera meaningful? No. The same with changing Faust's study, in the first scene, to a dissecting room and having one of the corpses on the tables turn out to be Mephistopheles; and with the striking innovations in the other scenes, which achieved only their intended purpose of drawing attention to themselves and away from the music.

Summer 1969 The notable and exciting performances I reported on last time—Colin Davis's and Giulini's with the New York Philharmonic, Abbado's *Don Carlo* at the Metropolitan—reached their climax in those in which Pierre Boulez, conducting the Philharmonic, repeated the demonstration of his phenomenal powers that he had given with the BBC Symphony in 1965. The marvelous sound of the wind chords, their precision of attack, shape and release, in response to unemphatic gestures that were like mere reminding signals—these testified to his possession of an ear in balancing the orchestra and a power of magnetic compulsion as phenomenal as Toscanini's and Cantelli's, which produced a marvelous clarity of orchestral texture like theirs. Moreover this extraordinary playing was done in a musical progression in which every sound fell into place naturally and inevitably, a statement of the work that resembled Cantelli's in the way it seemed not to be produced by human effort but simply to come into being and assume its emerging shape of itself.

It was in this matter-of-fact way that Boulez got the Philharmonic to produce—as if it were the easiest thing in the world—the unbelievably precise, beautiful-sounding and powerful playing it did in a performance of Stravinsky's *Sacre du Printemps* which had not only clarity, continuity and tension like those of Stravinsky's own performance, but the additional incandescence of a virtuoso orchestra's operation under a virtuoso conductor. It was one of the high points in a lifetime's experience of such operation; and it provided one of the high points of my musical experience, making me aware with new impact of the magnitude of Stravinsky's work, and leaving me newly moved by those concluding words in his account of it—that whereas Schönberg, Berg and Webern, in their innovations, "were supported by a great tradition . . . very little immediate tradition lies behind *Le Sacre du printemps*. I had only my ear to help me. I heard and I wrote what I heard. I am the vessel through which *Le Sacre* passed."

The quiet matter-of-factness of Boulez's operation was deceptive in more ways than one: not only in the fact that it was made possible by hard work at the rehearsals, but in the fact that the man who gave this appearance of simplicity and matter-of-factness in his conducting reveals complexity and eccentricity in his quoted ideas about music, in the music he himself has composed, and even in the programs he conducts. The program that ended with Debussy's *La Mer* began with *Jeux,* which the superb performance couldn't make anything more than the succession of mannerisms of the matured Debussy orchestral style that it is. And it included Alban Berg's Violin Concerto, which communicated as little to me this time as when Koussevitzky first performed it in the thirties, and Varèse's *Intégrales,* a work in another idiom I find uncommunicative. And *Le Sacre* ended a program which opened with five beautiful Purcell Fantasias for strings, but then offered Stravinsky's Symphonies of Wind Instruments, which impressed me as an ugly piece when Stokowski first played it in the early twenties, and has impressed me in exactly the same way whenever I have heard it again; and Webern's Six Pieces Op. 6, in which I could appreciate the subtle orchestral coloring and the occasional atmospheric effect of the phrases I found expressively meaningless. One hopes that in later visits Boulez will relax his zeal as a proselytizer of the bad twentieth-century music (the good has been accepted) and apply his powers to the good music of the two centuries before the twentieth.

Berg is for me the composer of the sound-track for the action of *Wozzeck;* and another great event of the season was the performance of this work that Colin Davis conducted at the Metropolitan—especially the orchestral performance that he made clearer-textured and more impassioned than Böhm's in the earlier productions. The cast was headed by Geraint Evans in the title role and Evelyn Lear as Marie—both excellent singing actors and effective in their parts, though Evans didn't produce the effect that Hermann Uhde did with his mere physical appearance—the enormous black eyes in the ghastly white face—and Lear was too piquantly beautiful and had too cultivated a diction for a coarsely sluttish Marie.

Giulini, returning to conduct the Philadelphia Orchestra in a Hurok subscription concert, employed its marvels of tone and sensitive execution in a performance of Schubert's Fifth, the best of his early symphonies, that had a suitable relaxed grace; a brilliant performance of the Overture to Rossini's *Semiramide;* and a performance of Brahms's

Second in which the orchestra demonstrated its high regard for him by executing with unfailing beauty of sound every italicized detail of what it must have regarded as a mistakenly overemphatic statement of the work. Giulini may think this is the right way to deal with Brahms; but it is the wrong way even with the pretentiously bombastic First Symphony, and certainly with the Second.

And Zubin Mehta, finally, conducted the Metropolitan's new production of *Il Trovatore* with the technical assurance and musical skill he had exhibited in his earlier *Aida*, *Otello* and *Carmen*, confirming my impression—after the performances of symphonic music I have heard on records—that he deals most effectively with opera. His authority appeared not to extend to Leontyne Price, who slowed down and distended the climactic phrases of Leonora's fourth-act aria as I cannot recall anyone else doing—though up to that point she had shown more regard for shape of phrase in the deployment of the voice that was agreeable and steady in the high notes in which it didn't have the luscious beauty of its lower range. Grace Bumbry's voice lacked the weight and dark color required for the role of old Azucena; James McCracken's quavering tenor made his Manrico almost as much a strain for the listener as for him; and though Sherrill Milnes, the Count di Luna, did some of the evening's best singing, his *forte* high notes no longer had the glow they had had in *The Barber of Seville* a few months earlier. My eye again had difficulty with Price in the role of a white character; and with Bumbry it had the additional difficulty of the absurdity of the enormous gray wig over the slim face and figure of a young girl. But these were minor as against the huge scenic constructions of Attilio Colonnello, seemingly molded out of halvah, which cluttered the stage, ranking with the other horrors presented at the Metropolitan of Rudolf Bing. The principals' costumes were passable; but the ones for the chorus had the Colonnello stamp—the most vivid in my memory being the quasi-Moorish affairs worn by the soldiers who in the encampment scene leaped to the front of the stage and menancingly pointed enormous red and yellow dinner candles at the audience. And one detail of present-day staging contrived by Colonnello with the director of the production, Nathaniel Merrill, calls for mention: during Ferrando's narration to the soldiers in the opening scene I became aware of creaking noises behind the backdrop, which were explained when backstage lighting revealed, on a high platform behind the backdrop, Azucena's mother being burned at the stake.

But in this sort of distracting gimmickry the Metropolitan is outdone by the New York City Opera, which began it twenty-five years ago and has carried it to its present high point in the monstrosities of staging contrived by Frank Corsaro. Between his *Faust* of last fall and his *Rigoletto* of last spring he published in *The Times* an article in justification of his practices that revealed a mind as irresponsibly vulgar as the taste revealed in his productions. The librettos of the operas, he contended, were bad originally; and there was nothing sacred about them that forbade the changes necessary to make them "apply to a modern experience," without which "there is no point in putting [the works] on," and for lack of which they have no interest for "the young people [who] are not going to the opera these days". It's true that the libretto of *Rigoletto* includes a great deal that is absurd to a rational mind; but it's also true that this libretto with its absurdities is the one Verdi chose to set to music, and that if one wants the music one must take the libretto with its absurdities. Specifically if one wants the music Rigoletto sings in his confrontation with the courtiers who abducted his daughter one must take with it the absurdity embodied in the words he sings—that this man, who in the presence of these courtiers mocked Monterone's anguish over the Duke's seduction of his daughter, now expects them to be affected by *his* anguish over *his* abducted daughter; that after denouncing them as the *"cortigiani, vil razza damnata"* that they are, he whimpers that they are all against him, and then, beginning to weep, appeals for their human sympathy. Evidently the young people who are the majority of the standees these days in the audiences that pack the Metropolitan for *Rigoletto* deal with this and the other such built-in absurdities of *Rigoletto* as everyone else does—by ignoring them and concentrating attention on the music that is their reason for being there. And actually those absurdities remain in Corsaro's production: what he does is to surround them with new—and, whenever possible, sensational and shocking—details of stage action which distract the mind that has learned to ignore and not be distracted by what it is familiar with.

As it happens, there is nothing absurd about the opening scene of *Rigoletto;* nor does it need any change to communicate what Verdi wants to establish about the Duke and his court. And clearly this *is* communicated credibly to the young people standing at the Metropolitan by what they see and hear going on at the elegant ball in Eugene Berman's marvelous *"sala magnifica nel palazzo Ducale";* whereas what Corsaro replaces it with—an orgy in which the participants tear each other's clothes off and roll on the floor in embrace, and this absurdly crowded onto the narrow raised platform on a small part of the large New York State Theater stage—distracts some spectators with thoughts of whether the dissoluteness of a sixteenth-century duke and his court did really exhibit itself in the form presented by Corsaro. Again, for the young people at the Metropolitan it is understandable that Rigoletto's reaction to Monterone's curse at the climax of the scene should be his frightened exclamation, "What do I hear! Horror!" and that his first words at the beginning of the next scene should be "The old man cursed me!"; whereas some spectators at the New York State Theater must wonder at Rigoletto's treating Monterone's curse, in the first scene, as a matter for laughter, and after this must wonder even more at his treating it in the next scene as a matter serious enough for him to get staggering drunk as he mutters, "The old man cursed me!" And they must be struck by his suddenly restored sobriety in his duet with Gilda, his suddenly renewed drunken state when he encounters the courtiers. Moreover the young people at the Metropolitan have learned to ignore in this scene such implausibilities as the house at the remote edge of town in which Rigoletto hides his daughter being located next door to Ceprano's palace, the comings and goings of the Duke and Rigoletto, the blindfolding of Rigoletto. But it is impossible for some spectators at the New York State Theater not to be struck by the implausibly complicated set with its profusion of entrances and windows, on which the characters' popping in and out reminds them of a Mack Sennett movie. The beginning of the next scene—the Duke's lament over his loss of Gilda as he sits alone in a large salon of the palace the next morning, followed by the courtiers' report to him of their having abducted her the night before and brought her to the palace—requires no change to be credible for the young people at the Metropolitan; but what Corsaro changes it into is questionable for some spectators at the New York State Theater. What they see there is the Duke in his student's disguise returning from Rigoletto's house in the middle of the night to what looks like a room in his private apartment and singing *Ella mi fu rapita* and *Parmi veder le lagrime* to the courtier in attendance as he exchanges his student's jacket for a dressing gown; and then the abductors reporting their abduction not just to him but to a gathering which includes court ladies and two leashed dogs to whom the Duke tosses bits of food. This is questionable for those who are aware that the words of the Duke's *Ella mi fu rapita* and *Parmi veder le lagrime* are unmistakably words addressed to himself, not to someone else, and who perceive that the court gathering in the middle of the night is not only improbable itself but incompatible with the subsequent action—Rigoletto's entrance in his jester's costume, the page's entrance with a message from the Duchess, Monterone's being led to prison—which indicates that the time of the scene is the morning after the abduction. And whereas the young people at the Metropolitan see Gilda rush to her father in the nightdress in which she was abducted, spectators at the New York State Theater are startled to see her come out of the Duke's bedroom resplendent in a costume of red and gold. As for the last scene, the young people at the Metropolitan see Gilda look through the specified crack in the wall to observe the Duke's dalliance with Maddalena; but spectators at the New York State Theater are offered the absurdity created by there being no wall, so that Gilda and Rigoletto are as visible to the Duke and Maddalena as the Duke and Maddalena are to Gilda and Rigoletto. Nor is this all: Corsaro has Gilda arrive with her father in a boat on the left, in which he later sends her away while he makes an exit at the back of the stage; but when she returns dressed as a man it is not in a boat on the left but on land on the right.

These distracting goings-on, the night I observed them, drew attention away from a musical performance conducted well by Gabor Otvös, with Louis Quilico a sonorous Rigoletto, Patricia Brooks singing well as Gilda, Pierre Duval having to strain for the Duke's high notes, and Robert Hale an impressive-sounding Sparafucile.

The Guarneri Quartet's concerts at the Y.M.H.A. and the Metropolitan Museum were outstanding occasions—with especially notable performances of Beethoven's Op. 18 No. 5 and Op 132; but there were some disquieting moments. In Beethoven's Op. 130 at the Y.M.H.A. I heard an expressive overloading of phrase that I was sure I hadn't heard in Cambridge a couple of years earlier, and that I couldn't go along with. Nor could I go along with the slowing down of the first movement of Beethoven's Op. 59 No. 2, at the Metropolitan, for an expansively expressive treatment of the second subject; and I

Winter 1970   173

found this treatment of the second subject even more objectionable
in the first movement of Mozart's K.499. Also it was a mistake in
my opinion, to conclude Op. 130 with the Great Fugue Op. 133 instead
of the finale that Beethoven substituted for it. Beethoven should have
the right to his second thought here as in *Fidelio;* and listening to
the Great Fugue I was struck by its lack of any relation to the movements
of Op. 130 in style, substance and expressive content; whereas the
finale Beethoven substituted for it goes with those movements perfectly.
I think other groups are right in performing Op. 130 with this finale
and the Great Fugue by itself, and the Guarneri Quartet would be
wise to do the same.

Winter 1970 The Guarneri Quartet's performance of Beethoven's
Quartet Op. 132 in Sanders Theater, Cambridge, last July confirmed
earlier impressions that the playing which in the beginning was completely straightforward has begun to include monkeying with tempo
which I find damaging to the performances. The most striking instance
this time was the enormous slowing down of the series of half-notes
following the series of quarter-notes in each of the statements of the
opening section of the great variation movement, with not as much
as a *sostenuto* in the score to justify it. I found the distended half-notes
impossible to accept each time in the opening section; moreover they
couldn't be slowed down in the first variation because the new dotted-
quarter-and-eighth rhythm continuing below them had to remain
unchanged; and the same thing happened in the second variation. There
was another striking slowing down in the finale—this one of bars 166-75,
in preparation for the return of the principal theme in its original
key. The *espressivo* in the score might justify a slight expansion of
the tempo, but not the Guarneri's enormous retardation.

In this sort of thing the Guarneri Quartet is revealing something
less than the flawless musical judgment and taste of its peers, the
Yale Quartet and the Quartetto Italiano. The Yale, composed of musicians in the Yale School of Music and led by Broadus Erle of the
unforgettable New Music Quartet, can be heard only on records—in
marvelous performances of Mozart's K.421 and Beethoven's Op. 127.
The Italiano has astonished music-lovers with recent recorded performances of Mozart, Beethoven and Schubert that have revealed an ability

the group didn't have twenty years ago to play this music as superbly as it plays its instruments.

The gala concerts with which the new Chamber Music Society of Lincoln Center inaugurated Alice Tully Hall in the new Juilliard School revealed the hall to be one that transmitted a natural and beautiful sound with sufficient volume at least as far back as row R, where I sat at the first concert. It opened with Bach's moderately interesting Trio Sonata in C, admirably performed by the violinists Pinchas Zukerman and James Oliver Buswell IV, with the cellist Leslie Parnas contributing an audible bass line, and Charles Wadsworth filling in on the harpsichord a harmony that was mostly inaudible even in the moderate-sized hall. Next, the baritone Hermann Prey, who had achieved a delightfully sung Papageno in the Metropolitan's *Magic Flute*, demonstrated in Schumann's *Dichterliebe* that his agreeable voice was not a medium for effective *Lieder*-singing. And as against the excessively reticent playing of the important piano part by the usual accompanist, Mr. Wadsworth's was enlivening to the point of occasional excessive vehemence—notably in *Ein Jüngling liebt ein Mädchen*. Such vehemence was damaging also at certain points in the excellent performance of Schubert's Quintet Op. 163 by Messrs. Buswell, Zukerman and Parnas with the violist Walter Trampler and cellist Pierre Fournier—for example, in the gigantesque *crescendos* in the sustained opening and closing sections of the slow movement; the exaggeratedly robust lilt of the finale. And at the second concert the Guarneri Quartet's dynamic and expressive overloading of the third and fourth movements of Beethoven's Quartet Op. 130 distorted their shape and destroyed their grace. Another thing wrong at this concert was to have the Beethoven quartet—which the Guarneri elected to conclude with the Great Fugue—followed by a work so inferior and trivial as Tchaikovsky's Sextet for strings, *Souvenir de Florence*. This poor judgment in program-making produced even worse in the group of seldom-heard works for the third concert: Beethoven's Quartet Op. 16 for piano and winds, Rachmaninov's Sonata for cello and piano Op. 19, and Mendelssohn's Piano Trio Op. 66—which is to say, an inconsequential early piece by the one major composer on the program, another such work by a fourth-rate composer, and an unfamiliar work by a skillful minor composer. And a number of programs of this kind were among the sixteen announced for the Society's subscription series.

What Shaw said about Berlioz—that he was one of those "who are poets and thinkers rather than musicians," but whose love of music causes them to "select music as their means of expression"—was not true of Berlioz, who had great powers of musical creation which happened to be set in operation by his susceptibility to poetic stimulation. But the New York City Opera's production of *Mefistofele* last fall demonstrated that it *was* true Boito—that he was a man of literary skill and ideas but no creative power in music who, setting his libretto, operated with the mere ability to use the available musical resources of his period competently but not, for the most part, interestingly. The few moderate successes in that use—notably Margherita's *L'altra notte* and some of her later phrases to Faust in the prison scene—count for little beside the major failure, the ineffective music for the opera's principal character. Except for the vocal inadequancy of the tenor Arturo Sergi's Faust, the musical performance conducted by Julius Rudel—with Norman Treigle's well-sung Mefistofele and Carol Neblett's agreeable-voiced Margherita and Elena—was good. But the stage production devised and directed by Tito Capobianco was another of those that offer a realization not of what the composer set down as embodying his intention in the work, but of what the director has thought up as embodying *his* idea of what the work is about; and I would object even if the realization—in the scenery of David Mitchell, the costumes of Hal George, the lighting effects of Hans Sondheimer, the direction of Capobianco, the choreography of Robert Joffrey—had been good; but an additional reason for objecting was that they were bad, and therefore a constant irritating distraction.

Spring 1970 Interest in the Beethoven *Eroica* that a Japanese conductor and orchestra would produce led me to the concert of the NHK Symphony of Tokyo under Hiroyuki Iwaki in Carnegie Hall, where I heard the most excitingly effective performance of the work since Toscanini's. In fact the two introductory chords followed by the *Allegro con brio* statement of the opening theme established immediately in startling fashion what continued to be evident thereafter—that this was the performance of a man who must have listened to the Toscanini performances of the *Eroica* on records and have been convinced of the rightness of the conception of the work they embodied. Moreover it was the performance of a man who operated as a musician in this work very much as Toscanini did—with similar subtle modifications of a steadily maintained tempo, similar continuity and cohesive tension in the shaping of the sound moving in time—and operated as a conductor with a similar control of a superb orchestra sensitized to his direction. But the performance was not a copy of Toscanini's: there was more than the faster tempo of the *Marcia Funebre* to make it unmistakably Iwaki's working out in sound of what he had come to feel himself as the right conception of the work.

Another such experience was provided by the Carnegie Hall concert of the Royal Philharmonic under Rudolf Kempe. A fast-paced performance of Strauss's *Don Juan* demonstrated the brilliance of sound and execution the orchestra had acquired under his direction; then a performance of Mozart's Piano Concerto K.271 offered a sensitively phrased orchestral context for shapeless and otherwise mediocre playing by Evelyne Crochet, who I would guess was the management's, not Kempe's, choice for soloist. And finally a performance of Mahler's Symphony No. 1 left one overwhelmed by the operation of conductor with music and orchestra—the evident contact of Kempe's mind with everything happening in the score and with the player or players who produced it in sound—and by the statement of the work this operation achieved.

The Carnegie Hall management made a poor choice for the first concert of its series *The Art of the Lied:* the tenor Ernst Häfliger, who had little left of his once beautiful voice, and who gave a demonstration of skillful manipulation of that little without disaster, rather than of art in the delivery of Schubert's songs (you wouldn't have known this from the tributes to Häfliger's voice in the press). But I hadn't come to hear Häfliger; I had come to hear the man "at the piano", Franz Rupp, whom Irving Kolodin thought he was complimenting by describing him as "the world's equivalent to Gerald Moore prior to Gerald Moore". Moore has managed to get the press and public to accept his estimate of himself as the uniquely great accompanist of all time; but it isn't true. One can hear on records Coenraad Bos's marvelous playing with Elena Gerhardt, and Rupp's with Schlusnus, Kreisler and Feuermann; and I wrote once about Rupp as an ensemble pianist what is not true of Moore: that the context Rupp created for the singing or playing of these others—exciting as playing of the piano and as playing of the music—revealed gifts of the magnitude of theirs and placed him among the greats of the musical world. And now again at Carnegie Hall it was the playing Rupp did with Häfliger that alone gave musical interest and distinction to the occasion.

At the concerts of Peter Pears and Benjamin Britten in Hunter College Playhouse also it was Britten's unusual playing of the piano parts of Schumann's *Dichterliebe* and Schubert's *Die Winterreise* that made the performances the arresting and fascinating ones they were—though what remained of Pears's once beautiful tenor voice was agreeable to the ear, free of its quaver of recent years, and skilfully deployed in sensitively inflected phrases. What was unusual in Britten's playing was what he found to point up and make meaningful that one hadn't ever been made aware of before. And if it produced a better result in *Dichterliebe* than in *Die Winterreise* this was because in *Die Winterreise* the pointing up was so intensified as to produce occasional distortion of shape and excessive vehemence. One result was the disappointment of my hope for a performance of *Der Leiermann* that would avoid what seems to me an error of most singers in this concluding song. That is, the frozen, numbed despair of the song seems to me to dictate the numbed manner in which it should be sung and played; and I find confirmation of this in Schubert's markings: the *pp* at the beginning is not modified at all in the vocal part; in the piano part it changes to *f* only after the last vocal phrase, and before this sets limits on the few dynamic stresses and expansions marked in the text. But most of the singers I have heard have sung the song with expressive warmth; all, except Hans Hotter, have made the last vocal phrase an impassioned outburst; and not only was Britten's playing too vehement, but Pears, before his final outburst sang the phrases in a mannered staccato that was obtrusively unsuited to their expressive character.

On the other hand, at Marilyn Horne's Carnegie Hall recital one heard the most beautiful female voice of today, and a use of it which constituted some of the greatest singing of today. The extraordinary range of the voice, from the high notes of a soprano to the low ones of a contralto (which Horne sometimes, mistakenly, makes into approximations of a baritone's); the absolute technical control of it evident in the sustained phrases of melodic writing, the astoundingly accurate fast coloratura passages; the musical intelligence that governs the use of it—these produced superb performances of the pieces by Purcell, arias by Handel and Rossini, and songs by Schubert, Debussy and Strauss on the program.

Another outstanding singer, Beverly Sills, made the New York City Opera's new production of *Lucia di Lammermoor* last fall a notable event. Her voice, as I have said before, no longer has its earlier loveliness, and is a little tremulous and edged; but it is still agreeable to the ear, and is deployed with a musical style, and in coloratura passages with a technically secure bravura, that produced a remarkable vocal performance in *Lucia*—one, moreover, that embodied the expressiveness of a dramatic performance more powerful than one usually sees in this opera. And I take nothing away from her achievement when I question one detail: her directing certain florid passages in the Mad Scene at Enrico (if I remember correctly) in the manner of accusations or denunciations, which they are not. I suspect this to be an innovation of Tito Capobianco, whose staging was another of those in which the directors of today feel privileged to recreate the composer's work in ways they consider necessary for understanding of what, actually, audiences have understood for a hundred years, and understand today, without any such help. Thus, audiences have known from their librettos what happens in the first two scenes of *Lucia* in the park of Ravenswood Castle: in the first, Normanno's reporting to Enrico the surreptitious visits of Edgardo to Lucia; in the second, Lucia's entrance with Alisa for the meeting Edgardo has requested. But Capobianco has the conversation of Normanno and Enrico take place in what the program describes as a courtyard of the castle but what looks like a basement storeroom, and introduces four mysterious gray-robed silent characters, one of whom receives from Edgardo, who appears for a moment in a doorway on the left, a letter which is then handed to Lucia, who appears for a moment in a doorway on the right. The letter presumably is the request for the meeting in the park, which Capobianco thinks is necessary, as Donizetti did not, for the audience to see actually being delivered. And an audience today should see what Donizetti wanted it to see, not what someone else thinks he should have wanted.

Of the other major roles, Edgardo was sung with no musical finesse by the tenor Michele Molese, Enrico and Raimondo more beautifully by Dominic Cossa and Robert Hale; and the singing was done in a bland orchestral context provided by Charles Wilson's conducting.

Aside from the opening scene Marsha Louis Eck's sets were well designed; and so were José Varona's costumes.

Like its inaugural concert, the two subscription concerts of the Chamber Music Society of Lincoln Center that I attended suffered from the participation of its eager-beaver-like director, Charles Wadsworth, whose St. Vitus dance at the piano was a visual concomitant of the obtrusive playing that wrecked the balance of the three instruments in the performance of Mozart's Trio K. 498 for clarinet, viola and piano with Gervase de Peyer and Walter Trampler, at the first concert, and dominated over the winds in Poulenc's Sextet at the second. It was when he was off the stage that one heard excellent ensemble performances: at the first concert Beethoven's rarely played but outstandingly fine Quintet Op. 29 for strings, performed by the violinists Yoko Matsuda and Charles Treger, the violists Boris Kroyt and Trampler, and the cellist Leslie Parnas; at the second Boccherini's Quintet Op. 17 No. 1, an unfamiliar work characteristically individual in its musical thinking, performed by the violinists Pia Carmirelli and Hiroko Yajima, Trampler, Parnas and the cellist Fortunato Arico, and Beethoven's String Trio Op. 9 No. 1, performed by Carmirelli, Trampler and Parnas. The first program was completed by the world premiere of a piece commissioned by the Society, Colgrass's *New People*, a setting of the composer's own poems, for mezzo-soprano, viola and piano, which I found not to be worth the work expended on it by Shirley Verrett, Trampler and Wadsworth and the attention of the audience; and songs of Granados and Nin. And the second offered five uninteresting Schumann duets sung by the soprano Veronica Tyler and tenor Anastasios Vrenios. The works of Mozart, Beethoven and Boccherini made these two of the better programs achieved by Wadsworth's idiosyncratic way of combining the familiar and the unfamiliar, which was to add to the few well-known masterpieces—Mozart's String Quintet K. 516 and Clarinet Quintet, Beethoven's Cello Sonata Op. 102 No. 2 and Schubert's Quartet *Death and the Maiden*—not some of the many other masterpieces that the concert-going public rarely hears—the many quartets of Haydn, the other string quintets of Mozart, the many quartets and quintets of Boccherini, the Quartets Opp. 29 and 161 and Octet of Schubert—but instead "rarely heard compositions requiring unusual combinations of instruments and voices", on the questionable assumption that any and all such compositions were worth performing and listening to. This produced the very first program, with Mozart's Clarinet Quintet as the one major work, and the rest a Pergolesi trio sonata, three folk song arrangements by Beethoven for mezzo-soprano, violin, cello and piano, Saint-Saëns's Caprice on Danish and Russian Airs for flute, oboe, clarinet and piano, and the new Colgrass piece. And it produced a number of others which also looked more interesting to the eye than they were likely to sound to the ear—some without even one major work by a major composer to balance the unfamiliar minor or inconsequential pieces.

Summer 1970 Something needed to be said—I wrote to *The Times*, which decided not to have it said in its pages—about the critical practice of writing about the ideas in one's head instead of the musical facts presented to one's ears, exemplified in several pieces of writing in *The Times*. Thus, Peter G. Davis had begun a report on the opening concert in the Guarneri Quartet's Beethoven series at the Metropolitan Museum of Art with a general statement that the group's "way with Beethoven is essentially lyrical and lightweight compared to, say, the gritty drama of the Budapest Quartet," and offers "a soft-grained, even-tempered . . . view of the music". And this idea in Mr. Davis's mind of the Guarneri way of playing Beethoven had not been affected by what the group actually presented to his ear in the very first work it performed: its more than ordinarily robust delivery of the sonorous chords which begin the Quartet Op. 127 and recur later in the first movement; its other attempts in later movements to impart bigness to the music that resulted in occasional excessive vehemence. All these didn't keep Mr. Davis from writing that "the performance was full of sensitively wrought details and elegantly turned phrases," and that "the composer's sinewy thought processes were obscured by an overabundance of expression." And Allen Hughes seemed to have worked out in his mind a basic idea for his review of Michael Rogers's piano recital—the idea that Rogers did "some of the smoothest piano-playing to be heard nowadays", the playing of "a well-bred pianist and musician" in which "there were no idiosyncrasies . . . to give it a personal stamp" and "not much indication of originality in his interpretative thought". And he didn't let this idea be affected by such facts of Rogers's actual

playing as the grandly proclamatory style of the opening page of
Schumann's Fantasy, the similar power in later pages of the first movement (to say nothing of the extraordinary continuity and coherence
Rogers imparted to the discontinuously episodic movement), the impassioned high points to which Rogers carried the quietly meditative writing within the coherent shape he created in the final movement.

But these lesser reviewers had been following the practice of their
superior, Harold Schonberg—for example in his Sunday article on
the damaging prevalence today, as a result of the influence of Schnabel
and Toscanini, of the principle of strict adherence to the composer's
printed notes, which produced uniformity and lack of individuality
in the playing of today's young pianists; as against the eighteenth and
nineteenth-century tradition that had required a pianist to add something of his own to the mere printed notes—which the young pianists
of today could, and should, learn about from the recorded performances
of Pachmann and Hofmann and their contemporaries. In all this Schonberg was writing about what existed as idea in his mind, not about
what was presented to his ear either by today's young pianists or by
the records of musicians of the past. Those records show that Pachmann
and Hofmann and their contemporaries did not play music with freedom
and with taste in that freedom, but inflicted on it the same distortions
and extravagances, for the same exhibitionistic purpose, as Tetrazzini
and De Lucia and the other singers of their period did; and that
Schnabel's and Toscanini's respect for the composer's text caused them
not to play like human metronomes but to keep their plasticity within
the limits of coherent shape, as singers like Rethberg, Bjoerling, Flagstad
and Steber did. As for today, the young pianists who respect the
composer's text do this in the same way as Toscanini and Schnabel;
and their doing so does not result in uniformity and lack of individuality.
Cliburn, Ashkenazy and Evelyne Crochet are indistinguishable as they
exist in Schonberg's mind; but the listener capable of hearing their actual
playing recognizes the striking differences between Cliburn's and Ashkenazy's performances of Chopin's B-minor Sonata, and between
Ashkenazy's superbly articulated performance of Mozart's Concerto
K.271 and Crochet's shapeless one.

Called on to review Rossini's *Otello* or Bellini's *La Straniera*, Schonberg
writes the ideas in his head about what he calls the formula operas
of Rossini, Bellini and Donizetti—with their unvarying succession of

"opening chorus . . . cavatinas followed by cabalettas . . . duets, trios and quartets, and a full ensemble to end every act"—which, for him, have little musical value, since they were written for the singers of the period to display their virtuosity and *bel canto* style; and which he says cannot be sung properly by the singers of today who, with few exceptions, don't possess that virtuosity and style. And intent on these ideas, rather than on what the works actually present to his ear, Schonberg dismisses each work as having little musical interest —does not, that is, hear and report the melodic beauty and dramatic force of much of the vocal writing in *Otello*, and what Rossini contrived for the orchestra in expressive support of that vocal writing; or the beautiful and affecting melodic writing that Bellini put into *La Straniera* to exhibit the singers' voices.

Schonberg's most ludicrous performance on this subject appeared not in *The Times* but in *Harper's*. (I find it inconceivable that there is another person who thinks and writes exactly like Schonberg in the record reviews signed Discus in *Harper's*, and must therefore believe they can be only by Schonberg.) A review titled *Old Operas and Real Music* dealt with recorded performances of Wagner's *Tristan*, the real music, and Rossini's *Semiramide* and Donizetti's *Lucrezia Borgia*, which, for Schonberg, were two formula operas of the period—*Lucrezia*, except for its well-known *Brindisi*, being "an awful opera . . . without an original idea or an original melody"—both with "vocal parts composed for a long-extinct breed of singer", and both "bearable if the singing is of an ultravirtuosic nature," but "murder otherwise". And though the recorded *Semiramide* wasn't "made any better musically" by Sutherland and Horne, they at least were capable of the virtuoso singing it required; whereas Caballé, who "obviously . . . is being set up as some sort of rival to Sutherland" in *Lucrezia*, was "not really a coloratura" but a lyric soprano, whose "coloratura passages are extremely labored," and who "technically . . . has no business in *bel canto* opera"; indeed "she may be in the process of losing both voice and reputation if she sticks to this kind of material. . . . She would provide an appealingly sung Mimi. But Lucrezia Borgia? Never."

These ideas in Schonberg's head about the two operas and the performances were ludicrously at variance with what was actually presented to his ear. In *Semiramide* one did hear every character, in every situation, sing in an extreme florid style devised not for expressive but for spectacular vocal effect; but in *Lucrezia*—except for the *Brindisi*, a set piece in bravura style for its special purpose, and the least valuable music in the opera—the characters sang melodic writing of high musical quality which amazed one with its Verdian dramatic force in the second-act confrontation of Lucrezia, her husband and her son, and moved one with its expressiveness in the concluding duet of Lucrezia and her son. This melodic writing included some intensifying florid elaboration at cadences; and these florid elaborations Caballé executed with the ease born of the same vocal control that deployed her agreeable-sounding voice in long phrases which exhibited her sense for their shape, their style, their expressiveness, or that spun it out in an occasional series of exquisite *pianissimo* high notes, or that projected the series with power. In *Lucrezia* it was only these short cadential elaborations that Caballé sang with ease; but at the Metropolitan later she had the insolence—in the face of Schonberg's pronouncement, which should have settled the matter—to sing the extended coloratura writing of *Sempre libera* in *La Traviata* with the same security and effectiveness, not with the "struggle" that proved to Schonberg "she isn't a real coloratura. She is a manufactured one, a coloratura *faute de mieux*."

The Metropolitan's new production of Bellini's *Norma* this year, with Sutherland in the title role and Horne as Adalgisa, provided another occasion for the Schonberg operation. In his head Sutherland "still has the most glowing, the richest and most sensuous-sounding voice, of any soprano before the public"; Horne's "big, strong, securely produced voice does not have the sensuous sheen of Sutherland's"; Bergonzi's singing as Pollione was "tonally beautiful and, as always, effortless"; Siepi, as Oroveso, "used his smooth voice with the knowledge of a great veteran"; and as for Bonynge's conducting, "his rhythm is flabby, and he was constantly throwing askew the metrical patterns with his accented upbeats." Actually, however, Sutherland never had that glowing, rich and sensuous-sounding voice; and the performance of *Norma* revealed a lessening of its former limited attractiveness: in addition to the drab lower range there was now a cold, metallic middle range; and only the top was still bright. Her use of it, moreover, included her excitingly accurate execution of florid passages, but also a greater amount of her mannered moaning. The performance revealed further that it is Horne who has that most glowing and rich female voice of today; and her deployment of it not only in florid passages as excitingly accurate as Sutherland's, but in equally exciting phrasing of sustained melody, provided the great singing of the occasion. Bergonzi's voice exhibited a loss of some of its former beauty, and a new strain in the production of high notes; Siepi's the roughness it has had for years. And Bonynge's conducting produced a performance that was musically sensitive and enlivened, coherently shaped and precisely executed.

The stage production was not as outrageous as some other recent ones at the Metropolitan; but it was bad enough. The couple of Stonehenge-like movable constructions designed by Desmond Heeley for all the scenes didn't provide a believable interior—or even exterior—for Norma's dwelling, and made the task of the stage director, Paul-Emile Deiber, more difficult; but it was Deiber who had Norma's children play the games in the background that distracted attention from the performance in the foreground.

There is also the New York City Opera in the critic Alan Rich's head that he writes about—"the most artistically significant venture of its kind in this country, and quite possibly in this world", which presents "opera as good, modern, exciting theater"*—as against the actual New York City Opera that has merely produced a greater number of worthless contemporary operas and a greater number of monstrosities of staging of operatic classics than the Metropolitan. It was the actual New York City Opera that presented Debussy's *Pelléas et Mélisande* badly designed, with Lloyd Evans's damaging innovations in scenery; badly cast, with Patricia Brooks a Mélisande who looked and acted an experienced woman of the world, Louis Quilico a Golaud who looked like Rigoletto, and André Jobin a Pélleas whom it was hard

---

* (1973) Right from the start in 1944, in Rich's head, the company's objective had been "opera as good, modern, exciting theatre, performed by bright young people who cared no less about what they did on the stage than how they sounded." And "the style [that] was bursting out all over that first night" in the performance of *Tosca* "blazed with explosive force" in the performance of *Carmen* the second night. This statement he supported by quoting from my *Nation* review the comment that I could not "recall ever having heard the title role sung as beautifully as it was by Jennie Tourel—with such loveliness of vocal sound and such musical phrasing." What he carefully did not quote was my further comment on Tourel's dramatic inadequacies, and on the "same contrast between musical excellence and dramatic absurdity in the entire performance"—the absurdity of "what that chorus of women looked like and did . . . the appearance and antics of Regina Resnik [Frasquita] and Rosalind Nadell [Mercedes]", and various details of the stage direction.

to accept as an innocent; and badly directed by Frank Corsaro. As for the music, it was sung best by Quilico, and paced well by Rudel, but the orchestral sonorities, for all their delicacy, needed a larger orchestra for adequate realization.

Ashkenazy, who the year before had astonished one with a volcanic performance of Beethoven's *Appassionata* Sonata, this year astonished one with the powerfully and grandly declamatory character of his playing not only in Beethoven's Concerto No. 5 *(Emperor)* but in his Concertos Nos. 3 and 4, at the three concerts of the London Symphony presented by Carnegie Hall. It was most striking in the opening movement of No. 4, which is in large measure quietly meditative; and I recall in particular the passage beginning four bars after the piano's entrance in the development: the series of two-bar statements falling away from an initial held chord, played usually in accordance with the *pp* marked in the score, was made by Ashkenazy into an eight-bar crescendo of dynamics and tension to the beginning of the energetic new episode. And with all its increased power the playing didn't exceed the limits of coherent shape and agreeable piano sound.

An additional point of interest was the operation of the orchestra's new principal conductor, Andre Previn, who in the concertos kept the orchestral context admirably in gear with the soloist's playing but evidently didn't feel obligated to make it as tremendous as that playing. The first concert opened with an unusually fast-paced performance of Berlioz's *Corsair* Overture; and since it was a performance conducted by someone whom Schonberg thought of as "still in the process of learning his trade", he reported that in this fast tempo "the winds had to scramble, and even the brilliant players of the London Symphony were not able to articulate"; whereas the actual playing amazed one with the seemingly effortless accuracy of the woodwinds and brass, the sensitive articulation and phrasing of the strings, in that impossibly fast tempo—a brilliant virtuoso achievement of conductor and orchestra. On the other hand the concert ended with a performance of Beethoven's Seventh in which the tempos were right and the movements proceeded, in these tempos, with continuity and coherence, but which didn't add up to a compelling statement of the work.

The performance of Prokofiev's rarely heard, and not very interesting, Symphony No. 3 that young Claudio Abbado produced with the Boston Symphony at one of its Carnegie Hall concerts, the performances of

Hindemith's Symphonic Metamorphoses of Themes by Weber, Prokofiev's Piano Concerto No. 3 (with Martha Argerich) and Stravinsky's *Oedipus Rex* that he produced with the New York Philharmonic in two of its concerts in Philharmonic Hall—these revealed again the gifts of ear for orchestral sonority and balance, of authority and magnetic compulsion, of feeling for continuity in tension and shape, that had been so impressive in his performance of *Don Carlo* at the Metropolitan the year before. And so one was unprepared for the defects of other performances at these concerts, and the deficiencies they revealed in musical judgment and taste, in mere self-discipline. The Boston Symphony must include a few players who know from personal experience the marvels of orchestral sound Koussevitzky achieved with that orchestra in Debussy's *Nuages* and *Fêtes* and Ravel's *Daphnis and Chloë* Suite—including the incredible ninth chord of the brass at the climax of *Lever du jour* in the Ravel piece; the sudden drop from a brilliant tutti, in the *Danse générale*, to magical sounds of distant horns. And these players could appreciate Abbado's failures—the climax of the procession in *Fêtes*, where one heard not a balanced texture but an unbalanced mass of noisy sound; the coarse brass chord at the climax of *Lever du jour;* the unmagical sounds of the horns in *Danse générale*. What impelled the audience to cheer and yell at the end was Abbado's whipping up of the tempos of *Fêtes* and the Ravel piece—concerning which Toscanini made the correct comment after the sensation created by Munch's performance of Berlioz's *Symphonie Fantastique:* "Is easy to make exciting in double tempo." And this way of "making exciting" was part of the pulling of Tchaikovsky's Fifth about that distorted its shape and expressive content. What remains to be added is that in four early choral pieces by Musorgsky for projected dramatic works he didn't complete it was astonishing to hear the Musorgsky idiom already unmistakably established and used with complete assurance.

After Abbado's uneven and undisciplined operation I could appreciate what Colin Davis's disciplined gifts produced with the Boston Symphony. In particular, after what Abbado did to the Tchaikovsky Fifth I could appreciate Davis's performance of the Fourth, in which, obeying every one of Tchaikovsky's many directions for changes of tempo and expressive shaping, he produced a superbly effective realization of the work that Tchaikovsky had imagined. The symphony ended the Philharmonic Hall concert that Davis opened with a delightfully witty performance of Stravinsky's Scherzo à la Russe; but in between he wasted his and the orchestra's talents and energies on the endless manipulation of meaningless substance in Tippett's Symphony No. 2. Similarly at Carnegie Hall, after fine performances of Mozart's impassioned Overture to *Idomeneo* and his Piano Concerto K.537, with undistinguished playing of the solo part by Ingrid Haebler, Davis devoted the rest of the concert to Elgar's boring Symphony No. 1. These works of Elgar and Tippett are for English audiences, and shouldn't be inflicted on Americans.

The Amadeus Quartet's recorded performances, ranging from moderately good to mediocre, didn't prepare me for the graceless plodding from one note to the next in Mozart's Quartet K.421, at the Metropolitan Museum of Art, which was the worst quartet performance I can remember hearing in a concert hall. Mozart's Clarinet Quintet K.581, which followed, offered the ear-ravishing tone and phrasing of the clarinettist Gervase de Peyer, and a little more sensitively phrased playing by the strings. But I decided not to risk the closing performance of Mozart's Quartet K.387.

Fall 1970 The last of the Lincoln Center auditoriums, the Juilliard Theater in the Juilliard School, was inaugurated with a performance of Stravinsky's *The Rake's Progress* by the Juilliard American Opera Center, a unit of the School created to prepare vocal students for careers in opera, and in this preparation to include their first experience in actual performance. In making Tito Capobianco its director the School added the Opera Center to the organizations at Lincoln Center—the Metropolitan Opera, the New York City Opera, the Chamber Music Society of Lincoln Center—that are directed by men who are in one way or another incapable of directing them properly. What disqualifies Capobianco is the idea he shares with other directors of today that the work created by the composer and librettist is material for the stage director to manipulate and amplify and change in the exercise of his own imagination. As it happened the staging of *The Rake's Progress* was not as damaging as some of the others contrived by Capobianco, and in fact was skilful and effective much of the time. But it did include an egregious example of what the directors of today feel free to do: at the point in the brothel scene where Mother Goose claims

Tom Rakewell for herself, Stravinsky, Auden and Kallman—having considered the various possibilities—decided to have her lead Tom out of the room; but Capobianco felt free to make a different decision—to have her remove her dress and spread herself on her back on the table, to have Tom undressed to his undershirt, lifted high, and deposited face down on her, and to have them lie in embrace. My contention is that—Stravinsky and his librettists having made their decision—no one, including Capobianco, has the right to make a different decision for them; and Capobianco's belief that a director does have this right makes him unfit for the position in which he will impart this belief, as principle and in practice, to young students who should have impressed on them the inviolability of the creative artist's work.

The performance took place on a Ming Cho Lee construction very much of the twentieth century, with its iron posts to which were attached the visible stage lights, and distractingly incongruous with the eighteenth-century scenery and costumes, the Hogarthian reproductions on the curtain and at the sides. Stravinsky's music was of a kind which—unlike Verdi's in the opera house and Beethoven's in the concert hall—Erich Leinsdorf's accurate time-beating was enough to make effective, earning the applause after each act. Less justifiably, his entrance to begin the performance—fresh from the latest of his fiascos, this one with the Boston Symphony—and his entrances for the later acts brought him prolonged ovations from the audience. (I recall the public of fifty years ago as being as undiscriminating as the public of today; but it didn't go into the frenzies of enthusiasm for the third-rate equally with the first-rate that the public of today goes into.)

Balanchine's new *Firebird* for Gelsey Kirkland included an entrance solo in which the inflections of the configuration of her lovely body were breathtaking but did not create the image of a powerful Firebird, and a characteristic Balanchine supported adagio which exhibited her exquisite lyrical dancing, not the struggle of a captured bird. This lack of essential dramatic characterization was increased by the new costume of light-colored filmy drapery that seemed designed mostly to reveal the long lines of her legs, and that was completed on top by half of a Chagall tricorne, as absurdly irrelevant in itself as the other Chagallisms of the production, and dramatically damaging as a replacement of the traditional headdress of plumes: when the Prince released her she didn't give him a plume with which to summon her in need; and when she appeared at the height of his struggle with Kastchei's Subjects it was without being summoned by his waving of that plume.*

After John Simon's conclusive demolition of George Steiner's pretensions as scholar and thinker, in a review of his *Death of Tragedy* in this magazine a few years ago, it has been astonishing and disheartening to see Steiner's similarly pretentious writing continue to be published—not only in *The New Yorker* but in more distinguished magazines. And the range of the pretensions has been extended to include music: a reader has sent me Steiner's review in *The New Statesman* of David Cairns's new translation of Berlioz's *Memoirs*, which is a piecing together of Steinerian inventions such as Simon demolished.

He begins with an imagined situation in 1950 which made Jacques Barzun's high claims for Berlioz in his *Berlioz and the Romantic Century* that year look eccentric—a situation in which "very few recordings of Berlioz's music were available." But it was in 1950 that Clough and Cuming completed their *World's Encyclopedia of Recorded Music*, which devoted two and a half double-column pages to recordings of Berlioz's works—evidence of considerable activity before 1950; and Turner's *Berlioz* and Wotton's *Hector Berlioz*—both in illuminating contact with the man and his music as Barzun's high-flown writing was not—had been published in the mid-thirties in England, where Hamilton Harty had performed Berlioz for years and had made recordings, available here in the thirties, of excerpts from *Romeo*, *The Damnation of Faust* and *The Trojans*, and the overtures. Also available here on records at that time had been Weingartner's and Walter's performances of the *Symphonie Fantastique*, an abridged *Damnation of Faust* and excerpts from *L'Enfance du Christ*. And Toscanini had begun to perform the excerpts from *Romeo* with the New York Philharmonic and NBC Symphony in 1928, *Harold in Italy* in 1929; he had performed the entire *Romeo* with the Philharmonic in 1942 and broadcast it with the NBC Symphony in 1947, and had recorded the excerpts that year; and Koussevitsky, who had begun to perform the *Symphonie Fantastique* in the twenties, had per-

* Ballet reviews of previous years appeared in *Ballet Chronicle* (Horizon Press, 1971).

formed *Harold* and recorded it in 1945. In short, in the twenty years before 1950 there had been sufficient performances, recordings and broadcasts of the major works for the musical public to have become familiar with them and for part of this public to have recognized their greatness. And what happened after 1950 was not, as Steiner claims, a reversal of his imagined situation, but a continuation of the actual situation: additional performances, recordings and broadcasts, and additional appreciation of the works.

Steiner attributes the alleged reversal in part to the efforts of writers like Barzun and Cairns and the conductor Colin Davis; and whereas I doubt that Barzun's high-flown intellectualism about Berlioz as a figure in the Romantic Century, in his pretentiously gigantesque book, won Berlioz any listeners, or that his worthless comments on the works as pieces of music increased anyone's appreciation of them, I can believe that Davis's superb performances of them and Cairns's perceptive writing about them did persuade additional listeners in England. Steiner recognizes that Berlioz's genius had something to do with it, but also "the way we now 'read' his art and presence"—which brings us to further Steinerian inventions. We "read" Berlioz's art and presence, according to Steiner, as listeners whose "awareness [and] habits of recognition" are penetrated with "the currency and authority of Wagnerian opera", but who on the other hand have seen "Wagner's politics and theories of music . . . recently . . . in need and receipt of strenuous apologia". And so "the simultaneous obviousness and ambiguity in the Wagnerian presence, together with the gradual distancing from us of Schoenberg—especially of that in Schoenberg which is a logical extension of *Tristan* and *Parsifal*—have given Berlioz a new character. He embodies an alternative possibility." But my own love of Berlioz's music—exactly like my love of Haydn's, Mozart's, Beethoven's, Schubert's, Verdi's, Musorgsky's, Debussy's, Mahler's, Stravinsky's —was a direct response to each work experienced in and for itself by a mind not at all concerned with any other music, and specifically not with Wagner's and Schönberg's; and what I know of a number of other people makes me certain that the members of the public who have come to love Berlioz's music have done so in similar direct response to what they have heard, not because it offered an alternative to Wagner.

When Steiner comes to the occasion for his review he makes the true statement that Berlioz "was one of the foremost musical critics of his century and his *Memoirs* are a masterpiece." But concerning Cairns's new translation of the *Memoirs* he is fulsomely inaccurate—the most important example being the statement that "Cairns's English pulses with vital élan; it is gay, histrionic, biting . . . as the original requires." The fatuous belief responsible for Barzun's mistranslation of Berlioz's letters and other writings was that writing in English today Berlioz would write with Barzun's prissy urbanity; and the unexpectedly similar belief responsible for Cairns's translation of the *Memoirs* —unexpected because of the intelligence evident in his excellent music criticism and his enlightening notes for the *Memoirs*—is that writing in English today Berlioz would write in the manner of a cultivated Londoner. Writing in English today Berlioz would produce the same rhetorically heightened and impassioned prose as he produced in French; this, therefore, is what a translator of his French must produce in English; and one finds that the way to do it is to adhere closely in the English to Berlioz's words, order of words and sentence structure in the French—as against Cairns's changing of all these, which produced not an English equivalent of the Berlioz original but a well-written paraphrase of it.

When I received the book I went straight to the moving concluding passage, of which the French is:

Je finis . . . en remerciant avec effusion la sainte Allemagne où le culte de l'art s'est conservé pur; et toi généreuse Angleterre; et toi Russie qui m'as sauvé; et vous bons amis de France; et vous coeurs et esprits élevés de toutes les nations que j'ai connus. . . . Quant à vous, maniaques, dogues et taureaux stupides, quant à vous mes Guildenstern, *mes* Rosencranz, *mes* Iago, *mes petits* Osric, *serpents et insectes de toute espèce,* farewell, my friends; *je vous méprise, et j'espère bien ne pas mourir sans vous avoir oubliés.*

"I end," says Berlioz; "I come to an end," Cairns has him say; and so thereafter to the final sentence. "As for you," says Berlioz to the "maniacs, stupid mastiffs and bulls"; "as for you," he repeats to "my Guildensterns"; for similar rhetorical effect he repeats "my" before each of the other names; and his closing hope is "not to die before I have forgotten you." But Cairns has him say instead:

For you, morons, maniacs, you dogs, you Guildensterns and Rosencrantzes, Iagos, Osrics, gadflies, crawling worms of every kind; farewell, my friends, I scorn you, and trust to have forgotten you before I die.

Nor is it only such an unusually emotional passage that Cairns rewrites in this damaging way. Recounting the hostility of French and Italian composers to Beethoven's symphonies when Habeneck introduced them to the Parisian public, Berlioz exclaims: "*Que d'abominables sottises j'ai entendu dire aux uns et aux autres sur ces merveilles de savoir et d'inspiration!*"—"How many abominable stupidities I have heard said to various people about those marvels of skill and inspiration!" —which Cairns changes to "I have heard them airing the most lamentable nonsense about those marvels of beauty and technical mastery."

Winter 1971 Thinking about the essential equipment of a critic—his judgment and taste—and how it was acquired, I remembered a statement a few years ago by the violist Nicolas Moldavan. Before he joined the NBC Symphony he had played in the Flonzaley and Coolidge Quartets; and he remarked that he would have been a better quartet-player if he had played *first* with Toscanini: "In a quartet you have four individuals; and if I feel like playing this passage a little broader I take my time; and the cellist takes *his* time; and so the music becomes distorted. What Toscanini taught me was that a piece of music has a frame, and you phrase and build within this frame." Learning this and other things of that kind by playing with Toscanini was the way Moldavan developed the musical taste that guided his operation as a performing musician; and it occurred to me that what he learned as a participant in Toscanini's performances could have been learned also by a listener to them. I did in fact, by listening to them, learn that a piece of music had a frame, and the performer had to phrase and build within that frame—which is to say, his every modified tempo and sonority had to be in proportion to what had preceded. And learning this and other such things by listening to Toscanini's performances and rehearsals was in effect a process of developing the judgment I applied to what I heard and reported on as a professional listener, a critic. Toscanini was not the only performing musician who taught me in this way: Schnabel, Szigeti, Casals, the Budapest Quartet, Rethberg, Schumann, Flagstad, Bjoerling were some of the others. Nor did their teaching result in my accepting only their performances. Toscanini's working within a frame, and in this way achieving proportion, continuity and coherence in the shape in sound he produced, established such proportion, continuity and coherence as some of the essentials of good performance, which I was able to hear when they were achieved by other conductors in performances different from his; and thus he provided me with criteria which enabled me to recognize good performances by conductors as different as Beecham, Cantelli, Colin Davis, and flawed ones by Stokowski, Koussevitzky, Furtwängler, Bernstein. And the same with Schnabel, Szigeti, Flagstad, Bjoerling and the rest.

But Moldavan's musical taste developed through his playing with Toscanini because he was capable of learning what Toscanini had to teach; and a listener's musical judgment would develop through his hearing great musical performers only if he too had the ability to learn from what he heard them do. Actually most non-professional listeners do *not* have this ability—which is why audiences that respond with cheers to the playing of Ashkenazy respond in the same way to the playing of Barenboim. And actually most professional listeners don't have it either—which is why they write about Barenboim as if he were another Ashkenazy. Realizing that what was true of most was true of one in particular enabled me to understand at last what had until then baffled me: how a professionally trained musician like Winthrop Sargeant, who had played in the New York Philharmonic a couple of years with Toscanini and acquired close-range experience of the plasticity and grace characteristic of his performances, could find in Szell's steely, graceless performances those which today most closely resembled Toscanini's, and could commend Mehta for not imitating Toscanini's rigidity as other young conductors did. Or how, after having heard all the great conductors of the past forty years down to Colin Davis and Boulez of today, he could write after Barenboim's pedestrian and coarsely played Beethoven *Eroica* and his vulgarly italicized Mozart *Prague* that he was "the most promising conductor of his generation", with "every one of the endowments that will . . . in all probability make him a very distinguished maestro." Or how, after having heard Schnabel's perfectly articulated and shaped performances of Beethoven, he could hear in Barenboim's undisciplined operation in the *Appassionata* the "extraordinary musical taste and intelligence" and the "infallible sense of form" that made Barenboim "one of the world's important artists of the keyboard". All these baffling statements, and the many others, I now understand: Sargeant has heard the greatest

musicians of the past forty years; but he learned nothing from them
that enables him to know today when he is hearing a good performance
and when he is hearing a bad one.

Spring 1971 Though the president of American Ballet Theatre told
the company's press representative that I had never said a good word
about the company and he didn't want me in the theater, and was
not persuaded otherwise by the press representative, a friend's ticket
enabled me to see the gala opening-night *Giselle* with Natalia Makarova
and to report that her deployment of her lovely body was exquisite,
and was made breathtaking at times by the slowness of some of the
movements—the slowness, for example, of her various extensions, notably the unfolding in the course of two great lifts in Act 2 (as against
the breathtaking impetus of Suzanne Farrell's extensions in the climactic
lifts in Act 3 of Balanchine's *Don Quixote*). Makarova was most impressive in this act, where for the most part she was called on only to
dance, and one's attention wasn't distracted from her marvelous dancing
by the face that was almost mask-like in its immobility in the reduced
light of the nocturnal scene. In Act 1, on the other hand, right from
the start, she had to act as well as dance, and to act with a face which
in the bright light of the daytime scene was disturbingly unlovely.
Though her dancing in this act was superb, her face made the acting
ineffective; and the mad scene was made ineffective by its lack of
clear development and structure.

At a number of points Makarova's movements were different from
what we have always seen, even—if I remember correctly—in the
Kirov performance with Kolpakova in 1961. Two such differences in
Act 2 call for mention: At the point where we have always seen
Giselle lifted by Albrecht, who has turned as he held her high in
the air, and has then lowered her until her left leg has rested on the
stage floor, with her left arm extended backward to complete the exquisite configuration of her body—at this point Makarova was lowered
instead to a standing position with a slight *plié*, which was less effective.
And at the point where we have seen a series of increasingly high
lifts reach a climax in the great lifts with retracted legs, Makarova
instead separated her legs in a split, which also was less effective.
The New York City Ballet's new male dancer, Helgi Tomasson,

delighted one with the beautifully clear style of his perfectly executed movements, and delighted Verdy with his absolutely secure partnering, which enabled her to operate with complete freedom. After their first *Nutcracker* she exclaimed: "He doesn't need another rehearsal; he only needs two more performances!" And at the second of these additional performances it was exciting to see her expand her movements and enrich them with the nuances that are uniquely hers.

An unfamiliar opera of Donizetti may, like *Lucrezia Borgia*, turn out to offer the operation of impressive powers in vocal and orchestral writing which amazes one with the moving expressiveness, the dramatic force, and even the stylistic freedom of its invention. But it may, on the other hand, turn out to be merely a product of a routine use of his style that does its job efficiently; and this is true of *Roberto Devereux*, except for the beautiful and subtly phrased melodic writing of Elizabeth's *Vivi, ingrato* at the beginning of the last scene. And it was in this aria that Beverly Sills, for whom the New York City Opera put on the work, did her only distinguished singing of the performance—quiet singing in which her voice was steady and quite lovely, her deployment of it in subtly inflected sustained phrases impressive in style and expressively moving. At other times—apart from the florid passages that were made spectacular by her accurate agility and brilliant style—her voice was tremulous and unpleasant to the ear, especially when her vehemence forced it to the point of sheer strident screaming, which I doubt that Donizetti had in mind. It was related to Sills's dramatic performance in the role of the queen, which impressed audiences and critics as great acting, but struck me as hamming of the crudest kind. Sills did succeed remarkably in getting herself up to look like the Elizabeth we have seen in portraits; but it was impossible for me to accept what she did—her screaming at Essex, her gesticulation that all but physically assaulted him—as what a queen, even a queen humiliated and enraged by the discovery that a lover whom she still loved now loved another woman, would do in the presence of her assembled court. I doubt that I would have found her similar behavior in an earlier scene believable even if she and Essex had been, as the libretto says they are, alone; but I certainly could not accept as believable her carrying on as she did in the presence of the pages and guards whom Tito Capobianco thought it effective

to place around the stage. Again, Nottingham merely singing his rage
to his wife in the presence of the guards whom he had summoned
to detain her would have been believable; but what Capobianco thought
up as an effective addition—Nottingham, in their motionless presence,
seizing his wife and throwing her about—was not. And the beginning
of the court scene gained nothing, for me, from Hans Sondheimer's
contribution of this kind with his lighting: the darkness in which the
lords and ladies conversed in song behind the spotlighted silent queen.
However, after the monstrous excesses of recent productions one
must concede the unusual restraint exhibited in this one of *Roberto
Devereux*, which—except for an implausible and gimmicky prison cell
—had good sets of the normal kind by Ming Cho Lee and good costumes
by José Varona; while the musical performance conducted well by
Rudel offered superb singing by Placido Domingo (Essex) and good
singing also by Richard Fredericks and Beverly Wolff (the Duke and
Duchess of Nottingham).

Janáček's *The Makropoulos Affair*, on the other hand, was taken by
Frank Corsaro as an opportunity to go all-out. The work is a Moravian
forerunner of Berg's *Lulu*, with its action, based on the play of Capek,
revolving around a woman who exercises an invariable and sometimes
fatal fascination on every man, young and old, whom she encounters;
and with music which, though it doesn't in the least resemble Berg's,
is as unattractive and uninteresting as his in its own way. That way
is an orchestral writing in which phrase follows phrase without continuity of musical thought and without relation to a vocal recitative
that has no expressive connection with the words. And I don't think
I would have received a different impression if the production had
been the normal one Janáček envisioned, and I had not had to fight
off the distracting Corsaro inventions that seemed to represent his determination to be "with it". The major new gimmick this time was films:
whereas Janáček had been content to let the audience read about the
happenings that had preceded the first act, Corsaro introduced the
act with a silent film of these happenings, in which, however, they
were comprehensible only if one had read about them in the synopsis
in the program, so that the film was superfluous. Worse still, at a
number of places where Janáček had been content with a mere reference
to something, Corsaro spelled it out in a film sequence in parallel
with the action on the stage that distracted one's attention from that

action and the music. And predictably one such reference to "certain erotic practices" was spelled out in a film of the nude torsos of a couple in constantly changing embrace. These and other distracting nonessentials were what engaged Corsaro's attention and effort, instead of something as essential as a set that would have some resemblance to the "backstage at the theater" referred to in the program and would meet the requirements of the action, as Patton Campbell's set did not.

The difficult and unrewarding singing that Maralin Niska was called on to do in the principal role she did well. And Gabor Ötvös conducted efficiently.

As for the Metropolitan, the first thing to say is that after the latest example of Bing's total lack of the artistic competence he pretends to, the new production of Gluck's *Orfeo ed Euridice*, it is good to know that in another year we will at last be rid of him. His successor's professional experience is that of an actor and stage and film director; but he works with a musical director in Stockholm and has said he will do so here; and with a musician handling musical matters, including the casting that Bing has reserved exclusively and often disastrously to himself, we may have an end of what wrecked the new *Orfeo*. A musician would have known that the Metropolitan had in Marilyn Horne the singer with the beautiful voice and the ability to shape Gluck's phrases that made her the predestined singer of the title role; but Bing, apparently incapable of hearing the unpleasant harshness of Grace Bumbry's voice and her inability to produce with it a musical and expressive statement of a single phrase in the opera, assigned the role to her; and this decision doomed the production even without the other things that damaged it—one of them the deteriorated voice of Gabriella Tucci (Euridice), the other the staging.

To see the difficulty of devising meaningful and interesting stage action for an opera in which so little happens, and how that diffficulty can be solved, one need only consider the scene in which Orfeo—his hand grasping Euridice's, his face averted from hers—is shown leading her back to earth, resisting her entreaties and despairing complaints, begging her to continue when she refuses to go any further, and, when he can resist her no longer, looking at her, which causes her to die. One need only, that is, consider how little of the sense of the scene is conveyed by the two singers lunging separately about the stage as they sing, and in these lungings repeatedly facing each other, so that the dramatic point of Euridice dying when Orfeo looks at her is lost; and on the other hand consider how clearly and powerfully the sense of the scene is conveyed by the *pas de deux* in Balanchine's ballet to Stravinsky's music, whose detail elaborates the essential point of Euridice's persisting in her attempts to get Orpheus to look at her and her dying when at last he does so. One realizes from this that the effective way to stage *Orfeo* is to choreograph its action for dancers on the stage and have the soloists and chorus sing with the orchestra in the pit—which is in fact what Balanchine did at the Metropolitan in 1936. But this is a project for a Balanchine; and Bing entrusted it instead to Milko Sparemblick, who, for no imaginable reason, choreographed for dancers on the stage only the music of the chorus in the pit, so that one saw on the one hand, as usual, Orfeo and Euridice lunging about the stage as they sang and making no dramatic sense in the scene of their journey back to earth, and on the other hand the contorted and ugly modern-dance-style movements Sparemblick thought up for the dancers to go with the chorus's singing in the first act, and the blander but equally uninteresting ones he contrived for the scenes in the Elysian Fields and the Temple of Love.

Rolf Gérard produced powerful sets for Euridice's tomb and the entrance to Hades, but achieved only a vast expanse of pink and gilt for the Elysian Fields. And Bonynge, who I was reliably informed conducted the first performance poorly, conducted the later one I heard with precision, animation, and enlivening rhythm and phrasing.

Mehta's orchestral performances on records have been far less impressive than his performances of Verdi at the Metropolitan; but they didn't prepare me for the Beethoven Ninth he produced with his Los Angeles Philharmonic in Carnegie Hall—the worst orchestral and musical operation I had heard since Barenboim's concerts with the London Symphony two or three years ago. The conducting movements one saw conveyed an assured mastery in the guidance of the orchestra and shaping of the music; but what I heard revealed that like his friend Barenboim, Mehta has no ability to achieve the balance in an orchestra that produces beautiful sound and clear texture, and no ability to phrase and shape coherently within the frame of a symphonic movement. What I heard, that is, was an opaque mass of coarse sound that was, as in Barenboim's performances, occasionally drowned by the thunder of the kettledrums; and an undisciplined dealing with the music like Barenboim's which produced shapeless statements of the work's four movements. But the conducting movements that conveyed assured mastery to the eye persuaded the audience that it was hearing a masterful performance which justified the storm of applause at the end—and not only the audience but a former orchestral musician who had played a couple of years under Toscanini, and who reported in *The New Yorker* only slight technical defects of string articulation and ensemble and kettledrum attack in the playing of the orchestra that Mehta had "trained admirably", and a performance of the symphony with "the solid authority that we expect from a maestro of experience who has studied his score carefully".

The next orchestral concert I heard was one in Philharmonic Hall by a much finer orchestra, the Boston Symphony, which played raucously last year in performances of Debussy's *Fêtes* and Ravel's *Daphnis and Chloë* Suite conducted by Abbado, but beautifully in performances conducted by Davis, and beautifully now under young Michael Tilson Thomas, demonstrating his possession of the ear for orchestral balance that Mehta and Barenboim lack. The evidence was the delicate sonorities he got from the orchestra for Webern's Six Pieces Op. 6, the clear textures he produced with it in Debussy's *Images: Gigues, Rondes de Printemps* and *Ibéria*. In addition one heard the operation of a first-class musical mind in his dealing with the marvelous Debussy pieces—the pacing and shaping that gave them unfailing continuity and coherence. It was a mind of his own, whose dealing with *Ibéria* differed from Toscanini's and Boulez's, managing to maintain continuity in a last movement much slower and more deliberate—and I thought less effective—than theirs, and slower than Debussy requests with his metronome marking shortly after the direction *Dans un rhythme de Marche lointaine, alerte et joyeuse*. This mind put together the program that offered on the one hand Bach's Brandenburg Concerto No. 3 and the Debussy *Images*, and on the other hand the Webern Six Pieces and Ingolf Dahl's Concerto for Alto Saxophone and Orchestra, which sounded like the solution of a problem set in an examination, "Write a concerto for alto saxophone and orchestra"—a solution which demonstrated the ability to devise things for the saxophonist, Harvey

Pittel, and the orchestra to do, but not to make them—in the words of W. J. Turner about some of Bach's solutions of problems—as expressive as they were accomplished.

The Fischer-Dieskau series sponsored by Carnegie Hall had a new point of interest: the participation of the pianist Barenboim. And in the first eight songs of the opening Schubert program, which were largely quiet, not only did Fischer-Dieskau delight ear and mind with the beauty of his voice and his subtly inflected deployment of it in the long-breathed phrases, but Barenboim produced what one hadn't heard from him before: phrases which proceeded from beginning to end with sustained continuity of tone, tension, inflection, outline. Moreover, in these quiet songs Barenboim was himself physically quiet. But with the final song of the first half of the program, the declamatory *Prometheus*, one began to hear and see again the Barenboim one had come to know before: the piano's forceful chords were finished off with impressive flourishes of the arms. And with Fischer-Dieskau's erupting *crescendos* in the more forceful and dramatic songs of the second half of the concert Barenboim felt free not only to similarly italicize his playing for the ear but to theatricalize it for the eye with the movements of head, body and arms that demonstrated, like Leonard Bernstein's, how deeply he was involved with, and affected by, the music. This increased as the concert approached its end, and attained its climax in the encore period, in the exuberantly blown-up performances by singer and pianist of *Der Musensohn* and *Abschied*.

The Wolf concert offered even worse excesses in many of the songs, among them the concluding *Abschied*. It is one of Wolf's humorous pieces, ending in a lilting waltz in which the narrator exults over the way his uninvited and unwelcome guest, propelled by a little kick, had tumbled down the stairs. And after Fischer-Dieskau's overdramatizing of the waltz Barenboim crashed it out on the piano with vulgar distortion, eliciting a storm of applause from the audience and an embrace from the singer.

Thus we are left with the strange fact that an artist with Fischer-Dieskau's highminded dedication and his musical intelligence and taste can surprise us not only by the italicizing that flaws some of his performances, but by participating in Leonard Bernstein's tastelessly distorted *Falstaff* and *Das Lied von der Erde* and now in the shocking performances with Barenboim, and by speaking of the pleasure he had in the collaboration with Bernstein and demonstrating such pleasure in his embracing of Barenboim.

Summer 1971 In recent years Violette Verdy has appeared in New York City Ballet productions with Peter Martins and Helgi Tomasson, whose expert partnering—in *Ballet Imperial, Swan Lake, The Nutcracker,* Tchaikovsky *Pas de Deux*—has given her the security that has enabled her to operate with complete freedom and effectiveness, and who in addition have provided her performances with the enhancing contexts of their superb dancing. But the New York audiences have had few opportunities to see what Verdy described to Dance Society a year ago: the special working relation that she and Edward Villella have achieved in their years of performing together. It is in their engagements outside of New York that they have been giving their great performances together of Tchaikovsky *Pas de Deux;* and it is of course outside of New York that they have had opportunities to perform in works not in the New York City Ballet repertory. It was in Boston that I saw them in *Giselle;* and in Washington, this year, that I saw them in the Bournonville classic, *La Sylphide.*

This work required Verdy and Villella to master—i.e. to feel at home in, and appear to be at home in—a style of dance movement and pantomine which was new to them, and which they were taught by a dancer famous for her performance in the title role, Elsa Marianne von Rosen. For Verdy the differences in the dance movements—as she described them in an interview with Selma Jeanne Cohen—were first their lightness, expressing the Sylphide's lightness of spirit that she said was timed into the music; and then the fact that "the hands are very soft, the elbows and shoulders . . . demure, and the head has all sorts of delicious angles." As for the pantomime, the gestures were those of a character charmingly irresponsible in her innocent wilfulness; and from my recollection of Toni Lander's performance I knew how difficult it was to make this character believable—how fatal to credibility "a false move, even just a misplaced accent" could be. And Verdy's achievement was not merely the dancing that she made enchanting with her lightness, with the softness of her hand movements, the demureness of her elbows and shoulders, the delicious angles of her head, but the flawless pantomime with which she made the Sylphide completely believable. For Villella the problem of the Bournonville style was what he described as the "little syncopations, little steps that have a slight difference in phrasing from the way we are used to doing them"; and what my eye noticed was the dazzling profusion of small leg movements and beats that he executed with precision and made as exciting as the powerful turns and leaps involving torso and arms, the powerful leg movements and beats, one usually sees him do. And his miming also compelled belief in the James one saw at the moment on the stage.

These two dancers performed in a context of excellent dancing by the soloists and *corps* of the National Ballet, with Andrea Price a charming Effie, Gerard Sibbritt an accomplished and amusing Gurn, and Frederic Franklin a striking Witch. The performance had stylistically harmonious scenic backgrounds designed by Robin and Christopher Ironside and obtained. I was told, from Ballet Rambert.

With the New York City Ballet a month later, when Verdy and Villella appeared together in the second of only two scheduled performances of Balanchine's *La Source*, he again made his physical power unobtrusive, using it to project himself about the stage with effortless grace and elegance in the intricate movements of his solos; Verdy, in her solos, again enchanted the eye with the subtle nuances of rhythm and inflection that are uniquely hers; and in their two *pas de deux* he added noble style to the skill with which he supported and presented her breathtaking unfoldings in arabesques and lifts. He also exhibited in these the deference that is a built-in stylistic feature of partnering; but at the curtain calls after the piece he chose to make an explicit personal gesture of homage to Verdy that was extraordinary and impressive in the mere fact of its being made, but acquired additional impressiveness from the manner of its making—its characteristic personal grace. Each time the curtain rose he kept his face turned to Verdy's as he brought her forward to the wildly applauding audience and as he stood holding up her hand in presentation of her to the audience to which she bowed; and only after she had turned to him and they had bowed to each other did he turn to the audience and accept applause for his own superb performance.

One sympathized with the marvelous Paolo Bortoluzzi and other impressive dancers of Maurice Béjart's Ballet of the 20th Century who performed in the ballets of his I saw at the Brooklyn Academy of

Music—*Choreographic Offering, Nomos Alpha, Actus Tragicus, Le Sacre du Printemps* (an outrageous misuse of Stravinsky's score)—which revealed Béjart as a choreographer with great pretensions and only slight gifts. And *Erotica* and *Bach Sonata* revealed his inability to do anything with Suzanne Farrell, after the marvelous things Balanchine had done with her for the New York City Ballet.*

In 1954 Boris Kochno published in France *Le Ballet*, in which 150 pages of text and superb photographs were devoted to the productions of Diaghilev and his Ballets Russes; and it was natural for me to think that Kochno's *Diaghilev and the Ballets Russes*, published here this year, was an English translation of those 150 pages with the same photographs. Instead it turned out to be a newly written book, with information about each of the Diaghilev productions from *Le Pavillon d'Armide* in 1909 to *The Prodigal Son* in 1929, and with different photographic documentation that was inferior and inadequate. This was most evident and important in connection with the early ballets in which Nijinsky appeared: as against the numerous exciting photographs of him in *Le Ballet* there not only are fewer in *Diaghilev* but they are less well chosen, less well reproduced, and in some instances reduced excessively in size.

When I referred a year ago to Marilyn Horne's as the most beautiful female voice, and her use of it as some of the greatest singing, of today, I momentarily forgot about the beautiful voice and great singing of Janet Baker, which her Hunter College recital this year served to remind me of. It is a more delicately lovely and flexible voice than Horne's; and much of the time the great singing—in the songs of Debussy and Fauré, for example—is a quiet flow of tone with subtle inflections in which one hears the operation of extraordinary and unerring musical intelligence and feeling and taste. But it is a voice capable of the physical power for the emotional or dramatic intensity of music like *Parto, parto* from Mozart's *La Clemenza di Tito*, whose phrases were

---

* One noted with interest that Clive Barnes—who had found Farrell's departure from the New York City Ballet unregrettable, and the dancers who replaced her preferable, praising Mazzo for avoiding in *Symphony in C* "the stylistic mannerisms of her predecessor . . . who here had an overfondness for kissing her knee"—wrote this year after *Don Quixote*, as though he had never written anything different, that Mazzo "lacked that effortless quality of perfect line that was Miss Farrell's," whom "no one will be able to replace . . . while her memory is still green."

superbly shaped by the same musical intelligence, feeling and taste. An additional gift for, and relish in, comedy was revealed in Schubert's *Die Männer sind méchant;* and, at the end, a command of the special style of the opening melodic writing of *Non più mesta* from Rossini's *La Cenerentola,* and of the bravura style in the later accurately executed florid passages.

Horne sang with delightful effect in Rossini's *The Barber of Seville* at the Metropolitan, and could be faulted only for a varied repetition of a section in her first aria that went far beyond any recognizable relation to the original. Figaro's entrance aria is traditionally an invitation to exaggerations and interpolations that Sherrill Milnes didn't resist; and in the second-act duet with Rosina he was unable to repeat accurately the little florid phrases of hers that he was supposed to repeat; but for the most part he used his fine baritone voice well. On the other hand Enrico DiGiuseppe's tenor not only couldn't manage the florid passages in the first act but was unattractive to the ear in its upper range.

As for the Metropolitan's new *Fidelio,* Florestan's dungeon is supposed to look as ruinous as it did in the production designed by Boris Aronson; but I don't see any justification for this appearance of crumbling ruin in the scenes in front of the Jailer's lodge and in the courtyard of the prison. And I question the German-Nazi-like uniforms and caps of Pizarro and the soldiers—especially since Don Fernando appeared in the final scene in eighteenth-century costume. There have been far worse things in the productions of the Bing era; but these were disturbing and distracting enough; and I should mention that they were decided on jointly by Aronson and the stage director Otto Schenck.

The Leonore in the performance I attended, Hildegarde Hillebrecht, sang well in everything but what is most important—the great recitative *Abscheulicher!* and aria *Komm' Hoffnung,* for which she lacked the power of voice and style they require. But one heard great singing by Jon Vickers in Florestan's *Gott! welch' Dunkel hier;* Edith Mathis's lovely light soprano in Marzelline's aria; good singing by John Macurdy, the Rocco, and William Dooley, the Pizarro. Regrettably one did not hear this singing in a whole created by great conducting: Böhm's pacing included going from the trio to the concluding section, in the first scene, with no change from the *Allegro ma non troppo* of the one to the *Allegro molto* prescribed by Beethoven for the other—which is to say, with none of the dramatic urgency and excitement in the concluding section that Beethoven intended.

I can express gratitude without the slightest reservation to the Juilliard School's American Opera Center for the production of Mozart's *La Clemenza di Tito* that provided an opportunity not only to hear the beautiful music sung well by the student soloists and chorus with the excellent student orchestra under Bruno Maderna's assured direction, but to do so undisturbed by what I saw: singers in rich eighteenth-century-Roman costumes designed by Hal George deployed with remarkable skill by Osvaldo Riofrancos on a permanent set of platforms and columns admirably designed by John Scheffler—with not a trace of the updating that has afflicted the staging of operas of the past in recent years.

The program of a Boston Symphony concert I attended in Philharmonic Hall exemplified ideas about program-making that Michael Tilson Thomas had described to an interviewer earlier in the season—the idea in particular, as I recall it, that programs should be made more varied, and in this way more interesting, with works for groups of different sizes and varying composition. It had occurred to me when I had read this that the audience was entitled to demand that such works be performed only if they were worth attention as pieces of music; and this thought recurred as I sat listening to Thomas's demonstration of how Bach could be boring with a small group of strings, winds and drums in his Suite No. 4 (but not in Nos. 2 and 3, which is why they are performed and No. 4 is not); how Schönberg could be boring with the entire orchestra in his Five Pieces Op. 16; and how Stravinsky could be boring with a small group of winds, percussion, solo string quintet, cimbalom and four singers in what my guest characterized as the "whimsy-whamsy" of *Rénard*. Only after these did Thomas perform something unusual that deserved the audience's attention—Act 3 of Tchaikovsky's *Swan Lake*. And only then were the extraordinary powers he had wasted on the earlier pieces employed in music worthy of them, producing a performance that was literally stunning not only in its tonal beauty and brilliant execution but in its unfailing musical rightness and the effect it gave to Tchaikovsky's marvelous writing in all its variety.

It occurs to me now that the variety Thomas wants doesn't require orchestras of different sizes: it can be achieved with the varying use of essentially the same orchestra by Haydn, Mozart, Beethoven, Schubert, Mendelssohn, Berlioz, Tchaikovsky, Brahms, Strauss, Mahler, Debussy, Stravinsky and Prokofiev.

Van Cliburn continues to give overwhelmingly great performances of the few great works he plays; and far from overwhelming the reviewers, he continues to elicit their condescension and denigration. His tremendous performance of Beethoven's *Appassionata* Sonata was characterized by a reviewer in *The San Francisco Chronicle* as a "miserable reading . . . plodding, coarse, dull and totally without direction"; and it was the same performance, if I remember correctly, that occasioned the contemptuous dismissal by a reviewer in *The Boston Globe.* These were assistant reviewers, who were echoing what the first-line writers have established about Cliburn not just in San Francisco and Boston but in New York. In a performance of Beethoven's Concerto No. 3 with the Philadelphia Orchestra this year he produced grandly impassioned and powerfully sculptured playing in which every note assumed the place allotted it in the emerging shape by a mind unfailing in its conceptual grasp of that shape and its control in achieving it. And his reward was Winthrop Sargeant's statement in *The New Yorker:* "I have admired Mr. Cliburn in the past for certain sensitivities to the Romantic style, and he is assuredly an able pianist. But his solo in this work was somewhat fussy, and, in the slow movement, almost unbearably spineless. I have always been an advocate of the Romantic style in *rubato*, but there is a limit beyond which simple incoherence sets in, and I think that Mr. Cliburn passed this limit."

One knew with Stravinsky, as one had known with Toscanini, that there would have to be an end; but miraculously the tiny, frail body continued to withstand the attacks of illness, and the powerful mind remained entirely unaffected by them. That was the difference: Toscanini's life had really ended, for him and for us, three years before his death, when he had been compelled to stop conducting; but the prose writing with which Stravinsky delighted those who found nothing to interest them in his recent music continued—with no lessening of intellectual force, personal vitality, verbal felicity and pungency— almost to the last moment of consciousness. In February there was an ostensible "Rap Session" with *The New York Review of Books* in which Stravinsky commented with his usual perception and humor on the general New York scene before getting to the new Boulez recording of Debussy's *Pelléas et Mélisande.** It is saddening to think that this is the last of such reports of what that ear and mind discovered in the music he went back to listen to in recent years.

And only a few weeks before his death he wrote a letter to *The Times* (published as inconspicuously as possible on a back page of the Sunday theater section) which began: "Clive Barnes's 'This Firebird Is For Burning' adds several cubits to the stature of his incompetence as a commentator on ballet." Mr. Barnes's dismissal of Stravinsky's criticisms of the original Fokine ballet with the statement "This was Fokine's ballet, not Stravinsky's, and Fokine knew best," led Stravinsky to write:

> . . . How can Mr. Barnes decide that Fokine knew better than I did, not knowing what I knew? And anyway, knew *what* better? I was at least there, I worked with Fokine. And I had been brought up on ballet since early childhood, hence may have had as keen appreciation of it as Mr. Barnes. And though this is boasting, I had a reputation with the dancers for a choreographic imagination. Finally, my letters, which are now being prepared for publication (and may this be the last addition of the sort), bear out my later criticisms in concrete terms. Not that any of this proves that Fokine did not know best, of course, but it certainly weakens Mr. Barnes's claims to know.

And later Stravinsky referred to Mr. Barnes's "facile reviews and the way they oscillate between the 'rave' for one kind of mediocrity and the 'roast' for another." Thus Stravinsky's last public act was another of his attacks on reviewers in which, though he spoke on his own behalf, he spoke also for those who fear to speak out for themselves—the Verdys, Villellas and Farrells, the Cliburns, Ashkenazys and Michael Rogerses—who in addition to all they have to endure in their working lives to give us their great performances, must endure in silence the irresponsible and damaging nonsense that editors allow to be written about those performances by the Barneses, Schonbergs and Sargeants. With this last action, as I said of an earlier one, Stravinsky earned the gratitude of his fellow artists and the admiration of us all.

Fall 1971 Jerome Robbins, as a choreographer, "shouted greatness almost with diffidence," according to Clive Barnes; and he may actually

* See page 90.

have felt some diffidence in relation to Balanchine during his first association with the New York City Ballet twenty years ago; but nowadays he makes his claims to greatness with the outward signs of full confidence in them: the signs backstage that one hears about, and the ballets eventually seen on stage, each a bigger Big Work asserting a claim to the position Mr. Barnes has declared his—that of Balanchine's successor when he eventually retires from the New York City Ballet.

The Big Work signalling his advent in the company as a major creator, and one in which he elected to demonstrate what *he* could achieve in the format of Balanchine's *Liebeslieder Walzer*, was *Dances at a Gathering* two years ago. And now we get the ostentatiously Bigger Work of that kind, *Goldberg Variations*. The special character of the Bach music was enough to make it a formidable, awesome choice for a ballet; but Robbins's decision to choreograph it with all repeats resulted in ninety minutes of the same alternation of good and bad as in *Dances at a Gathering:* the good the occasional successful achievement of Robbins's limited gift for dance invention; the bad the unattractive results of the attempt to transcend that limitation with a straining for novelty, and the resort to show-biz humor or pretension to profound meaning.

The musical season's concluding high point was the recital at the Metropolitan Museum of Art at which Ashkenazy performed Beethoven's Sonatas Op. 81a *(Les Adieux)*, Op. 57 *(Appassionata)* and Op. 111. I have reported the increased intensity and power of his dealing with music in recent seasons; and in the *Appassionata* and Op. 111 this time he operated with a demonic intensity that was overwhelming (as against the power of this intensity, what is overwhelming in Cliburn's performance of the *Appassionata* is the power of its grandeur). It was an intensity which didn't entail the slightest loss either of conceptual grasp of the music or of the control that kept the greatest piano sonorities agreeable to the ear. And the conceptual grasp was that of someone with an unfailing sense for continuity and coherence and proportion in shape; someone, moreover, whose shaping of the music revealed thinking of his own in an occasional unusual feature. One such feature occurred in the first movement of the *Appassionata* after the opening section of the recapitulation in F minor that ended in a pause on the dominant: the *fortissimo* statement that followed proclaimed its shift to F major with a tremendous broadening of tempo that I couldn't recall having heard before. And another was the treatment of the first two variations in the slow movement of Op. 111: in the face of the directions about dynamics and tempo in the printed text that indicate a rather quiet progression which is suddenly broken in on by the *forte* of Variation 3, Ashkenazy created in the first two variations a build-up of intensity—with a steady crescendo in sonority and acceleration in tempo—to a climax in the *forte* of Variation 3. It was unquestionably not what Beethoven had in mind; but, just as unquestionably, when done with Ashkenazy's musical understanding and taste it was something one found valid and convincing.

When the first edition of Willi Apel's *Harvard Dictionary of Music* appeared in 1944 I wrote that it was the only good book we had got from the German musicologists in this country, but that it contained an article on music criticism by one of the worst of them, Hugo Leichtentritt, whose muddled mind revealed itself to be completely without understanding of the practicing critic's operation, to be filled instead with schematizations miles removed from the realities of that operation, and to be insufficiently acquainted with the field and its literature, with the result that he was unable to evaluate the actual operation of the critics he mentioned, and didn't even mention critics as outstanding as Bernard Shaw and W. J. Turner. I published a reader's complaint that the bibliographies referred one to obscure and inaccessible European periodicals, mostly German; only later did I discover that the bibliography for Concerto included the worthless book of Veinus but not Tovey's great essay in Volume 3 of his *Essays in Musical Analysis*, and the one for Conducting included Wagner's *On Conducting* but not Berlioz's *The Orchestral Conductor*.

From what I have just said it is understandable that I began, in the new edition, with the article on music criticism, and found that John Reeves White, conductor of Pro Musica Antiqua, had retained parts of Leichtentritt's article that should have been omitted with the rest, and had corrected some of Leichtentritt's errors and omissions but not others—not the omission of W. J. Turner's criticism, and not the statement that musical journalism had begun with Hanslick's writing in the Vienna *Neue Freie Presse*, when in fact Hanslick's writing had been preceded by Berlioz's in the *Journal des Débats*. As for Mr. White's additions, they included the statement "Perhaps the critic's main duty is to become involved in the strongest artistic currents, of both composition and performance, and develop a keen sense of public taste"—which indicated to me a lack of understanding of what the critic's task is and what it requires for its achievement. Though the book with the 1947 Harvard symposium, *Music and Criticism*, was included in his bibliography, Mr. White seemed either not to have read, or not to have remembered, or not to have understood E. M. Forster's definitive statement in it of the primary aim of criticism: to consider the work of art "as an object in itself, an entity, and tell us what it can about its life." In other words the critic was concerned not with "artistic currents" but with the particular object before him; he was not concerned with public taste but employed his own perception to discover the life in that object, his own judgment to evaluate it. Not understanding this, Mr. White found in Shaw's writing not the perception and judgment that made him a great critic but only "brilliant invective and enthusiasm" and the "lively style" that "still makes delightful reading." For the same reason he thought it sufficient to ascribe "great diversity of views" to the American critics he mentioned, saying nothing about the value of those views—i.e. which were, and which were not, the views of writers able to perform the critic's task of perceiving and evaluating what happened in the objects before them. And for the same reason he included many poor books (e.g. Paul Rosenfeld's *Discoveries of a Music Critic* and Max Graf's *Composer and Critic*) with the few partly good ones *(Music and Criticism* and Virgil Thomson's *The Art of Judging Music)* in his bibliography. (The bibliography for Concerto again had Veinus's book but not Tovey's essay; the one for Conducting again Wagner's treatise but not Berlioz's.)

In the new article on ballet I found that Ingrid Brainard named the famous first three Stravinsky scores for the Diaghilev company and the later *Les Noces,* but not *Pulcinella;* and that she mentioned Prokofiev's early and forgotten *Chout* but not his more consequential and enduring *Prodigal Son* for the last Diaghilev season. She had Balanchine beginning his collaboration with Stravinsky in this country with *Jeu de Cartes* in 1937 and producing with him *Agon* twenty years later, leaving unmentioned Balanchine's historic choreography for Stravinsky's *Apollo* in the Diaghilev season of 1928, and in this country his choreographing of Stravinsky scores for *Le Baiser de la Fée, Danses Concertantes, Orpheus, Movements, Variations, Rubies.* She also left unmentioned Balanchine's collaboration with Prokofiev in *Prodigal Son* and with Rieti in *Le Bal* in the last Diaghilev season, and in this country his choreographies for scores by Hindemith, Schönberg, Ives, Webern, Schuller, Xenakis and others. She mentioned Leonard Bernstein's *Fancy Free*, but didn't say it was a collaboration with Jerome Robbins, that the two had collaborated again in *Age of Anxiety*, and that Robbins had choreographed scores by Copland, Morton Gould and Stravinsky. She didn't mention the brilliant Lew Christensen collaboration with Virgil Thomson in *Filling Station*, and Ashton's collaboration with Thomson in the historic first production of *Four Saints in Three Acts*. And her bibliography, incredibly, didn't include Denby's *Looking at the Dance*.

A new article on broadcasting of music—attributed to Ross Allen of Indiana University, with revisions by William H. Cavness of WGBH, Boston—turned out to be incomplete, inaccurate and misleading. It began with the statement that "it was not until large networks were established . . . that broadcasts of serious music became available to a wide audience"—to which it failed to add that the large commercial networks which broadcast the great orchestras and the Metropolitan Opera in the thirties and forties stopped doing so years ago and offer no serious music at all today, leaving the Metropolitan to be broadcast over a Texaco ad hoc hook-up of AM and FM stations, and some of the orchestras to be broadcast live by individual stations in their cities and from tapes by a few individual stations elsewhere. Instead the article went on to speak of the broadcasts of the Sunday afternoon concerts of the New York Philharmonic as one of "the two series that have endured the longest and secured the most loyal group of listeners" —as though the Sunday afternoon Philharmonic broadcasts were still being heard; whereas in fact CBS had stopped broadcasting the concerts even before the Philharmonic moved them to Monday evenings a few years ago, and though for a time they continued to be broadcast live and from tapes by a few individual stations, these broadcasts also stopped two or three years ago.

So with the later statement that "since the early 1930's all the networks have made significant contributions in music performances designed especially for radio listeners," to which the article failed to add that all the contributions of this kind—the series of the NBC Symphony and NBC-TV Opera Theater, the CBS Invitation to Music, the CBS

Symphony, the ABC Symphony—had ended in the late forties and early fifties. And the large fact which the article failed to make clear was that even in the golden thirties and forties the commercial networks gave the public for the most part only the performances and repertory of the celebrated American orchestras and the Metropolitan Opera; and that even with the few additional programs of their own they didn't achieve anything comparable with the British Broadcasting Corporation's planned presentation of the entire literature of music—the entire literature of the orchestra, the string quartet and other chamber groups, the voice, the piano and other solo instruments, the less familiar music of the past, the music of today.

The article on the phonograph and recorded music by Philip Lieson Miller of the New York Public Library's Music Division in the first edition had been an informative and adequate account of developments in both until the early forties; but his account of developments since then in the second edition turned out to be incomplete. The 33⅓ rpm long-playing disc, he wrote, "made the older 78 RPM discs obsolete," but "fortunately many of the older discs have been transferred onto LP discs"—which gave the impression that the transferred recorded performances had remained available on these LP discs; whereas what he failed to add was that in a comparatively short time they had disappeared again, this time from the LP catalogues. And when he described the development and introduction of the stereo disc he failed to mention that it made the mono discs obsolete and resulted in the loss of the many superb performances on those discs, only a few of which had been reissued on lower-priced records. In addition, he described the advantages and disadvantages of magnetic tape in the recording process without mentioning the possibility it had offered of altering the original sound, and the most notorious examples of such electronic manipulation—RCA's monstrously falsifying "enhancements" of Toscanini's recordings. And finally there was Mr. Miller's bibliography, which began, rightly, with the Clough and Cuming *World's Encyclopedia of Recorded Music*, a useful reference work that enabled one to find out what had been recorded until 1957. With this work that went as far as 1957, the revised *Gramophone Shop Encyclopedia of Recorded Music* that stopped with 1948 lost its practical value; and presumably it was included in the bibliography merely as the first work of its kind. But then it was puzzling to find in the bibliography the obsolete 1950 record guides of David Hall and Irving Kolodin and 1956 guide of Harold Schonberg with their evaluations of records no longer available today, but not the very first book of that kind, which I published in 1938, and not, on the other hand, the most recent and least obsolete book of that kind, which I published in 1967.

On the way to the article on the phonograph my eye caught the one on operetta, which stated that "during the late 1920's the sentimental operetta began to change (e.g. Jerome Kern's *Showboat*, 1927) into what is now called a 'musical comedy,' 'musical play,' or simply 'musical,' " but which failed to name any of the other outstanding examples of the genre by Kern, Vincent Youmans, the Gershwins, Rodgers and Hart, Irving Berlin and Cole Porter in the twenties and thirties. Only the Gershwin *Of Thee I Sing* and 1940 Rodgers and Hart *Pal Joey* were mentioned, as examples of the introduction of political and social satire; Porter's 1948 *Kiss Me Kate*, as an example of the more unified format devised by Rodgers in the 1943 *Oklahoma* and 1949 *South Pacific;* and Berlin's 1946 *Annie Get Your Gun*, which "continued the more traditional vein." Of later works the Frederick Loewe-Alan Jay Lerner *My Fair Lady* was mentioned, but nothing by Harold Arlen. And the bibliography didn't include the Gershwin, Kern, Rodgers and Hart, and Porter song books.

My final discovery was that Wilder Hobson, whose *American Jazz Music* offered the best introduction to the jazz heard until the Second World War, wasn't included among those whom John Wesley Work of Fisk University cited in his article as reliable chroniclers of this early period, and that Hobson's book had been removed from the bibliography in which it had been included in the first edition. What commanded Mr. Work's respect was the pretentious schematizations of Rudi Blesh, not the mere accurate perception of Hobson.

All this seems to me to add up to an inordinate amount of intellectual sloppiness in these few articles of a work of scholarship published by so eminent a press. And I won't pretend that I'm surprised by it.

Winter 1972 One of the musicians who gave me his recollections of Toscanini for *The Toscanini Musicians Knew* was the bassoonist Hugo Burghauser, who played in the Vienna Philharmonic for a number of years before he was elected its chairman in 1933. I continued to visit him; and he turned out to be an inexhaustible source of interesting information which had the unique value of coming from an actual participant in the incidents he described. It was he who told me what must have been galling for George Szell to remember in later years—that when Toscanini, in the greenroom after Szell's first rehearsal with the NBC Symphony in 1941, berated him for a method of rehearsal which Toscanini considered to be mistreatment of his orchestra, Szell dropped to his knees, embraced Toscanini's knees, and exclaimed, "Forgive me, Maestro!"; and when, amazed, I asked Burghauser how he knew this, he answered with a spreading of upturned hands, "I was there." (He had just come to this country; and as someone who had known Szell in Europe he had attended the rehearsal and was visiting Szell in the greenroom.) And another incident which Burghauser could tell me about because he had been there seems to me worth reporting here.

Burghauser had been talking about the conductors who did hear every note in an orchestral tutti, and did therefore catch the occasional wrong note, as against the conductors who did not. He had recalled how Richard Strauss, when he heard something wrong from, say, the third horn, would not stop but would merely give the player a look, leaving it to him to correct the mistake in his part with the full score later; whereas Toscanini would stop to correct the mistake in the part immediately. This had led Burghauser to recall Toscanini's first orchestral rehearsals of *Tristan und Isolde* in Bayreuth in 1930, at which he corrected mistake after mistake in the printed parts that had gone uncorrected by all the conductors who had conducted *Tristan* in Germany until then— "which," Burghauser had remarked, "was for Furtwängler, a man of great vanity, an unbearable humiliation, and the reason for his antagonism to Toscanini."* And then he had recalled the incident I am about to report.

---

* *(1973)* What Burghauser described was not the first such "unbearable humiliation" which this "man of great vanity" held Toscanini responsible for, nor the beginning of his "antagonism to Toscanini". The triumphs of the ascendant Furtwängler in Germany in the early twenties had led to a first guest engagement with the New York Philharmonic in January 1925—another triumph with orchestra, public and press that had led to his being re-engaged for two months of each of the following two seasons. And arriving in New York in February 1926 in the expectation of a repetition of the triumph of the year before, he had encountered instead the lessened responsiveness to him of an orchestra, a public and a press still overwhelmed by the performances Toscanini had

It involved the composer Schönberg, who chose to be out of step with the world and complained all his life about the world's refusal to get in step with him. To those who found his music not only ugly but pointless in its ugliness Schönberg insisted that every note in the texture of a work of his was part of what he had heard in his mind and what had to be heard by the listener; and he complained that on the rare occasion when a work was performed it was performed inaccurately, and that as a result listeners didn't hear what he had composed. What Burghauser recalled was the occasion in the twenties when Schönberg was rehearsing a small Vienna Philharmonic group for a performance of his *Kammersymphonie*, and at one point the clarinet-tist Polatschek (whom Koussevitzky later brought to the Boston Symphony) leaned over to Burghauser and whispered that he had just discovered he had by mistake been playing a clarinet in B-flat instead of the clarinet in A in the score, and that Schönberg hadn't noticed it. This led Burghauser to suggest to his fellow wind-players the experiment of playing wrong notes to see if Schönberg would hear them; and Schönberg, it turned out, did not hear them.

Musicians, like all other artists, dislike and despise critics. Nor is this true—as Harold Schonberg has contended in *The Times*—only of the solo performers who get unfavorable reviews which some of them deserve: it is true also of the great singer or pianist who is praised for a performance he knows went badly, and feels contempt for the critic who didn't hear this. And orchestral players, though not directly affected by reviews, have the same feeling: they acquire in their rehear-

conducted in *his* first guest engagement in January. For Furtwängler, accustomed to triumph after triumph, this failure in 1926 was not merely a disappointment but an "unbearable humiliation" brought about somehow by Toscanini—the first of such "humiliations" responsible for his antagonism to Toscanini, which he revealed soon afterwards in the incident described by Rudolf Serkin. In Zürich in 1926 Toscanini conducted his La Scala Orchestra in a performance of Brahms's Second which for Serkin was an "incredible revelation"; but Furtwängler, said Serkin, was shocked by some things in it, and at a private reception after the concert "embarrassingly and painfully told Toscanini in violent terms what he thought." Toscanini listened, in Serkin's words, "like a little boy"; then he answered: "When Steinbach [a celebrated conductor contemporary with Brahms, whose performances of Brahms's works were considered authoritative] came to Turin [in the 1890s] and conducted the Brahms Second Symphony, after the first rehearsal he turned to the orchestra and said: 'I have nothing to do. Who is your conductor?' And the answer was 'Toscanini'."

sals and concerts with conductors a knowledge of the capacities and the failings of each that makes them feel contempt for the lack of perception the critics reveal in what they write. It was Burghauser who, at Barenboim's first appearance as a conductor in New York with the London Symphony, explained the occasional nervous movements of his hands in his lap by saying: "As an orchestral musician I felt a vicarious anxiety with the player who had to decide which of the contradictory indications of the conductor's two arms to obey." And he was bound to feel contempt for the man who wrote in *The Times* the next day that Barenboim had "the clearest, most incisive of beats. . . . His left hand is independent, busy but not fussy, supplementing and not echoing the right."

But this dislike and contempt for critics that celebrated soloists and obscure orchestral players talk about to each other they are tight-lipped about in public. No matter how inaccurate, how injurious in its inaccuracy, how personally offensive even, the review may be, the soloist endures it in silence, aware of an angered critic's power to inflict further injury. Even Glenn Gould, who prefers talking nonsense on anything anywhere to playing the piano marvelously in the concert hall, was silent about Harold Schonberg's personally offensive and vulgar ridiculing of him: ". . . So then the Gould boy comes out, and you know what, Ossip? . . . The Gould boy played the Brahms D minor Concerto slower than the way we used to practice it. (And between you, me, and the corner lamppost, Ossip, maybe the reason he plays it so slow is maybe his technique is not so good.)" So with orchestral players: they talk about the critics' nonsense contemptuously or indignantly among themselves; but they don't write protests to the newspapers. As unprecedented, therefore, as Stravinsky's sensational published attacks on Winthrop Sargeant and Paul Henry Lang several years ago and on Clive Barnes last spring was an action by orchestral players a couple of years ago which received little attention in the press outside of the city where it occurred, and was not understood correctly by many of those who did read about it there.

That action was the Boston Symphony Members Association's sending the orchestra's trustees and management a telegram in which it declared *The Boston Globe's* music critic, Michael Steinberg, *persona non grata* and asked that he not be welcomed to the orchestra's concerts; and its informing *The Boston Globe* of this in another telegram. Even in Boston—where *Globe* readers had read the Steinberg review which impelled the orchestra to its action, and were given parts of the texts of the two telegrams with statements by the orchestra's management that the issue was not Steinberg's critical judgments but the personal offensiveness that had nothing to do with criticism—Steinberg and *The Globe* were able to persuade a number of people that his right to freedom of critical speech had been attacked. And in New York, readers of that newspaper of record, *The Times*, were not given the texts of the Steinberg review and the orchestra's telegrams that were essential for a correct understanding of the incident and its significance, but were merely told in a summary account from the *Times* Boston correspondent that Steinberg had written "a highly critical review of a performance by Carlo Maria Giulini", which had caused the orchestra to demand "that Mr. Steinberg be denied admission to concerts until he apologized for recent reviews," and that "Mr. Steinberg's musical scholarship has not been questioned" but "one source close to the orchestra said that Mr. Steinberg's style and manner displayed a 'personal arrogance that becomes offensive' "—not enough for a correct idea of the realities of the incident.

The Giulini performance was one of Brahms's Fourth, concerning which Steinberg wrote:

> If Danny Kaye or Victor Borge were to conduct a performance of the Brahms 4th just like the one Carlo Maria Giulini conducted Friday afternoon in Symphony Hall, one so raging and overwrought, one with its upbeats so stretched, with such crazed dislocation of tempo, and accompanied by a similar visual production with such prodigality in expressions of tragic suffering and deep knee-bends, the audience would have been in stitches. . . . The performance, instead of being the first ever fully to explore the comic possibilities of the Brahms 4th, proceeded from nothing more uncommon than opportunism and meretricious vulgarity.

As it happened, I had reported concerning Giulini's performance of the Brahms Second with the Philadelphia Orchestra the preceding season that "the orchestra demonstrated its high regard for him by executing with unfailing beauty of sound every italicized detail of what it must have regarded as a mistakenly overemphatic statement of the work"—the significance of this being that orchestral players are suspicious and cynical about conductors and on the alert for the slightest sign of personal exhibitionism, so that the beautiful playing the Philadelphia men had done in Giulini's misconceived Brahms Second had been evidence of how completely he had convinced them of his sincerity and dedication. Clearly he had convinced the Boston Symphony men as completely; and while they didn't question Steinberg's right to his disapproval of the excesses of Giulini's overemphatic performance of the Fourth, they did question Steinberg's right to *his* excesses in his report on the performance—his intemperate description of it, his ridiculing of Giulini's awkward conducting stances and movements, and above all his attributing Giulini's performance to improper and ignoble motives. It was this "unwarranted, cruel and hostile attack on our illustrious guest conductor, Mr. Giulini", which the Boston Symphony players were right in thinking had "gone far beyond the scope of musical criticism", that impelled them to request the exclusion of Steinberg from their concerts. And the same position was taken by the orchestra's manager in his reply to the telegram, in which he said the management also was offended by "the immoderate and unwarranted tone" of Steinberg's writing; and by the president of the orchestra's board of trustees in a letter to *The Globe*, in which he said he had hesitated to write because he was a strong believer in independent criticism and had often defended Steinberg against his detractors, but now felt that his "undisciplined and irresponsible reviews"—including the one that had "excoriated and ridiculed Giulini"—were damaging to Boston's musical life. But *The Globe's* editorial reply was that

> A music critic who pleased everybody would not be worth his salt, nor would a critic who pleased no one. A critic must criticize when that seems to him warranted, but always within the bounds of fairness and good taste. The quality of the performance is what should count. Personalities should play no part, whether in criticism of the performer or of the critic himself. Above all, the critic's right to criticize must be protected when he comes under attack.

And most of the published letters which this comment introduced were from readers whom Steinberg and *The Globe* had succeeded in getting to believe what was not true—that his right to criticize had been attacked by the Boston Symphony's players, management and trustees.

It was at this very time that I received a telephone call from someone who said he was taking the liberty of calling me to find out to whom among the *Times* executives he should address his demand for a confrontation with Harold Schonberg in this executive's presence concerning a false statement by Schonberg in his review of a concert the day before. The concert had been one at which Artur Rubinstein had played concertos with an assembled orchestra; and Schonberg in his review had spoken of the poor quality of this orchestra; whereas in fact, said my caller, the orchestral contractor for the concert had assembled a group of first-rate players who had tried their best but had been frustrated and defeated by the conductor's inability to provide the guidance they had to have for precise execution as a group. I told my caller I didn't think he would be able to get to any of the important executives at *The Times;* but if he did, he must realize, first of all, that Schonberg was *The Times's* music critic because these executives lacked the understanding of music that would have enabled them to know he shouldn't be; and that lacking this understanding they would assume *The Times's* music critic had been right in what he had said about Rubinstein's orchestra. And in the second place, even if my caller were able to convince the *Times* executive he spoke to that Schonberg had been wrong, the *Times* position to the public was that anyone it selected to speak with its authority in his field was qualified to do so, and therefore no *Times* executive could possibly, even in private conversation, admit that a *Times* writer had shown himself to be *not* qualified to do so. The most my caller could hope was that *The Times* might publish a letter; and—disappointed but convinced by what I had told him—he said he would write one. If he did, *The Times* didn't publish it.

I had spoken to him not only with *The Boston Globe's* editorial in mind, but with an experience I had just had myself with a *Times* executive. Schonberg had never replied in print to anything I had written about his writing; but in the article in which he contended that the musicians who attacked critics were the ones who got unfavorable reviews, he argued that freedom of criticism was part of the free exchange of ideas, and added that this didn't mean critics should themselves be immune from criticism: "Bernard Haggin thinks that I am a disgrace to American music criticism, and I think that he is a sour, pedantic old maid of a critic who was left at the altar many years back and has since been taking it out on everybody else." In a letter (not for publication) to the managing editor of *The Times*, A.M. Rosenthal, I said it was as legitimate for Schonberg to evaluate my writing as for me to evaluate the writing of other critics; but it was amazing that a paper as concerned with propriety and decorum as *The Times* permitted in its columns the personal offensiveness of Schonberg's review of Glenn Gould's performance of the Brahms concerto and now of his statement about me; and with such writing—whether about Gould or about me or about anyone else—Schonberg disgraced *The Times*. Also, I had never made a proposal to the *Times* music department; and so my low estimates of the *Times* music critics' writing hadn't represented the emotions of a rejected suitor. It would require the text of Mr. Rosenthal's reply, which cannot be quoted without his permission, to convey the contemptuous tone in which he wrote that it was pretty obvious that Schonberg and I didn't care much for each other; and that in Schonberg's place he would have ignored my criticisms since he was the best music critic in America and didn't have to defend himself. In reply to this I got Bernard Shaw to write from Purgatory:

Dear Mr. Rosenthal:
"Editors, by some law of Nature . . . are *always* ignorant of music, and consequently . . . an editor who can tell at a glance whether a review, a leading article . . . or a news paragraph is the work of a skilled hand or not . . . will let me inundate his columns with pompous platitude . . . bad grammar, bad logic . . . every conceivable blunder and misdemeanor that a journalist can commit, provided I do it in the capacity of his musical critic . . ."
                          Yours,
                          Bernard Shaw
                          (Music in London, Vol. 3, pp. 238-9)

And I added a postscript from me: "Thank you for making it clear why Mr. Schonberg was able to fill the columns of *The Times* with his arrogant personal offensiveness to Glenn Gould: it's pretty obvious that you and he have a lot in common."

I too could say "I was there" to the people who have been haranguing us about the pianists of the distant past—Hofmann, Godowsky, de Pachmann, Busoni, Rosenthal, Lhevinne—having been giants who in their dealing with their instrument and its literature reduced the pianists of today to insignificance. That is, I could say that whereas most of these people know those pianists only from phonograph records

I heard them in the concert hall. Godowsky, for example, was said last year by Harold Schonberg, who knows his playing only from records, to "[make] every other pianist sound like a peasant". And I could say that I heard Godowsky in Carnegie Hall in January 1914 in performances of a trio and sonatas of Beethoven with Ysaye and Gerardy; that I heard him again that year or the next in a recital in Aeolian Hall, and still remember the performance of Chopin's Etude in thirds that testified to his mechanical mastery of the piano; that even at that date I was able to perceive the absence in this mechanically perfect playing of the enlivening phrasing of the music I had heard in the playing of Hofmann and others; and that by 1921 I had heard enough to be shocked by Godowsky's rattling off Beethoven's Concerto No. 4 as if it were a Czerny exercise. I *could* cite these recollections of the living Godowsky's playing against Schonberg's extravagances about the performances on records—but I don't: I am entirely willing to judge, as Schonberg and the others do, by what is to be heard on records. The electrically recorded performances, according to Schonberg, show a startling change from the "calm, pluperfect kind of piano playing, a little lacking in tension", on the earlier acoustic records to a new "passion, depth, involvement"; but I heard nothing of this kind last year in the performance of Beethoven's Sonata Op. 81a *(Les Adieux)* reissued on an International Piano Library record: it was merely an intelligently conceived, smoothly executed performance, with none of the powerful note-to-note continuity of tension and outline in the building of coherent structure that one hears in the performance recorded by Cliburn, whom Schonberg and his colleagues continue to treat with condescension, when not with contempt, but whom I continue to find one of the greatest musicians I have heard play the piano, a real giant towering above most of Schonberg's giants of the past.

On a Victrola record I heard last year performances by another Schonberg giant, Lhevinne, that confirmed the impression I got of his playing at his first New York appearance in the twenties (the last I attended): that it exhibited remarkable digital facility but no ability to impart musical significance to the notes that were produced in dazzling profusion.

And I also heard last year several records with performances by Hofmann that were offered as incontestable evidence of his having been the greatest of those legendary pianists who in the early years of this century exhibited a mastery of the resources of their instrument, and a mastery of the correct style of performance of nineteenth-century Romantic music, that are not to be heard today. From 1914 I continued to hear Hofmann year after year, sharing the general view of him as the greatest of the time; but by 1933, when I reported in *Hound & Horn* on the last concerts of his I attended, I had come to think he provided the worst example of the corrupting influence of the virtuoso career.

> Playing the same [limited group of] works all these years, Hofmann has found relief or interest in playing them differently, in putting more and more "interpretation" into them. There survive certain performances—of Beethoven's Sonata Opus 111, the slow movements of the Sonata Op. 101 and the "Emperor" Concerto—that are still unequaled in their simplicity, clarity and power. Only a detail here and there betrays the tendency which made hash of the Händel-Brahms Variations, the Chopin B flat minor Sonata and parts of the Beethoven Sonata Opus 101 and Chopin B minor Sonata. These works he used as an acrobat would have used a trapeze: to exhibit to gaping audiences his powers of "interpretation". I mean this sort of thing: playing a phrase with a scheme of dynamics the direct opposite of what Brahms prescribed and in direct opposition to the tendency of the phrase; repeating the phrase (or the entire exposition in a sonata) with a different scheme of dynamics; picking out one note from each of a series of accompaniment chords, and bringing out these notes as a counter-melody which Brahms or Chopin never dreamed of; and various other businesses which combined to produce some of the most abominable playing I have ever heard. I can see the reviews if it had been a young pianist: ". . . youthful excesses of which it is to be hoped time will cure him". But of Hofmann it was ". . . heights of inspired musicianship".

From some of the records I heard last year I learned how much worse the playing got to be after 1933. The 1935 and 1938 performances on a Victrola record, described as "object lessons of their kind", were lessons instead in how the pieces should not be played: in the brisk, brittle treatment of the *Allegro maestoso* opening of the first movement of Chopin's Sonata Op. 58, the hurried, nervously mannered delivery of the *sostenuto* melody of its second subject, I didn't hear a correct playing of this music; nor in the performances of Chopin's Waltz Op. 64 No. 1 *(Minute)* and Berceuse in tempos too fast to achieve anything but dazzlingly fast passage work and figurations; nor in the performance of Chopin's Nocturne Op. 15 No. 2 in an incessantly and senselessly mannered style which didn't leave one bar undistorted and produced a whole without coherent shape. These were not performances which had anything to teach about the right style for Chopin to Rubinstein, Lipatti, Cliburn, Ashkenazy, Harasiewicz, Pollini. And it was in these pianists' recorded performances of Chopin's Concerto No. 1 that one heard subtleties and elegances of phrasing, not in the Hofmann performance of the late thirties on an International Piano Library record, in which the reviewers reported hearing those subtleties and elegances that set Hofmann apart from all other pianists: what his performance actually offered in the opening *Allegro maestoso* movement was an excessively hurried and wilfully, erratically mannered delivery of melodic phrases that destroyed their melodic shape and grace.

On another I.P.L. record was another excessively hurried performance that was destructive of the expressive character of Beethoven's Concerto No. 4. But then I came to an I.P.L. record with a number of Hofmann performances transferred from Brunswick acoustic records of the early twenties, one of which was a beautifully phrased and shaped Chopin Nocturne Op. 15 No. 2. The shapeless 1938 performance of this piece I had heard on the Victrola record was, then, an appalling distortion of what Hofmann had recorded for Brunswick at a time when he was still playing the piano as a great musician.

But even in the years when he was a great pianist and musician Hofmann didn't reduce Schnabel or Lipatti or Artur Rubinstein or the outstanding young pianists of today to insignificance; nor did the other pianists of the distant past that are alleged to have done so. As I said here once before, de Pachmann, Busoni and their contemporaries were not pianists who operated with freedom controlled by taste in the correct style for nineteenth-century music which they knew and pianists of today are ignorant of; they were pianists who felt free to inflict on whatever music they played the same tasteless distortions and extravagances, for the same egotistic purpose, and with the same lack of concern for anything but that purpose, as Tetrazzini, De Lucia and the other singers of that period. And the distinguished young pianists of today—Cliburn, Ashkenazy, Rogers—who operate with respect for the composer's text do so in the same way as Rethberg, Bjoerling, Flagstad and Steber: they don't, as Schonberg and

Winthrop Sargeant ask us to believe, merely play the printed notes with no concern for expressiveness like undistinguishable human metronomes, but shape—each in his own unmistakably different way, representing the exercise of his personal taste—the progression of notes for expressive purpose with a plasticity in tempo and sonority which they keep within the limits of proportion and coherence that the Busonis and de Pachmanns cared nothing about.

There is one more record to mention of those I heard last year—the Victrola with Rachmaninov's unbearably distorted performance of Chopin's Sonata Op. 35, but also his performances of smaller Chopin pieces, which were made exciting not only by his arrestingly incisive way of playing the piano, but by the arrestingly incisive operation of his mind—notably in the pointing up of details in the Waltzes that were played with enchanting grace. These, certainly, were the performances of a superb pianist and musician; but they didn't reduce Lipatti's wonderful performances of the Waltzes to insignificance.

Spring 1972 In a *New York Times Magazine* article about the remarkable twenty-seven-year-old conductor Michael Tilson Thomas, Leonard Bernstein was reported to have said to Thomas on one occasion, "You're *me* at that age"—which fortunately was not true. What Bernstein had in mind was the fact that young Thomas, like the young Bernstein, had the gifts which enabled him, without rehearsal, to substitute effectively for William Steinberg in the second half of a Boston Symphony concert, as Bernstein had substituted for Bruno Walter in 1943. But with this similarity there are dissimilarities which make Thomas's operation and the performances it produces strikingly different from the young Bernstein's. And this difference provides an occasion to point out that the mere possession of gifts—even gifts as impressive as Bernstein's—doesn't guarantee value in what they produce. It isn't only Bernstein who has demonstrated this: before him it was demonstrated by the even more impressively gifted Stokowski; and now it is being demonstrated by the far less impressively gifted Barenboim.

Gifts must be used; and value in the result depends on how they are used—more specifically, whether the use is controlled by the discipline that is the rarest of artistic gifts, and the crucial one. A couple of years ago, as the great ensemble pianist Franz Rupp listened to a tape of Michael Rogers's performance of Schumann's Fantasy Op. 17, he turned to me repeatedly to nod his appreciation of how Rogers, in an acceleration of tempo or a build-up of intensity, had sensed exactly where to begin to slow down the one or diminish the other. The discipline that manifested itself as a sense for measure and proportion in such details revealed itself further in the conceptual grasp of the movement as a whole in which all the details were in such correctly proportioned relation, and in the control which held the fingers to the realization of the detail of this imagined whole in the emerging shape in sound. An outstanding example of this disciplined operation can be heard on the new RCA record with Cliburn's tremendous performance of Beethoven's *Appassionata* Sonata; and it is especially impressive for anyone who heard Barenboim's undisciplined performance of the work a few years ago—its preoccupation with the detail of the moment without regard for the moments before and after.

As with Barenboim, so with Bernstein. I recall a Bernstein performance of Mahler's Second years ago in which—at the point in the *Andante moderato* second movement where the lilting opening section returns with a new counter-melody of the cellos—Bernstein, giving all his attention to the counter-melody and visibly demonstrating his intense feeling about it, lingered over it without regard for the fact that the slowing down destroyed the lilt of the section and its forward momentum. This was one of the countless times when the lack of discipline evident in the platform exhibitionist's demonstration of his intense emotional involvement with the music showed itself also in details of performance that were not in coherent relation with their context. And I cannot imagine anything more strikingly unlike all this than the unfailingly disciplined operation of young Thomas that produces the coherently related details of the emerging shape in sound in his performance, and that is evident in his manner of producing them with the orchestra: his involvement with the music is something one has to infer from his complete and intense concentration on his task.

The discipline I've been talking about is what is usually referred to as taste; and the difference between Thomas and Bernstein is that Thomas's performances have exhibited an unfailing musical taste which the young Bernstein didn't have at the beginning and the older Bernstein didn't acquire.* That is the answer to those who hear in Barenboim's performances the failings of immaturity which experience will eradicate: I can't see Barenboim's lack of discipline correcting itself anymore than Bernstein's did.

Thomas has told an interviewer, "I like to hear things I have never heard before"; and what he likes to hear he likes to perform for others —which is unfortunate for the people who attend concerts to hear music worth hearing, and would want even the out-of-the-way music on a program to be works of value, like the infrequently played Symphony K.338 of Mozart of which Thomas produced a marvelously paced and phrased performance with the New York Philharmonic, or works of interest like the *Seven Early Songs* of Alban Berg that preceded the Mozart symphony, and not Ruth Crawford's Andante for String Orchestra, an arrangement of a movement of a string quartet which the program described as "long admired by musicians", but in which I found nothing to admire, or Carl Ruggles's *Men and Mountains*, which I found as uninteresting now as at its première in 1924. Fortunately the Crawford and Ruggles pieces were quite brief; and before them there was a fine performance of several movements from Handel's *Water Music*.

For Pierre Boulez too programs are not the simple matter they may appear to be to the people who attend the concerts, but are complicated by Boulez's thinking on the subject. He thinks, for example, that just as a museum doesn't limit itself to Rembrandt's masterpieces but exhibits "other paintings of the same period that form the background to his work and help you to understand more precisely why that particular work [of Rembrandt] is a real masterpiece," so the concert should offer Telemann as well as Bach—to which one can answer that the greatness of Bach's D-minor Concerto for clavier is apprehended directly from that concerto and only from that concerto, not from anything

---

*Nevertheless it was inevitable that the immaturity ploy would be used with Thomas; and the perfectly conceived and perfectly achieved performance of Tchaikovsky's engaging but unprofound Symphony No. 1 he recorded with the Boston Symphony provided Irving Kolodin with the opportunity to demonstrate his possession of the experienced ear and mature mind that could detect the inadequacies and failures of youth: "There are, understandably, rawness, unfinished edges, a tendency to ride not merely the surface but the surface of the surface rather than to dig into the underlying substance."

outside of it, not even from Bach's own uninteresting Clavier Concerto in F minor, and certainly not from the boring concertos of Telemann; so that there is no need of being bored at a concert by Telemann to be excited by the D-minor of Bach. It is clear that Boulez is not, like E. M. Forster, interested in the particular work of art considered and experienced as an entity for the life that can be perceived in it; and this appears again in his contention that an orchestra's season should not be like a series of individual menus of which one recalls particular works and performances, but should have an over-all profile that stays in one's memory, "so that one can say, ah yes, that was the year of so and so." For the New York Philharmonic, then, this was to be the year of Liszt and Berg—the unfamiliar works of each that Boulez apparently felt would cause the Philharmonic audiences to recall the season with pleasure. In theory one welcomes the opportunity to hear a work by a famous composer that one hasn't heard; in practice one is guided by one's feeling about the works of his that one *has* heard; and the considerable amount of Liszt's music I had heard, not only the trashy exhibitionistic pieces for piano but some of the attempts at serious writing, had given me the view I discovered Bernard Shaw had expressed—in the statement that "[Liszt's] devotion to serious composition seems as hopeless a struggle against natural incapacity as Benjamin Haydon's determination to be a great painter"—and a strong disinclination to hear more. As it happened, Shaw's statement was occasioned by his hearing the oratorio *St. Elizabeth* and the *Dante Symphony*, two of the works of Liszt that Boulez thought Philharmonic audiences should hear, and that I for one, thought I could leave unheard. I cannot imagine the people in those audiences recalling with pleasure some day that this was the year of Liszt.

The New York City Opera's new *Carmen* is still another of the monstrosities produced in recent years by director-designer teams whose recreative renewal of old operas would make the works unrecognizable and, I am sure, unacceptable to their original creators. Thus, José Varona devised for the first act of *Carmen* a stage-filling clutter of new scenic details which obscured the essentials of the scene specified in the libretto, but which made possible the unending counterpoint of happenings thought up by Tito Capobianco that drew attention away from the essential action and singing of the principals—one example being the corner of a house that Varona placed in the center, with a balcony on which Capobianco placed an old woman engaged in some handiwork who every now and then got involved with a person on the stage. Other such innovations included the commanding officer of the relief guard entering on a horse, and Carmen making her first entrance barefoot on a mule; but although able to think up unnecessary details of that kind, Capobianco was unable to deal competently with essentials, such as the fight between the two groups of factory girls, which provoked laughter even from the undemanding opera audience, or Joy Davidson's dramatic operation as Carmen, which made me laugh when the audience was impressed. Her voice, moreover, and her use of it were as undisciplined as her acting, contributing to the musical deficiencies of the production that began even before the curtain rose with Julius Rudel's whipping up of the Prelude, and continued with his coarse-grained treatment of the music thereafter. Michele Molese's Don José helped neither the dramatic nor the musical performance; but Joanna Bruno, the Micaela, looked like a young village girl and used her fresh voice with musical taste; and Robert Hale was an excellent Escamillo.

On the other hand the production of Britten's operatic comedy *Albert Herring* was one of the company's all too rare successes—as the work is one of Britten's. He is England's one outstandingly gifted composer; but the gift that is most evident is the resourceful craftsmanship that, like Bach's, can produce writing which goes through the motions of saying something but actually says nothing—writing which, in W. J. Turner's words about Bach, is not "as expressive as it is accomplished". *Albert Herring* has such arid writing which merely carries the words and action without any expressive relation to either—a notable example being the love duet of Sid and Nancy overheard by Albert in the second act. But at a number of points there is real and brilliantly successful invention for the words and dramatic situation—like Lady Billows's grand announcement to Albert of his election to be King of the May, Miss Wordsworth's rehearsal of the children's song of homage for the coronation party, the speeches at the party, the dirge for the supposedly dead Albert. In these the music heightens the effect of Eric Crozier's words; and his delightful libretto amuses one in some of the other places where Britten's music does not.

The performance I attended was a very good one even without the right singer for Lady Billows. She must be excessively grand in appearance and manner, and able to proclaim the high notes of her announcement to Albert with assurance; but the New York City Opera's Judith Anthony was unimpressively dumpy and shrewish, and her high notes in the announcement to Albert were strident screams.

The important news about the Metropolitan is its acquisition of another remarkable young conductor, James Levine, who revealed, in a performance of Verdi's *Luisa Miller*, control, authority and discipline which held the orchestra and singers to a shaping of the music with the required Verdi *espansione* within the limits of proportion and coherence. As it happened, the performance had Placido Domingo and Adriana Maliponte singing the young lovers with fresh and beautiful voices and sensitive phrasing.

The designer of the Metropolitan's new *Tristan und Isolde* is Günther Schneider-Siemssen, whose idea of the bridge for *Die Walküre* into the future was the hollowed-out base of an enormous tree that he substituted in the first act for Wagner's room in Hunding's hut. This time he is content to provide for Act 1 of *Tristan* the curtained-off space on the deck of a ship that Wagner specifies—a realistic set made singularly beautiful by the translucent sails, which make possible the impressive dramatic moment when Isolde, turning, is transfixed by the silhouette of Tristan on one of them. But they make impossible Brangäne's drawing of the curtains, specified by Wagner, to reveal Tristan looking out at the sea, with Kurvenal at his feet and behind him the sailors and knights who, at the end of Brangäne's confrontation with Tristan, join in Kurvenal's offensive reply: instead Brangäne goes up to a ramp in front of the sails on which Tristan is pacing back and forth attended by Kurvenal, and Kurvenal's reply is joined, for no apparent reason, by an unseen chorus. Later the drinking of the love potion results in the disappearance of the ship of the real world in swirling colored mists in which Tristan and Isolde are seen isolated in the world of their own emotions—a new and effective handling of this difficult scene, which is, however, not enough for Schneider-Siemssen or August Everding, the stage director: the lovers' exalted emotional state must be demonstrated by their physical ascent to a high point in the stage space. Consistency would require them to remain at that high point while they continue the musical outpouring of their exaltation; but this would necessitate their instantaneous descent to the level of the real world at the moment when that world breaks in on them. Such an instantaneous descent is of course impossible; and what actually happens is that while the ear hears the lovers still singing at their high point of exaltation, the eye sees them descending to where they must be when their exaltation will be interrupted—which makes no sense.

This happens again in the second act. Again Schneider-Siemssen provides the scene Wagner specifies, and a beautiful one, even if a little semi-tropical for Cornwall. When the lovers begin their duet *O sink hernieder* the garden of the real world disappears and they are seen isolated in the world of their exalted emotional state, which again is demonstrated by their physical ascent to a high point in a space of swirling lights. And again while the ear hears the crescendo of their exaltation the eye sees them descending to where they must be when the real world will intrude itself on them. An additional detail which makes no sense is that Brangäne, who belongs to the real world that disappears during the lovers' duet, is made visible when she sings from her lookout during intervals in the duet—this in the face of Wagner's direction that she be invisible at these times.

It is only at the end of the third act that Isolde—removed from the real world to a high point in space for her final exalted utterance—can remain there to the end of that utterance, when she sinks lifeless upon Tristan's body. And this happens to be the only effective detail in the act. After the beautiful realistic sets for the first two acts Schneider-Siemssen reverts to his bridge-into-the-future style for the third, producing—in place of the castle, the garden, the tree for the wounded Tristan to lie under, the crumbling wall, the gate that Wagner specifies—an abstract construction whose two parts on the two sides of the stage, looking like the two blades of a gigantic excavator, narrow as they curve from the front of the stage to the back and center where their two narrow ends overlap. In the space between the overlapping ends are invisible steps to a ramp beyond which are the sea and sky. It is on the ramp that the characters—the Shepherd, Brangäne, King Marke, Moralt, the soldiers—have to make their entrances; and on the way down to the stage they disappear for a few moments in the space between the overlapping ends of the set. And in addition to the awkward and ineffective entrances caused by the set there are questionable details in Everding's staging. When the curtain rises Kurvenal is sitting not beside the sleeping Tristan, as Wagner and good sense direct, but on the opposite side of the stage from him; and instead of remaining by Tristan's side in their later exchanges he jumps up and away from him for each reply. If this represents William Dooley's idea rather than Everding's direction, Everding can be faulted for not correcting it. And the same may be said of Kurvenal's arm movements in moments of excitement that are absurdly like a bird's flapping of its wings.

Of special interest in the performance I attended was the Tristan of Helge Brilioth, in whom some had heard the promise of a new Wagnerian *Heldentenor*. His voice turned out not to be heroic either in size or in quality: it was a little dry in *piano*, rather metallic in its brighter *forte*, but without luster or warmth; and in the last act he seemed to have increasing difficulty in producing the sounds that were increasingly unpleasant. Whereas in both of Birgit Nilsson's recorded *Tristans* I had found the timbre of her voice not pleasant to listen to, at the Metropolitan now its cool, bright sound was agreeable to the ear, and in moments of great amplitude it acquired a glow and sheen. And it held out to the very end—the final exquisitely sustained *"Lust"*.

As for Erich Leinsdorf's shaping of the work, it was epitomized in his dealing with the very first statement of the Prelude, which was begun in an extremely slow tempo by the cellos, and completed in a faster tempo by the winds; his hurried shortening of the silence between this statement and the next; his similar dealing with the statements and silences that followed. I once heard Pavel Tchelitchev say to someone about her painting of a group of buildings: "It isn't only the forms that are important in a painting, but also the spaces between the forms." And one can say that for the opening section of the Prelude to *Tristan* to have coherent shape and sense it isn't only the phrases that must be exactly right in time values but also the silences between the phrases. Those time values of phrases and silences are right in Furtwängler's recorded performance, and in Toscanini's; but they were not right in Leinsdorf's performance; and his lack of the sense for tempo—the ability to set a right basic tempo and maintain it with modifications that are in right relation to it—continued to be evident in the rest of the Prelude. It was evident again in his moderately animated tempo for the Prelude to Act 3 instead of the moderately slow one prescribed by Wagner. And in the task of providing the orchestral context for the singing he was merely efficient where Furtwängler is in addition sensitive. In all it was the usual—i.e. technically proficient, musically mediocre—Leinsdorf operation; and, not surprisingly, he received the usual ovation each time he stepped onto the podium. But with the ovation before the third act there were, surprisingly, deep-throated boos from three of today's youth seated in front of me.

The Joffrey Ballet's performance of *Petrushka* that I saw this year was improved by the excellent Petrushka of Gary Chryst and Ballerina of Rebecca Wright; and with Geoffrey Holder's Blackamoor, Yurek Lazovski's Showman and good dancers for the exciting ensembles of the last scene, the choreographed essentials that combine with Stravinsky's music in a singular and great work of art were impressive even in the context of the usual confusion of the crowd scenes on the insufficiently large stage of the City Center. The program this time credited only Lazovski with supervision of the revival; and the omission of Leonide Massine's name presumably accounted for the disappearance of a couple of choreographed crowd sequences in the first scene. This time I was able to talk afterwards with Lazovski, who confirmed my impression that the knowledge of the work he had acquired from his participation in the last productions supervised by Fokine had enabled him to stage the choreographed parts of the ballet for the Joffrey company with complete accuracy. ("I told this to Clive Barnes," he said.) The crowd scenes were another matter: they had never been choreographed by Fokine, Lazovski said; and there wasn't much a touring company could do with the supers assembled only a couple of hours before the performance. (Diaghilev, he said, had used for the crowd whatever members of his company were available and even personal friends.)

Summer 1972 The first time I heard Debussy's *Pelléas*—performed in New York by the Chicago Opera with Mary Garden as Mélisande in 1918—a man standing next to me exclaimed during the first intermission, "Where are the arias?!"; and after the first tower scene he moaned, "Oh, what Puccini would have done with that!" I'm content not to hear the arias Puccini would have written; what I miss is the first-rate melodic writing of someone like Berlioz (since the opera in question is French) that would hold my attention and enable me to ignore the Maeterlinck play as I do the dramatic action of *Il Trovatore* or *Aida;* and I find intolerably boring the five acts of monotonous recitative that only rarely attains expressiveness. Certainly I recognize the marvelous orchestral writing; but I recognize too that it is writing for the play and recitative which have to be taken with it; and some of the best of it is the interludes between scenes, when the bored audience finds relief in talking. All this made me inclined to skip the Metropolitan's new production of *Pelléas;* but the enthusiastic report and urging of the young critic Harris Green persuaded me to go; and it turned out to be something I'm glad I didn't miss. Having mentioned the orchestral writing as the one valuable element in the work, I begin with the superb realization of it in all its subtlety and occasional splendor by Colin Davis with the excellent Metropolitan Orchestra. Before the performance began I was struck by the beauty of the forecurtain even in the lighted theater; when the theater was darkened the forecurtain turned out to be one of several scrims whose rising revealed the first scene—scrims made of a translucent fabric which reflected light; and with this fabric and Rudolph Kuntner's lighting Desmond Heeley created a number of scenes of extraordinary beauty and atmospheric effect—two exceptions being the vaults below the castle and the bedchamber of the last act. In these scenes one saw the stage action devised by Paul-Emile Deiber that was remarkable in the economy of the means which achieved impressive dramatic significance, and that included an effective innovation in the additional significant movement which prolonged a few of the scenes into the beginning of the orchestral interlude (with the incidental beneficial result that the audience remained silent during those moments of the interludes). In this stage action one saw evidence not only of Deiber's skill but of the gifts of the performers he had worked with. And with full appreciation of the major contributions of Thomas Stewart's Golaud and Barry McDaniel's Pelléas and the lesser ones of Giorgio Tozzi's Arkel and Lili Chookasian's Geneviève, I consider the outstanding and overwhelming contribution to have been Judith Blegen's Mélisande, one of the most extraordinary things I have seen achieved on the stage of an opera house. I have seen dancers use their bodies with expressive effect, but never an opera singer whose body even when motionless presented the compelling image, and in movement exercised the powerful dramatic effect, that Blegen's did—whose mere turning of her head had the expressive force Blegen's had, or whose darting now this way, now that in a desperate attempt to escape Golaud's inexorable grasp wrung one's heart as hers did. With her few quiet movements in the early scenes, her desperate ones in the scenes of Golaud's brutality, she created a Mélisande who was believable, convincing, agonizing—what no one had succeeded in doing before in my experience, and least of all the Mary Garden of 1918 with her mannered flutterings and self-conscious posturings. Thus it turned out that an opera of little interest for me provided one of the rare occasions when the work together of designer, director, conductor, singers and orchestra achieved a notable example of the combined artistic operation of operatic performance.

I happen not to have seen any of Tennessee Williams's plays, and don't know whether the original action of *Summer and Smoke* fleshed out with his own dialogue would have seemed to me dramatically plausible and effective, as Lanford Wilson's libretto for the new opera of Lee Hoiby, produced by the New York City Opera, did not. But in an opera the fleshing out of the action that makes it plausible and effective is done by dramatically expressive music; and though one heard words being sung to musical sounds—which was evidence for Hoiby that he had composed an opera, and for the captive subscription audience that it was hearing one—I didn't hear in the endless succession of sounds to which the words were being sung even one phrase that had relevant expressive point in the dramatic situation or any intrinsic interest or value in itself. In this it was exactly like Hoiby's earlier *Natalia Petrovna*, which the company had produced in 1965; and thus it was still another in the long series of worthless American operas on which the company has persisted in wasting its financial and artistic resources and its audiences' money and time, in accordance with the erroneous belief that one must produce bad American operas to get the eventual good one.

What made Hoiby harder to endure was the overwhelming demonstration of real creative power that had been provided only a few days earlier by a five-hour concert performance of Berlioz's *The Trojans*. The conductor, John Nelson, was someone I had never even heard of; and I was therefore unprepared for the mastery of the work and

of his performing forces that he revealed in a performance astounding
not only in itself but in the effect it gave to the music. A year ago,
reporting on a performance of passages from the first two acts, I said
these were the less interesting acts of a work that was not, as had
been claimed recently, Berlioz's greatest. For me his greatest was the
incandescently beautiful writing in parts of *Romeo and Juliet*, *The Damnation of Faust*, *Harold in Italy*, *Les Nuits d'Eté*; and in *The Trojans* the
one example of such writing was the septet of Act 4. What I discovered
this time was that in addition to the great writing of that kind Berlioz
produced great writing of another kind—the grandly eloquent dramatic
writing for voice and orchestra that one hears in *The Trojans*. And
the attention that was seized at the beginning by the powerfully expressive passage of the low strings leading to Cassandra's first recitative
was held thereafter by the operation of a mind that was at every moment
active in response to the situation and word. Nor was it only I who
heard this, but an audience which completely filled Carnegie Hall
(I was able to hear the performance only through the kindness of a
friend with an extra ticket); which didn't indulge in the usual indis-
criminate and prolonged screaming after arias, but applauded perceptively at other places too and stopped applauding when the conductor
wanted to go on; which stayed until the end, a little after midnight,
and then stayed on to applaud and cheer; and which—after deserved
ovations for Clarice Carson, the Cassandra, Richard Cassilly, the
Aeneas, and Evelyn Lear, the Dido—revealed its understanding of
the conductor's achievement by giving him the biggest ovation of all.
In every way, then, it was the most notable musical occasion in many
years.

People have occasionally exclaimed to me: "Why did Balanchine
. . ." or "Why doesn't Balanchine . . ." do this or that; and I have
had to say: "I don't know." I am myself, on occasion, unable to understand his doing what he has done, or even what he has said about
what he has done; in my years of watching and occasionally listening
I have acquired no knowledge of the working of his mind that is responsible for what he does and says; and in this situation I do the only
thing I can do, which is to describe what he presents to my eye on
the stage and say what I think about it.

Thus, I can offer no explanation of Balanchine's staging Fokine's

Chopiniana (better known by its later name *Les Sylphides*) in the way
he did. There occurs to me the statement attributed to Hindemith—that
music had a face; and if one didn't like it one shouldn't play it; but
if one played it one shouldn't change it. The original Fokine work
that Balanchine promised—what, in his book about the great ballets,
he calls "the second production", presented in St. Petersburg on April
6, 1908, and later presented in Western Europe by Diaghilev—had
a face: the face of a romantic ballet performed "in the light of the
moon" by "dancers in long white dresses"—dresses whose flow and
swirl was part of what one saw as the dancers' leaps and turns. If
Balanchine didn't like that face—didn't like the romantic moonlight
and long white dresses—he shouldn't have produced the work; if he
produced it he shouldn't have changed it. The movements that were
performed in short practice costumes like those of *Concerto Barocco* were
not the movements of Fokine's *Chopiniana;* they were the movements
of what the program note described as a "recension . . . offered . . .
as a testimony of approximate efficiency in a context of its contemporary
vitality", and what looked as skeletal and unattractive as that note
suggested. (The mere removal from the Fokine work of the encrustation
of sixty years' changes, corruptions and "layers of sentiment or senti-
mentality" that "have tended to dull the force, logic and ingenuity
of this academic masterpiece" would have produced not the seemingly
desirable restoration of the original one would expect, but, according
to the note, "a pious museum restoration" which the pejorative "pious"
and "museum" made unthinkable for stage presentation.)

But Fokine's work wasn't changed only by being performed in practice
costumes; it was changed also by being performed by the particular
dancers in those practice costumes. At a rehearsal for an out-of-town
performance once I saw Violette Verdy, in thick, fuzzy rehearsal tights,
make the arabesques and turns of the slow middle section of the C-
sharp-minor Waltz excitingly grand with the way her large movements
filled out time and space. But Balanchine, in his production, chose
to have the Waltz performed by Kay Mazzo, who had repeatedly demonstrated her lack of the ability to fill out time and space with such
impressive movements in supported adagios; and the practice costume
exposed and accentuated this inadequacy, as it did also the excessive
size of von Aroldingen's body. Many of the questions about Balanchine
have concerned dancers: it has been difficult to understand his assigning

dancers to roles they clearly were unsuited for, his not assigning to roles the dancers who seemed predestined for them. *Chopiniana* raised such questions: why Mazzo was assigned to a role which required her to do what she had clearly demonstrated in *Diamonds* and *Don Quixote* she could not do; and why the role was not given to the dancer who had repeatedly demonstrated in breathtaking fashion her ability to do the very thing Mazzo couldn't do—Verdy.

Difficult to understand also were Balanchine's additional changes in *Don Quixote* this year, which damaged the scene in the village square. The rising curtain revealed not the villagers who used to perform a perversely accented folk-style dance, but von Aroldingen and Peter Martins with a group of girls in ballet costume, who danced *Pas Classique Espagnol*. It was a good ballet piece, with an outstandingly fine solo for Martins; but as a ballet piece it had no dramatic relevance, was danced to some additional atrocious music by Nicolas Nabokov ("Why does Balanchine . . . ?"), and necessitated the omission of the sinister beggars' dance in which Don Quixote used to get absurdly involved. On the other hand, the marvelous *Pas de Deux Mauresque* in Act 2, in which Suki Schorer used to dance with piquant charm, was electrifyingly pointed up by Gelsey Kirkland's extraordinary clarity and sharpness. Nor was this the only or most impressive achievement of her special kind: the same clarity in the movements that seemed merely to come into existence in their unfailing perfection, as if human effort were not involved, made hers the most remarkable performance of the lead role in *Concerto Barocco*—and in particular the second movement's supported adagio—that I could remember.

As for the questions people ask in their annoyance at the increased cluttering up of the programs with the pretentious and empty works of Jerome Robbins, I continue to think Balanchine, recognizing the gifts that produced *Afternoon of a Faun* and *Les Noces*, feels obligated to give Robbins the opportunity to exercise those gifts, even though they produce works I cannot imagine Balanchine respecting—like the latest of them, *Watermill*. "And he takes forever" were the concluding words of Verdy's description to an interviewer of Robbins's manner of working with dancers, as against Balanchine's. These words about the rehearsals apply also to the completed pretentious ballets —whether the forever is the eighty or ninety minutes of constant movement of *Goldberg Variations*, or now the sixty minutes of *Watermill* in which the comparatively little that is done is magnified by the enormous slowness of the doing.

The small group of instrumentalists began to produce the tinkly, wispy sounds of Teiji Ito's score derived "mainly from religious ceremonial and theatrical music of the Orient"; the curtain rose on a completely dark stage; and after a couple of minutes there gradually became visible three tall constructions of long tufted stalks, a sliver of new moon, and a single black-cloaked figure standing with back to audience. For a few minutes this figure remained motionless; then slowly, slowly, slowly it turned toward the audience, revealing the face of Villella, who for another few minutes stood motionless again, looking, looking, looking into space, then slowly, slowly, slowly turned back toward the moon. What I recall next is Villella moving slowly, slowly, slowly to the right, stopping, slowly casting off his cloak, facing the audience in his black shirt and trousers and sandals, slowly withdrawing one bare foot, then the other from the sandals, slowly pulling the shirt over his head and tossing it away, slowly removing the trousers and flinging them toward the shirt, and facing the audience, finally, naked except for the male dancer's supporter. He had been seen similarly naked in Balanchine's *Prodigal Son*, but in a dramatic situation, after his despoilment by his companions; and attention had been held by the movements wonderfully imagined by Balanchine for that situation; whereas now in *Watermill* there was no evident reason for his nakedness, and for several minutes he did nothing but stand motionless, looking, looking, looking into space, and presenting for the spectator to see only the beauty of his body. This was difficult enough for him to carry off; but there was in addition one curious detail: whereas in *Prodigal Son* the despoiled Villella had been left with a purplish loincloth, in *Watermill* he was left not similarly with a bit of theatrical costume, but with the supporter that is never seen, and that, being seen now, drew attention to itself. That Villella did carry it off with an appearance of unself-consciousness in his quiet projection of strength and dignity was evidence of powers which deserved better employment than they were given in this ballet.

My next recollection (I cannot recall everything; nor does this seem necessary) is of Villella still standing motionless and looking out into space, seemingly oblivious of the boys who entered from both sides with what looked to me like colored balloons (but to someone else like unlighted lanterns) at the ends of long poles, and who after a few minutes withdrew—all without any evident point in relation to Villella. Then, alone on the stage, he slowly, slowly, slowly made movements which showed his body in a number of beautiful configurations—after which he sank down to a sitting position in which he seemed lost in thought. It may have been in this position that he ignored the three or four successive groups of boys who trotted onto the stage and around it like the group of boys in the last movement of Balanchine's *Rubies*, and then trotted off. Then, for no evident reason, Villella began running as fast as he could across and off the stage, first from right to left, then from left to right, and after several such crossings suddenly came to a stop, facing a group but not communicating with it. Later, Villella, lying in the stage shrank together in fear when a demon in the form of a ferocious animal attacked a boy who was similarly stretched out near him. Still later Villella remained either seated or stretched out on the right side of the stage as a girl, in a wide robe with her hair confined in a large headdress, entered on the opposite side, released her long hair from the headdress, shed her robe, and stretched out on her back in her black leotard; at which point a boy approached and bent over her, lifted her into his arms, and began with her a series of slow acrobatic involvements similar to those of the erotic *pas de deux* in Balanchine's *Bugaku*. The involvements ended with the two bodies in embrace rolling over two or three times, then separating and lying motionless. When, after a few moments, they began to rise, Villella began to rise with them; and as the boy left the stage Villella approached the girl, entwined an arm with hers, and, sinking toward the stage, possibly laid his head in her lap (I'm not sure of this) before stretching out on the stage alone, apparently in sleep; whereupon the girl picked up her robe and left. Finally a few girls entered to engage in play with some of the long tufted stalks; and after a time Villella, rising, picked up two of the stalks dropped by the girls and began to manipulate them. Eventually he dropped them; and picking up his cloak and wrapping it around his body, he moved slowly, slowly, slowly off the stage as it slowly, slowly, slowly became completely dark and the curtain fell.

With the predictable roars and cheers of approval there were this time a few boos. And encountering Harris Green outside, I discovered that he had been one of the booers: "We now have the *ballet* of the absurd," he commented. (Irving Howe told me later that he had booed—something he said he had never done before.) But the next day we learned in Clive Barnes's review that the boos had come from the fools who hadn't appreciated "a fantastic ballet . . . that attempts to question the art of the ballet and, indeed, our concept of the theater" with its experiments with a theatrical time longer than realistic time, and that "seems to make a new statement about dance, rather in the way Vaslav Nijinsky tried in 'L'Après-Midi d'un Faune' many, many years ago"; the fools who hadn't recognized in the things they had thought meaningless a ballet concerned with "a man of mature years looking back on the patterns of his life and the shadows of his destiny". To this I, a man of mature years looking back on the *Faune* in which I saw Nijinsky in 1916, can reply that its new statement about dance was made in a way completely unlike Robbins's—in a singular work of art that was immediately clear and overwhelming in impact even for a spectator aged sixteen.

"A ballet that attempts to question the art of ballet"—a prime example of what for Mr. Barnes is impressive writing and thinking—became, in a Sunday article a week later, "not a ballet" but "a theaterpiece . . . performed by trained dancers". And this—which happened to be true of *Watermill*—didn't keep Mr. Barnes, a few paragraphs later in the article, from describing the work as "a ballet that extends ballet", which it couldn't be and do if it was "not a ballet" but "a theaterpiece . . . performed by trained dancers". Nor, it would seem to me, could ballet be extended by "a ballet that attempts to question the art of ballet". But one must keep in mind that in these pronouncements Mr. Barnes's concern was to sound impressive, not to make consistent sense, or any sense at all. And there was no sense in the pronouncements about Villella's performance—that although he was an extraordinary technician Villella, like Nijinsky and Bruhn, was "often at his best when faced with a theater rather than a dance"; that *Watermill* had provided in Villella's career the something new that *Petrushka* provided in Nijinsky's; and that his performance in it was "the finest thing he has done". I don't know what Villella thinks of what he is required to do in *Watermill* and won't embarrass him by asking; but I do know what it has meant to him as a dancer to have achieved, in his dancing, mastery of the special styles first of *Giselle*, then of *La Sylphide*, then of *La Source;* and I would doubt that he thinks standing and moving about naked with dignity for an hour amid the goings-on in *Watermill* is a greater achievement.

It was after the preceding comments on *Watermill* had been written that someone told me what had been said of it by an experienced non-professional spectator. "It was beautiful—the changing moon, and so on," she had said. "And it was empty: it was like a ritual, but a ritual without a doctrine"—which strikes me as a remarkable perception not only about *Watermill* but about the entire Robbins operation.

Fall 1972 The various happenings last year in celebration of Virgil Thomson's seventy-fifth birthday ended with the Juilliard School's production of his new opera, *Lord Byron.* I had looked forward to another work in which Thomson would use his idiosyncratic method as attentively and freshly and effectively as in his earlier *The Mother of Us All;* but the very few good passages I heard in *Lord Byron*—among them some phrases sung early in the second scene by Thomas Moore and Augusta Leigh, and the final piece sung by the shades of the poets—which confirmed my recollection of the high quality of *The Mother of Us All*, also removed doubt concerning what I heard in most of the new opera: vocal writing that was a mere shapeless doodling of notes to carry the words to which it had no expressive relation; frequent bizarre-sounding orchestral contrivance with no relation to what was being sung; excruciatingly discordant choral writing with no precedent in Thomson's earlier operas that I could recall, and no reason I could discover for it in this one. Those few good passages also made it clear that the poor quality of the rest of the music couldn't be explained by the feebleness of Jack Larson's libretto, but had to be taken as representing the present state of Thomson's musical powers. Among these powers one must include the judgment that produced the choice—as the vocal medium of the work's darkly passionate protagonist—of a high light tenor voice, employed much of the time in its cruelly taxing highest range (I think Grayson Hirst was unwise to sing in a work that imposed this strain on his beautiful voice). The musical performance I heard was conducted effectively by Gerhard Samuel, except for the momentary breakdown at a dramatic high point in Act 3; the stage performance directed adequately by John Houseman had unimpressive sets by David Mitchell and remarkably unattractive costumes for the women by Patricia Zipprodt; and Alvin Ailey's choreographic evocation of Byron's dissolute life abroad, a danced interlude, was ludicrous.

One would have thought that Zeffirelli's spectacular and costly fiasco with Samuel Barber's *Antony and Cleopatra* would have ended his activity at the Metropolitan. But Mr. Bing's parting gift, to remind us of him for years after his departure, was a new staging of Verdi's *Otello* by Zeffirelli, with his sets and Peter Hall's costumes, which provided yet another confirmation of Haggin's Law that you can't keep a bad man down. Unlike Eugene Berman, the great designer of the beautiful sets of the Metropolitan's 1963 *Otello*, Zeffirelli decided the time had come for him to replace the ideas and decisions of Boito and Verdi with new ones of his own; and the results were ugly sets and stage action which at times obscured the essential dramatic point and at other times introduced points thought up by Zeffirelli that would have outraged Boito and Verdi. The musical performance gained by the fresh and beautiful voices which Teresa Zylis-Gara, the Desdemona, and Sherrill Milnes, the Iago, used in well-shaped and expressive phrases; but Otello's part calls for a free outpouring of powerful tenor sound which James McCracken's curiously constricted-sounding voice cannot produce; and his opening *Esultate!* was reduced in volume and impact by Zeffirelli's innovation of having Otello's ship appear at the back of the stage and Otello sing from its deck, instead of his entering after landing, as the score directs, and singing from the front of the stage.

Goeran Gentele, talking to a *Times* interviewer about his plan for a Piccolo Met similar to the Piccolo Scala of Milan for small-scale productions of suitable operas, old and new, pointed out how much better it would be for a young composer with no experience in writing opera to begin, and even to fail, with a small-scale work than with one on the scale required by a huge theater like the Metropolitan; and how, on the other hand, the Metropolitan, which had an obligation to do something about contemporary opera, could do it if it involved such a small-scale operation of the Piccolo Met. This was realistic and sensible; but then Gentele was reported to have said that it was "of the utmost importance to do something to change the image of the Met. We must add a contemporary aspect. We must do our best to attract a young public that does not come to the Met now, and we must do so by offering this public opera of its own time at a price it can pay"—which was neither realistic nor sensible. There is a young public interested in opera, and a young public that is not interested. The Metropolitan doesn't have to change its image of producer of the operas of Gluck, Mozart, Beethoven, Rossini, Donizetti, Bellini, Verdi and Wagner, among others, to attract the young public that is interested in them: this young public is already there in the standing room and cheaper seats, as it always has been; and no doubt it will also be at the performances of the Piccolo Met. But I find it improbable that the young public which does *not* come to the Metropolitan because it is *not* interested in the great operas of the past will be drawn to the Piccolo Met by an interest in the operas of today.

The major event of the New York City Ballet's spring season was a week-long Stravinsky Festival, conceived as a celebration, an homage, which—Balanchine said to me during a chance encounter—would show Stravinsky's entire life as a composer in the progression of works, and for this would include seldom-heard early pieces like the Symphony No. 1 and even, if it could be obtained, a piano sonata Stravinsky wrote as a child. And I couldn't imagine the mental process by which Balanchine had arrived at the decision that a demonstration in Stravinsky's music of his entire life as a composer required the inclusion of his inconsequential juvenilia but not of the first monumental products of his matured powers—*Petrushka* and *Le Sacre du Printemps*. Or the decision to include—in addition to the later outstanding *Pulcinella* and *Apollo*—the less consequential *Chant du Rossignol*, Octuor, Serenade in A, the extremely unattractive Piano Concerto, but not the toweringly great *Le Baiser de la Fée* (the complete ballet score, not the abridgment for concert performance titled Divertimento). Or the decision to include —with the still later charming *Danses Concertantes* and impressive *Orpheus*—the unattractive Violin Concerto, Duo Concertant and Symphony in Three Movements, but not the delightful *Jeu de Cartes*.

In this matter I felt most strongly about the omission of *Le Baiser de la Fée*. *Petrushka* and *Le Sacre* are performed frequently; but I can recall no concert performance in New York of the entire score of *Le Baiser*, and only one or two performances of the portion of it that Stravinsky made into a concert piece with the title Divertimento; and so the concert public is unaware that *Le Baiser* is the one later orchestral work of Stravinsky with a magnitude of scale and content which is comparable with that of *Petrushka* and *Le Sacre*, though achieved in a different way. It doesn't have the originality that is overwhelming in the other two; it is in fact one of the works that unperceptive critics have called imitations of other composers—the works in which Stravinsky found it interesting to have his mind operate with the thematic substance and style of this or that composer of the past, as Beethoven did with Mozart and Brahms with Haydn. But in *Le Baiser* Stravinsky's reworking of fragments of Tchaikovsky's piano pieces and songs, in contexts of his own invention in styles that are his extensions of Tchaikovsky's style, produces his most beautifullly wrought, most expressive and affecting, most dramatically imaginative writing—writing which attains the magnitude I mentioned that, in the end, is overwhelming. I acquired my own awareness of the greatness of *Le Baiser* through hearing it with the ballet that Balanchine made for his first American company in 1937, that was performed later by the Ballet Russe de Monte Carlo, and that was last performed by the New York City Ballet in 1950-51. It was a wonderfully imagined and powerfully moving dramatic ballet; and I have never understood his decision to drop it and his unwillingness to revive it. When I said this last spring to one of the company's management I was told the reason was its failure in 1950—the reason also for his not reviving his delightful ballet *Jeu de Cartes*. *My* recollection was that the audiences had enjoyed both these ballets; and when I asked Tanaquil LeClercq, who had danced in *Le Baiser*, what *she* remembered, she confirmed that "the audience *did* like both ballets. Not super hits . . . but nice applause, a few 'Bravos' once or twice." But it isn't only the unwillingness to revive the original ballets for *Le Baiser* and *Jeu de Cartes* that is baffling; it is Balanchine's not including the two scores in the festival with new choreographies, as he did *Danses Concertantes* and the Violin Concerto—his omitting *Jeu de Cartes* entirely, and his making a new choreography not for the whole of *Le Baiser* but only for "excerpts from the 'Divertimento' version" that is itself only part of the score.

I was able to attend only the first four performances and a couple of dress rehearsals; and in the limited available time I can write only briefly about what I saw. In some instances the choreographic celebration was no more interesting than the music it celebrated—the extreme example of this being the chaos John Clifford produced on the stage for Stravinsky's amazingly undisciplined as well as wholly derivative Op. 1, the Symphony in E flat. John Taras exhibited experienced competence in what he devised for the Piano Concerto, *Scènes de Ballet* and *Le Chant du Rossignol*, a spectacular with very little dancing, and produced something more excitingly effective with his use of the silhouetted dancers in the special style of *Ebony Concerto*. And competence was exhibited also in the experienced Todd Bolender's piece for Serenade in A, the younger Richard Tanner's for the Octuor. As for the more impressively gifted Robbins and Balanchine, in the columns of *The New York Times* during the preceding year Robbins had been providing the New York City Ballet with the creativity Balanchine had ceased to provide; but that hadn't been what I had seen on the stage of the New York State Theater, and it wasn't what I saw at the festival. The sensation of the opening performance was not the enjoyable *Scherzo Fantastique* that Robbins produced with his limited vocabulary and imagination for classical ballet; it was the *pas de deux* that Balanchine produced for the Aria I of the Violin Concerto—one that continued the series of acrobatic supported adagios of *Agon*, *Episodes* and *Rubies*, but was as astoundingly different from them as they had been from each other, and, like them, held one spellbound with its unending originality and power. And this would have been so if instead of *Scherzo Fantastique* the Robbins piece had been the later *Dumbarton Oaks*, a larger-scale and more elaborately contrived classical ballet, light in character and pleasant to watch; or, on the other hand, if it had been *Requiem Canticles*, a modern-dance-style piece for dancers in black leotards, whose movements didn't have for me whatever meaning or effect they were intended to have, and whose character can perhaps be conveyed by its ending—with most of the dancers crouched around the three or four who stood motionless with heads thrown back and mouths wide open as the curtain fell. Or even if it had been the delightful *Circus Polka*, performed not by the elephants for which the music was written, but by successive groups of smaller and smaller girls whom Robbins, playing the Ringmaster, marshalled into various arrangements in which they charmed one with their precisely executed ballet movements and poses.

Balanchine produced another overwhelming supported adagio for the Aria II of the Violin Concerto, and yet another fascinating one for the lilting middle movement of the Symphony in Three Movements;

and though he demonstrated again with these pieces that his powers operate most impressively in the manipulation of two linked bodies in adagio, he also produced superb invention for the large ensembles in the animated outer movements of the two works. And the second evening he offered a masterly and delightful new choreography for *Danses Concertantes*, in which, however, there were not the witty details in Lynda Yourth's dancing that I had seen in 1945 in Danilova's—details suited to the elegantly formed and styled Danilova that wouldn't even occur to Balanchine for the stockier-bodied and cruder-styled Yourth. (That says something important to Balanchine about his rejection of "stars" and preference for malleable young dancers. Danilova, in the rehearsals I observed, was a "star" only in her possession of extraordinary gifts that Balanchine could use to obtain what he cannot obtain from his young dancer today.)

It seemed at first that Balanchine, the next evening, was using the music of the third scene of *Le Baiser de la Fée* for a new classical *pas de deux* which, considered in and for itself, was charming, but which was less satisfying to someone who remembered the playful details of the beginning of the *"grand pas classique"* (as Balanchine referred to it) of the Boy and his Bride in the 1937 ballet, so closely related to the playfulness of the clarinet and flute in the music; the climactic supported *arabesque penché* related to the impassioned melody of the violins; the exquisite conclusion related to the delicate chatter of the woodwinds; the Bride's capricious solo. But this scene provided no music for the male dancer's solo that customarily precedes the girl's solo in such pieces; and for this Balanchine used music he should not have used—the eerie and violent music for the *pas de deux* in which the Fairy takes possession of the Boy at the end of the second scene. I can't imagine that Stravinsky would approve of this dramatically meaningful music being used for the leaps and spins and other feats of a male dancer's solo in a *grand pas classique*. And it seems to me that Balanchine's dealing with *Le Baiser* constitutes a failure in his obligation to this great work—an obligation which he can fulfil only by choreographing the entire score.

As baffling as Balanchine's dealing with *Le Baiser* was the further revision of *Firebird* that increased the damage done to it by the 1970 revision. His original streamlined version of the ballet for Stravinsky's streamlined 1945 version of the score preserved the essentials of the

story in the flame-colored costume of the Firebird, her powerful entrance solo, the *pas de deux* in which she was the struggling captive of
the Prince, and her gift to him, when he released her, of the plume
with which he later summoned her to his aid. But his first revision
two years ago eliminated these essentials; and the further revision for
the festival had the Firebird made up to look like the sinister woman
who lived down a manhole in Charles Addams's cartoons, and costumed
like a Chagall character in white robes with enormous white wings
and a bouquet of red roses which she kept transferring from one hand
to the other as she made her way, hampered by her robes, through
a necessarily unlively entrance solo and a *pas de deux* in which she
was more often separated from the Prince than held by him. At the
end of the *pas de deux* she gave him not a plume but her bouquet,
which later he presented to the Princess; and in his hour of danger,
therefore, he had no plume with which to summon the Firebird but
she appeared without being summoned. (This *Firebird* Clive Barnes
pronounced "much improved"—which revealed again how little his
writing has to do with what he professes to be writing about.)

In conclusion, it is one thing to read fantasying pronouncements
in *The Times*, but quite another thing to read in a printed article on
the company by Lincoln Kirstein, issued with the announcement of
the plans for the Stravinsky Festival, the unrealistic and—coming from
him—astonishing statement: "At the birth of the New York City Ballet
some twenty-five years ago, as well as over the last few seasons, Jerome
Robbins has occupied a place no less important than Balanchine." One
need only look at the company's repertory twenty-five years ago and
its repertory of recent seasons to know that what Kirstein wrote is
as untrue about twenty-five years ago as about today. The festival
demonstrated again that creative powers of the nature and magnitude
of Balanchine's are still not exhibited by anyone else today, including
Jerome Robbins.

Postscript 1973 Someone suggested that Kirstein's statement was not
what he himself believed but what he thought the public should be
persuaded to believe in anticipation of Robbins's eventual succession
whenever Balanchine would become inactive. The suggestion assumed
Kirstein's acceptance of the necessity of such a succession, which I

do not accept. What Kirstein considered imperative in 1934 was to make possible the operation of Balanchine's creative genius in this country, not Robbins's; what he should consider imperative now is the continued existence of the ballets that Balanchine's genius produced. And the way *not* to achieve this, it seems clear to me, is to give one choreographer the dominating position in the company that is now Balanchine's, which will result in this choreographer's ballets displacing and replacing Balanchine's. What *is* required instead is an administrative group that will include, in its management of the company's affairs, the commissioning of new works by choreographers of the period—this in consultation with the production staff that will preserve the existing repertory and assist in the preparation of the new ballets.

My report on what I saw of the Stravinsky Festival left no space for comment on the season of repertory that preceded the festival—comment on dancers, since there were no new works. When Balanchine attacks stars and the star system he uses "star" in only one of its meanings —to designate virtuoso dancers with glamorous personalities who he says are interested only in exhibiting their virtuosity and personalities in the stellar roles of *Giselle*, *Swan Lake* and *The Sleeping Beauty*, not in working in the new choreography he is constantly producing, and whom he therefore says he has no use for and no need of. What he never speaks of is the other meaning of "star", to designate the possessor of the extraordinary artistic capacities that great performances of those roles require. And the fact is that as a choreographer who devises movements for what he senses as each dancer's particular capacities, he has produced some of his greatest dance invention for the extraordinary capacities of stars. In the last Diaghilev seasons he produced it in *Apollo* and *The Prodigal Son* for Lifar, Danilova and Doubrovska; in the forties, with the Ballet Russe de Monte Carlo, he produced it in *Danses Concertantes* and *La Sonnambula* for Danilova and Franklin; and I can add that the Danilova who starred in *Swan Lake* and *Coppélia* worked, at the rehearsals I observed, with complete dedication to achieve what her special gifts stimulated Balanchine to invent in his two ballets. In the fifties, with his own company, Balanchine had use for a star, Erik Bruhn, whom he engaged twice as guest—not for the personality that Bruhn seemingly wasn't interested in exhibiting, but for the capacities as a dancer and artist that he placed at Balanchine's service in performances of the Poet in *La Sonnambula* which no one in the company has equalled; in effortlessly brilliant performances of the solo variation in *Divertimento No. 15* that others had struggled with ineffectively; in superb performances in the Balanchine versions of *The Nutcracker* and Act 2 of *Swan Lake,* and in one of the new Balanchine pieces in *Pan-America.* Moreover, Balanchine brought into his company Violette Verdy and, more recently, Peter Martins—both stars whose capacities Balanchine had use for, and who have continued to perform also in *Giselle* or *Swan Lake* or *The Sleeping Beauty* outside of his company. And finally Balanchine's own principal dancers, though listed strictly in alphabetical order, have included several who have been recognized as, in effect, the company's stars—the possessors of the special capacities that Balanchine has used in the extraordinary invention of, among other works, *Liebeslieder Walzer* (Verdy), *Bugaku* (Allegra Kent), *Don Quixote* (Suzanne Farrell), *Emeralds* (Verdy, Mimi Paul), *Rubies* (Villella, Patricia McBride), *Who Cares?* (D'Amboise, McBride, Marnee Morris). Nor has Villella been only one of these stars of the New York City Ballet's performances: he has made featured appearances outside of the company, some of them with Verdy in *Giselle* and *La Sylphide.*

What, then, Balanchine shuts out of his mind when he says (according to Lincoln Kirstein) he is interested only in capacity for movement, is that the capacity for movement he is interested in—the ability not merely to execute the difficult movements he invents, but to execute them with apparent ease, clarity, precision, projective force, and with the subtleties of timing and phrasing constituting the style, different with each dancer, that heightens the movements' beauty and effect—is of a kind and magnitude which, when exhibited by a dancer, is recognized as that of a star. And when Balanchine insists (according to Kirstein) that the role is more important than the dancer, he shuts out of his mind the importance to the role of the dancer whose individual capacities for movement he has used in it—the fact that to have the role he must have the dancer he devised it for. True, there have been instances in which the role has been taken over by another dancer who has made the movements beautiful and effective with the differences in their appearance produced by this dancer's different style: Farrell did this with the Diana Adams role in *Liebeslieder Walzer;* Gelsey Kirkland with the McBride role in *Rubies.* But in other instances such substitutions have resulted in loss: no other dancer has achieved an equally effective alternative to Kent's own performance of the movements Balanchine devised for her in *Bugaku;* one sees none of Verdy's grandeur of style, her subtleties of rhythm and phrasing, in *Liebeslieder Walzer* and the Tchaikovsky *Pas de Deux* when Sara Leland takes over her role in the first or even McBride in the second; Jean-Pierre Bonnefous provides an inadequate alternative for D'Amboise's perform-ance in *Who Cares?;* and what Balanchine devised for Farrell's deploy-ment of her lovely tall body in *Don Quixote* and *Diamonds* has none of its beauty and effect when performed by Kay Mazzo.

What is important about D'Amboise's performance in *Apollo*, then, is not that it differs from Lifar's original performance in 1928: all the performances since then have differed from his and from each other. What is important is that Conrad Ludlow's and Villella's and Martins's performances have been, in their different ways, beautiful and moving, whereas D'Amboise produces a damaging distortion of the role that I cannot get myself to look at. But for reasons one cannot imagine it is D'Amboise whom Balanchine has preferred, and who was to have appeared in all of last spring's performances. Special circumstances, however, resulted in Martins's doing a couple of them, which luckily I saw; but at these I discovered that whereas a few years ago the work had had Farrell as Terpsichore and other suitable dancers as Calliope and Polyhymnia, now it had Mazzo as an insignificant Terp-sichore and Karin von Aroldingen and Gloria Govrin as her ineffective associates. And in the Stravinsky Festival, with D'Amboise back in the title role, Stravinsky's beautiful score for this work was celebrated with a performance by unsuitable dancers.

All this illustrates further what I wrote last year about the difficulty in understanding some of the things Balanchine does and says. After years in which he has denounced stars while he used their special capacities, he is now putting dancers *without* those capacities—Mazzo, von Aroldingen, Leland—into roles he originally made for dancers *with* them.

Index

251

ACKNOWLEDGMENTS

I am indebted to Harris Green, for help in deciding what to put into the book, and the staff of Horizon Press, for another collaboration of a kind that is unique in my experience.

DATE			